Rocking Your World:
The Emotional Journey into Cr

C000144442

ABOUT THE BOOK

Rocking Your World: The Emotional Journey into Critical Discourses is an introductory text that emerged from the belief that we often learn best through personal narrative and story. This collection of real stories connects critical theory and critical pedagogy with personal transformation. It is an experiential primer in how to navigate a developing appreciation of how silent (and sometimes not so silent) machinations of power align themselves along axes of gender, race, class, sexual orientation, and global position (amongst others) to both conceal and perpetuate injustice and oppression.

In this book, twelve authors share personal reflections of how various critical discourse communities have impacted their lives. They explore a range of professional, family and social barriers to personal growth as teachers, professional researchers and everyday people; they give us glimpses into the impact of positionality, the balance between activism and intellectual rigor, the obstacles to teaching critically, and more.

This book would be an ideal complement to traditional texts and would provide countless opportunities to generate the kind of personal introspection and dialogue that can make studying critical pedagogy and other critical discourses a transformative experience. It is a must read for any teacher or student interested in the power of critical theories to transform how we see the world in which we live.

TRANSGRESSIONS: CULTURAL STUDIES AND EDUCATION

Scope
Cultural studies provides an analytical toolbox for both making sense of educational practice and extending the insights of educational professionals into their labors. In this context *Transgressions: Cultural Studies and Education* provides a collection of books in the domain that specify this assertion. Crafted for an audience of teachers, teacher educators, scholars and students of cultural studies and others interested in cultural studies and pedagogy, the series documents both the possibilities of and the controversies surrounding the intersection of cultural studies and education. The editors and the authors of this series do not assume that the interaction of cultural studies and education devalues other types of knowledge and analytical forms. Rather the intersection of these knowledge disciplines offers a rejuvenating, optimistic, and positive perspective on education and educational institutions. Some might describe its contribution as democratic, emancipatory, and transformative. The editors and authors maintain that cultural studies helps free educators from sterile, monolithic analyses that have for too long undermined efforts to think of educational practices by providing other words, new languages, and fresh metaphors. Operating in an interdisciplinary cosmos, Transgressions: Cultural Studies and Education is dedicated to exploring the ways cultural studies enhances the study and practice of education. With this in mind the series focuses in a non-exclusive way on popular culture as well as other dimensions of cultural studies including social theory, social justice and positionality, cultural dimensions of technological innovation, new media and media literacy, new forms of oppression emerging in an electronic hyperreality, and postcolonial global concerns. With these concerns in mind cultural studies scholars often argue that the realm of popular culture is the most powerful educational force in contemporary culture. Indeed, in the twenty-first century this pedagogical dynamic is sweeping through the entire world. Educators, they believe, must understand these emerging realities in order to gain an important voice in the pedagogical conversation.

Without an understanding of cultural pedagogy's (education that takes place outside of formal schooling) role in the shaping of individual identity--youth identity in particular--the role educators play in the lives of their students will continue to fade. Why do so many of our students feel that life is incomprehensible and devoid of meaning? What does it mean, teachers wonder, when young people are unable to describe their moods, their affective affiliation to the society around them. Meanings provided young people by mainstream institutions often do little to help them deal with their affective complexity, their difficulty negotiating the rift between meaning and affect. School knowledge and educational expectations seem as anachronistic as a ditto machine, not that learning ways of rational thought and making sense of the world are unimportant.

But school knowledge and educational expectations often have little to offer students about making sense of the way they feel, the way their affective lives are shaped. In no way do we argue that analysis of the production of youth in an electronic mediated world demands some "touchy-feely" educational superficiality. What is needed in this context is a rigorous analysis of the interrelationship between pedagogy, popular culture, meaning making, and youth subjectivity. In an era marked by youth depression, violence, and suicide such insights become extremely important, even life saving. Pessimism about the future is the common sense of many contemporary youth with its concomitant feeling that no one can make a difference.

If affective production can be shaped to reflect these perspectives, then it can be reshaped to lay the groundwork for optimism, passionate commitment, and transformative educational and political activity. In these ways cultural studies adds a dimension to the work of education unfilled by any other sub-discipline. This is what Transgressions: Cultural Studies and Education seeks to produce—literature on these issues that makes a difference. It seeks to publish studies that help those who work with young people, those individuals involved in the disciplines that study children and youth, and young people themselves improve their lives in these bizarre times.

Rocking Your World:
The Emotional Journey into Critical Discourses

Andrew H. Churchill
McGill University, Canada

SENSE PUBLISHERS
ROTTERDAM / TAIPEI

A C.I.P. record for this book is available from the Library of Congress.

ISBN 978-90-8790-649-8 (paperback)
ISBN 978-90-8790-650-4 (hardback)
ISBN 978-90-8790-651-1 (e-book)

Published by: Sense Publishers,
P.O. Box 21858, 3001 AW
Rotterdam, The Netherlands
http://www.sensepublishers.com

Printed on acid-free paper

DEDICATION

This book is dedicated to Kristin without whom the journey would be infinitely less interesting and not nearly so much fun.

TABLE OF CONTENTS

FOREWORD

If it's important, you are going to have to pay

I have had the good luck over the last three decades to be blessed with smart, committed, and very brave doctoral students. Andrew Churchill fits all three of these categories. The first night I met Andy in my Introduction to Critical Pedagogy class at McGill University, he was asking hard, thoughtful, and challenging but respectful, questions about critical pedagogy. By the third night of class, buoyed by his readings of the critical pedagogical texts assigned, he was asking even better questions–ones that I and many of my professorial and activist colleagues in the field had not asked. I was impressed. In the years that have followed that introduction, my respect for Andy has never diminished as he continues to push the envelope of critical pedagogy in creative, pragmatic, sensitive, and intellectually rigorous ways. He is very humble and didn't want me to write such an introductory paragraph to his book, but I did anyway.

As I gained deeper insights into Andy's talents and commitments, I was fascinated by his ideas concerning unique and compelling ways to introduce a group of students to critical theory. Andy's engagement with critical pedagogy had rocked his world and had raised numerous questions about issues of selfhood and the purpose of teaching and learning. As I listened to him talk about these affective dynamics, it became more and more apparent that he had an excellent book floating around in his head. As a major professor or dissertation director, I find that student publication should be an essential part of the doctoral experience and try to create opportunities for all my students to publish their research in journals and chapters. That said, I am very careful about suggesting that a student take on the larger challenge of writing or editing a book, for you don't want to divert a scholar from focusing attention to the pursuit of the degree. In Andrew Churchill's case there was no question that his best intellectual, programmatic, and vocational interests were well served by undertaking this project. The power of this book is testimony to the worth of the undertaking.

I have focused on Andy's talents, but in no way do I want to exclude the brilliance of the contributors to this book. They are an amazing group of diverse students/ scholars who provide fascinating insights into the questions Andy has asked about the impact of critical discourses and the issues that emerge once the critical tsunami is unleashed. Watching the interactions between Andy and the authors has been an enjoyable and edifying process. This book illustrates the process of scholar-activists at work, engaging one another in difficult and often very personal and emotional questions about, their role in their profession and the world, the nature of identity and questions concerning their dignity, as well as the constitution of being itself.

What makes a compelling introduction to critical discourses? How do we engage students in the domain of criticality? Why should we? These are both affective and cognitive questions, pedagogical and ideological inquiries. While Andy and the contributors focus on narrative and the affective dimensions of the process, they all understand that there is no way to separate the personal story from the theoretical, the cognitive from the affective. Andy could not have formulated his compelling questions, issues, and processes of engagement without a profound understanding of critical theory. Too often, narrative based research can be inexcusably vacuous if it is not accompanied by a rigorous knowledge base and a wide range of socio-cultural, political, economic, and psychological insights. Thus, the book works to bring these divergent but ultimately inseparable domains together in the effort to engage students in thinking about what the critical journey might entail.

As you may know, I intensely believe in the power of the impassioned spirit of critical pedagogy. I understand that there was something profoundly special about Paulo Freire and many of the scholars/activists who have followed (or preceded) him in the wide realm of the critical with its concern for social justice, the end of human suffering, and a teaching and learning process that leads to individual and social transformation. Don't get me wrong, I don't believe in this power blindly nor do I romanticize the domain. I understand that many acute mistakes have been made by individuals pursuing these goals and by people operating under the flag of critical pedagogy. This is why I speak of an evolving critical pedagogy that learns from diverse peoples in differing historical and socio-cultural locations.

This is why I insist on a humble critical pedagogy that is courageous in its undertakings but aware of its all-too-human fallibility. Such a humility and its concurrent willingness to listen to others often runs counter to the arrogance of too many academics and social activists. I am far too depressed by my encounters with peoples from these domains that feel far too certain about the righteousness and correctness of their causes. The last thing in which I want to be involved is an infallible critical pedagogy–or an infallible "anything" for that matter. The critical pedagogy the authors of this book put forward is one that, if anything, asks questions of itself. In asking questions of itself, it induces us as critical pedagogues to ask questions of ourselves. Such a process can be painful, but it is necessary if we want to do good work in the world.

Thus, we are faced with the contradictions between acting bravely against injustice and subjecting ourselves to questions around the complexities of such actions in our own lives. There is a delicate balance here, a tightrope to be walked. If we move too far to one extreme, we can become "un-self-reflective" kamikazes who fight every battle and lose our voices and our efficacy as agents of justice in the process. On the other extreme, we can become intellectual navel-gazers who wallow in our angst about taking a stand. After doing critical work for four decades, I certainly make no claim to know how to walk the tightrope. I have told my colleagues and students over these four decades that everyday I assess how well I performed my criticality. Some days I feel I acted too quickly, spoke up too loudly against what I saw as an injustice. Other days I feel that I should have acted when I didn't, I was too reflective and let an excellent moment for intervention pass me by. It's a daily struggle–we never get to a point of perfect equilibrium. I have now achieved a universal critical consciousness and need go no further in my studies and deliberations–not!

Recently, while dealing with criticism of work that I have done while concurrently re-reading Paulo Freire's *Pedagogy of Hope*, I had a less-than-profound but potentially important realization. As Paulo described some of the abuse he had to endure for his work for social justice and the success of his seminal book, *Pedagogy of the Oppressed*, I realized that we have to pay a price for anything we do that is important in the struggle for a critical pedagogy and social justice. It wasn't as if I didn't already understand this rather obvious point, but there was something about the timing that placed the notion in a new light. If we're not ready or willing to make such a payment, we're probably not ready to engage in a critical pedagogy. In order to put oneself on the line for critical principles, pedagogies, ideologies, and actions that challenge the status quo, we must have our minds right. This point is central to this book. We must be ready to have our world rocked not just with the insights we initially gain in our critical encounters, but we must be ready for the explosions that will follow us as we live out our criticality throughout our lives. In this context we must avoid the pitfalls of self-righteous martyrdom on one level or nihilistic cynicism on another. Both are unacceptable and will certainly undermine our efforts to make a difference. And both are easy traps in which a criticalist can become ensnared.

This difficult part is necessary to the critical conversation. But there is also much joy and reward to take from work in critical fields. We can become better human beings than the ones we now are. We can play a role in helping people who are oppressed by race, class, gender, sexuality, ability, etc. gain new forms of empowerment. We can help change the consciousness of the privileged and help them redirect their lives in the service of social justice. In an era of cynicism and selfish acquisition, we can help create alternative realities and ways of being. I will never let the "difficult part" of cultural work undermine my commitment to try to do what is right. I will never let my deliberations about the complexity of criticality stop me from calling out an injustice, even if I don't take advantage of the initial opportunity to do so. I will never let careerist ambition or a desire for recognition and status stop me from being true to myself and to those in need. And I will never assume that I have lived up to these brash pronouncements.

Andy and the authors of this book rock our world. If you are just entering into the zone of criticality or if you are a teacher/professor/activist in the critical cosmos there is something here for you. I am so proud of Andy and the authors and am thankful I could be a part of this project. The "price we pay" for our critical work–whether from having our world rocked or as blowback from rocking the world of others–is in the end worth the good that we can do. I challenge you to develop the guts that it takes to engage in and endure the vicissitudes of the process. I can think of no better way to spend your life.

Joe L. Kincheloe
Canada Research Chair of Critical Pedagogy
The Paulo and Nita Freire International Project for Critical Pedagogy

ACKNOWLEDGEMENTS

First and foremost, I wish to acknowledge the authors of this edited collection who each took risks in pushing their writing beyond the purely intellectual to share the personal stories about how critical discourses have impacted their learning, thinking, teaching and being in the world.

As this is a book about the journey into critical discourses, I also want to acknowledge the people who have helped me along my own journey. Though this group is, not surprisingly, dominated by the McGill community, I want to first acknowledge Jeff Beedy, (headmaster of the school where I worked before coming to McGill) and that school's community of educators. This is where the seeds of my wanting to think differently about schools were initially sown. At McGill I want to acknowledge my fellow graduate students with whom I have struggled in classes to understand assigned texts, formed study groups to further explore areas of interest, and developed writing groups to hone our own voices. I want to especially recognize the graduate student group affectionately known as "Critical Theory for Dummies" which gave me the initial courage to pursue this project. My colleagues are my best teachers and my inspiration.

I also want to thank the professors with whom I have worked most closely. Shaheen Shariff, with whom I do research on cyber-bullying, has nurtured my confidence to begin presenting and publishing, and unselfishly has given me the space to do so. Bronwen Low was my first professor at McGill, and it was in writing reflection papers in her class that I began to challenge the ways I had been conceptualizing issues in education. Anthony Paré has helped me immensely to become a better writer and teacher as well as a more thoughtful thinker. Shirley Steinberg has helped broaden my perspective beyond schools. Last, but certainly not least, I want to acknowledge Joe Kincheloe. Joe is an outstanding supervisor, a wonderful teacher and a friend. It is his care that has allowed this book to come to fruition. Not only did he nurture the initial idea, but he has spent countless hours walking me through the process of editing thus giving me the confidence to complete this project. It would be an understatement to say that without him this book would not have been possible.

I also want to acknowledge the support of my family. As will be discussed in this book, challenging our thinking and our histories is not easy work and often impacts our relationships with the people we hold most dear. I am deeply indebted to my parents, siblings and extended family who unconditionally support my growth–even when this growth challenges their worlds as well.

Finally, I want to acknowledge Kristin McNeill, who, during this journey, agreed to marry me. She has been, and continues to be, amazingly supportive of me and the work I try to do. In this particular case, she also brought her considerable editorial talents to bear spending countless hours reading and re-reading the chapters of this book making shrewd suggestions about how to sharpen arguments and clarify explanations.

Part I: Introduction and reflections

ANDREW H. CHURCHILL

1. THE EMOTIONAL JOURNEY INTO CRITICAL DISCOURSES

Appreciating the challenge

The challenge of understanding critical discourses is a multi-faceted and complex one, much like critical discourses themselves. In this book, twelve authors share reflections about how critical thinking has impacted their lives. It is our hope that this sharing will help you better understand and appreciate the power of critical discourses to change (or continue to change) how you see the world.

To begin, I want to discuss three ideas from which this book emerges. The first has to do with the very real emotional impact these discourses often have on the personal aspects of our lives. The second has to do with exploring the challenge of how we learn. And the third explores how we can remain open to challenging how and what we believe. These are by no means exhaustive of the topics covered in this book, but they are a good starting point.

ROCKING YOUR WORLD

This book is first and foremost based on a simple premise: critical discourses demand that students ask themselves questions about how they see and participate in the world. These questions often lead students to see the world in new ways and confront previously unconsidered issues. These new ways of seeing the world challenge basic assumptions. Much like a stone dropped into a still pond, this creates a ripple, disturbing one's basic beliefs. But unlike the stone causing a ripple, critical discourses may have an effect more like a tsunami transforming the landscape into something significantly less recognizable–*rocking worlds*.

The authors in this book have been affected by a wide variety of critical discourse communities as they each discover or further develop their own more critical gaze on the world in which we live. This book is a collection of their stories. Specifically, these stories focus on deconstructing the emotional components of this journey and reflect on how an increasingly critical understanding of the world changes each author's life. In order to explore both developing a more critical gaze and the affective and emotional components of this journey, I want to share a reflection.

This story is about me–a middle class, white man who, as an adult, has begun for the first time to reflect on his own personal culpability in supporting the power structures that oppress others. Critical discourses, including critical theory, critical pedagogy, race studies, historiography, and media literacy–to name just a few–

A.H. Churchill (ed.), Rocking Your World: The Emotional Journey
into Critical Discourses, 3–9.

have played important roles in helping me develop a more critical gaze. This new perspective forces me to consider how issues of power align themselves along axes of gender, race, class, sexual orientation and global position (amongst others) to shape the world in powerful and complex ways. One way I have come to appreciate this impact is by reflecting on how developing a more critical gaze has changed how I see a very specific place in the world–a place that no doubt elicits strong feelings in many people: Ground Zero.

Like most people, I remember the exact moment when I learned of the planes crashing into the World Trade Center in New York on September 11, 2001. When the first airplane hit, I was in an administrative meeting at a high school in New Hampshire where I was working at the time. This meeting, along with everything else happening on campus at that moment, was immediately interrupted, and an emergency meeting was called. We gathered as a community in our school auditorium, and on the 20 by 20-foot movie screen normally reserved for Saturday night movies, we watched replays of the horrible scenes of the planes flying into the buildings and their collapse. Like everyone, I remember how surreal the moment felt.

Just two months later, I went to the actual site. I was visiting New York as field experience in my MBA program. Typical of most MBA trips, the schedule included a visit to Wall Street. In the aftermath of 9/11, getting anywhere near Wall Street was impossible. Instead, we visited a commodities trading floor in mid-town. We passed through extensive security, which included rigorous personal identification, metal detectors, and individual interviews just to get into the building–an attempt to create an oasis inside the building from the feeling of insecurity that permeated the streets outside. At one point, we had to evacuate the building because of a fire alarm. I remember the controlled panic as we rushed down the stairs and outside–unsure of what we would see upon emerging from the darkened stairwell into the daylight. The culture of fear was palpable.

The next day was unscheduled, and I, along with several classmates, headed to Ground Zero. The site became increasingly surreal as we got closer. The first sensory clue was the smell: a pungent stench of smouldering plastic, rubber and steel. We passed a stream of exhausted soot-covered firefighters. Finally, we arrived at the awful wreckage of an entire city block crumbled in on itself.

I remember sobbing. Overwhelmed by the destruction before me and struggling in my personal life–in the midst of a divorce, dissatisfied with a job I used to love, anxious about the future–this moment became one of unfettered grief and anguish. At the time, I could not separate my own personal struggles from the tragedy before my eyes. I was simply overwhelmed. I also remember being angry–angry and vengeful. I felt that the people responsible for this pain should be punished. At that moment I supported George Bush's reaction: "America was targeted for attack because we are the brightest beacon for freedom and opportunity in the world …. This is a day when all Americans from every walk of life unite in our resolve for justice and peace" (Bush, 2001 as cited in *The Greatest American Speeches*).

Fast forward to March 2008 when I revisited Ground Zero. In the time between, I had left my job, moved to Montreal, had become fully ensconced in graduate school and was happily married.[1] This trip to New York was for an academic conference. It was springtime, and the city was in full bloom.

Once again I was deeply moved. The scene was totally transformed. Instead of the smell of burning wreckage, there was the pure smell of welding steel. Instead of battle-weary firefighters, I saw busy and energetic workers in hard hats. Ground Zero was no longer a death trap but a bustling construction site. New buildings were being built and, in the hours I watched, I felt I could actually see them rising to the sky.

Yet, despite the productive activity and the lightness of my spirit, I didn't feel hopeful. Instead, I felt a very real sense of outrage and a heavy sense of foreboding. I think the outrage was multi-faceted. As I looked at the young kids and teenagers being paraded through the site by their parents, this reconstruction project felt more like a sales pitch for the War on Terror, exemplified by the slowly climbing Freedom Tower and the characterization of "its illuminated mast evoking the Statue of Liberty's torch" ("Freedom Tower," 2008). This was not the sombre reminder of tragedy which I had envisioned. On a different note, having just seen a documentary on the lack of basic rebuilding in New Orleans after the hurricanes, I was struck by the grandeur of the Freedom Tower plans. Additionally, I was outraged that my country's response to the tragic death of over 3,000 civilians was to wage a war that has resulted in the deaths of hundreds of thousands civilians in other countries–as well as thousands more of our own citizens. Finally, a sense of foreboding made me wonder, "if we are building such a memorial for a single isolated event, what could be built in the Middle East in the aftermath of American bombings of their cities?"

I felt as if something had been taken from me. I had wanted to come to Ground Zero to acknowledge the tragedy of that moment and to pay my respects. Instead, I wrestled with a different perception: that the rebuilding had been warped to justify political agendas. I was also mad that I was thinking this way; in essence, I was irritated by my developing criticality. Why wouldn't it leave me alone to just sit quietly in this sacred place?

I share this story because I think my conflicting reactions to this place offer an interesting example of how critical discourses have changed the way in which I see and experience the world around me. What for me had once been a knee-jerk reaction to what I perceived as an attack on democracy and my country's attempt to secure justice and freedom has shifted to a more complex and self-reflective viewpoint–one which attempts to question the complexity of the role that the United States, imperialism and the West occupies in the world.

I also share this story because of the ripple effect that has been created from my articulation of feelings about 9/11. For example, I worry about how sharing these feelings may disturb my relationship with the mother and four children of my university fraternity brother who was killed fighting in Iraq. How can I question the rationale behind this "war on terror" without questioning the commitment of my friend who died in a job he took to serve his country? In this questioning, how do I avoid desecrating his memory and in the process jeopardizing my relationship with his family and my fraternity brothers whom I see at the annual fundraiser for his kids' education? This is the very real ripple effect that is caused by questions that critical discourses demand of me. These questions rock my world.

REJECTING DISEMBODIED KNOWLEDGE

Unfortunately, most current introductory texts dealing with critical discourses do not typically acknowledge this affective impact of the learning process. Instead, most texts rely on an academic discourse genre dominated by scholarly intellectual argument. In not considering the ambivalence that new perspectives create within the identities of students new to critical discourses, common introductory texts treat critical theory as if it were a finite body of intellectual knowledge that can simply be imparted to students. This treatment of knowledge and learning is what Paulo Freire in *Pedagogy of the Oppressed* (1970) famously names the "banking model of education" which he argues is the very thing that most needs changing. *Rocking Your World* is inspired by Freire's idea, and, juxtaposed with common introductory texts, focuses on how criticality impacts our being in the world.

This focus is accomplished by the frequent use of self reflection and personal narrative reflecting the commitment of many critical discourses to broaden traditional pedagogy beyond simply intellectual arguments. It thus reflects a methodology consistent with many of its theorists. These theorists include a wide array of researchers critiquing the epistemological assumptions embedded within a 20th century view of science that assumes the world can be understood by breaking it into discrete component parts and isolating individual variables. Many of these same theorists also challenge traditional views of pedagogy which position schooling as a process whereby teachers impart concrete knowledge to their students, who can then be tested for how accurately they regurgitate this information.

While understanding the nuances and details of these critiques is not necessary to understand the rationale behind this book, it may be helpful to consider a few examples. Joe Kincheloe, in a recent paper entitled "Critical pedagogy and the knowledge wars of the twenty-first century" (2008), claims criticality demands we not only reconsider epistemology (ways of knowing and constructing knowledge), but also ontology (ways of being in/with the world). Megan Boler, in her book *Feeling Power: Emotions and Education* (1999), challenges teachers to embrace a "pedagogy of discomfort" which recognizes "how emotions affect how and what one chooses to see, and conversely, not to see" (p. 177). James Paul Gee, whose recent work focuses on literacy and computer games, rejects the debate that literacy learning is either an expressive process or a natural process (the former a rationale for whole language and the latter for phonics); instead, he suggests it can be most accurately understood as a cultural process whose outcome is as dependent on how one perceives oneself as it is on the efficacy of a particular teacher or pedagogy (2004). Similarly Alfred Tatum's literacy work with African American males demands that literacy theory move beyond pedagogical strategy that focuses solely on the cognitive. In his recent paper, "Toward a more anatomically complete model of literacy instruction" (2008), Tatum asserts that we must begin paying attention to the relationship and responsiveness gaps between readers and educators if we wish to close the achievement gap of many African American males in schools. Finally Francisco Varella, who follows in a Vygotskian tradition of psychological inquiry, offers the importance of enaction which brings to the foreground the importance of *being*–what Kincheloe might call ontology (Kincheloe, 2008)–in the learning process (Varella, 1999). While I could cite countless others, it is enough to appreciate that a range of scholars has suggested the importance of moving beyond traditional, intellectual modes of scholarship and pedagogy. It is this call to broaden academic discourses on which the approach of this book is based.

While the preceding paragraph will be one of only a few places in this book easily recognized as traditional scholarship with its referencing of intellectual conversations using complex and scholarly nomenclature, this does not mean this book should be considered non-scholarly. In fact, what the preceding references show is that bringing this kind of balance to scholarly writing, teaching practices, and processes that help students construct knowledge is exactly what numerous critical academics suggest needs to be done. This approach embraces identity transformation as central to developing a critical appreciation of the relationship among power, knowledge production and the stratification of societies along the lines of gender, race, class, sexual orientation and global position (and others). By focusing on both the affective and cognitive intellectual journey, this book embodies ways of knowing that many critical discourse communities espouse. In so doing, I hope students will enter into an engagement with criticality that reflects the epistemological stance of critical pedagogy.

REMAINING OPEN[2]

One of the challenges of writing (and reading) these stories is not falling into the trap of creating new binaries (situations that are defined by choices of either/or) or meta-narratives (generalizations used to simplify complex social phenomena), both of which critical discourses are committed to eradicating.

For instance, the hypothesis central to the conceptualization of this book is that the affective or emotional component of learning should not be excluded by the rational, logical or intellectual manner in which most introductory texts are written and to which traditional academic scholarship usually speaks. Notice how this creates a binary where the emotive and affective are now labelled as being illogical or non-intellectual because one is juxtaposed against the other. In this example, using this language to highlight the importance of the emotional aspects of this book serves to undermine the very hypotheses that I am trying to put forward–that emotional and affective aspects of our knowledge development are not separable from the intellectual. That this book deals with knowledge development in a holistic way is not intended to reject a traditional cognitive academic mode of learning. Instead what this book is attempting to offer is a more complex, nuanced perspective on our learning processes–one that does not pit one mode of learning against another as if the two are separable and somehow mutually exclusive: a false binary.

A second important issue in this collection of stories is the rejection of the idea that there is one singular truth. This, it seems to me, is one of the cornerstones of the post-structuralist critical struggle. There are truths and there are knowledges (even though the latter in this plural form is not recognized in most dictionaries). This is one of the great epistemological shifts that we must attempt to make. We must come to understand that what we once understood as truth becomes an infinitely complex web of multiple understandings. Earlier I talked about the need to reject binaries and meta-narratives and, at some level, this is also what we are trying to do when we reject the idea of there ever being a singular truth. In rejecting this concept, we are also rejecting our almost hard wired need to essentialize–that is to identify the essence of something. In thinking more critically, we must learn that for every moment we try to create a binary that helps us understand something more clearly, or create a meta-narrative that distils an argument into its essential components, at that very moment, we are potentially buying into the idea that there is one truth. In that act of believing in a singular truth, we are creating closure in a way that disallows the possibility for other truths to also be known, understood and acknowledged. We must be careful to recognize that there can actually be multiple truths and attempt to structure our understanding and actions with this knowledge, or we will create closures that prevent us from remaining open to the infinite complexity of our world. At the same time we must not allow this fluidity of truth to paralyze us from taking action. There is in fact suffering and injustice in the world that should not be allowed to be interpreted out of existence.

A final issue which has been important for my emerging appreciation of critical discourses is the idea that "knowledge does not age well."[3] For me, this is a simple yet powerful thought. It recognizes that at one point scientists "knew" the world was flat and, more recently, that Pluto was a planet. Knowing the problem such "facts" face over time forces me to consider what it is that I know today which may make me laugh tomorrow for having believed. I have come to think of this by its postmodern term as epistemological humility; that is, we should always be suspicious of both what it is we think we know and also how we decide we know things. I actually find it strangely comforting to believe that not only *what* we know but also *how* we know will change over time. Somehow this allows for unimaginable possibilities because it acknowledges that we cannot yet know how to imagine them. For me, these possibilities include thinking about how various peoples in the world treat each other as well as our planet. While I find issues of widespread poverty, environmental destruction, global warfare, rampant materialism, and excessive individualism to be exceedingly scary components of our modern existence (and have a hard time imagining their solutions), I find it comforting to believe that solutions will emerge as we actively try to engage in addressing and thinking about these problems.

Acknowledging how critical discourses can help direct us towards a more complex understanding of the intellectual spaces in which we work and the human spaces in which we live is the basis of this book. This acknowledgement allows us to embrace a more holistic and less disembodied view of knowledge and, rather than trying to make sense of things by breaking them down into discrete parts, instead we make sense of them by embracing their interdependence. This resistance to appreciating the infinite complexity of our world in search of easily understood meaning-making is one of the challenges of critical discourses and is one of the many things that the authors of this book struggle with as they share their journeys into criticality. I hope (and believe!) you will enjoy reading our stories and learn much from them.

NOTES

[1] I position these experiences within certain moments of my life because circumstances had changed since 2001. First, I had spent three years in graduate school with a significant amount of my studies devoted to reading and learning about a variety of critical discourses. Second, I was a much happier person. This combination was integral in the way in which I experienced Ground Zero and illustrates how we create meanings of things based on where we are–intellectually, emotionally, physically, spiritually, etc. at a particular moment in time. This acknowledgement of the contextualized nature of how we make meaning is an important realization in our journey towards a more critical appreciation of the world and thus part of the journey towards criticality.

[2] I owe this commitment to "not forming closures" to Jeff Beedy, the headmaster of the school where I worked for eight years. He would challenge our students, faculty, leadership team and trustees to remain open to all of the possible alternatives, knowing that once people form closure, the potential for understanding dramatically decreases.

[3] This quote is from a conversation with Joe Kincheloe about knowledge and its limitations.

REFERENCES

Boler, M. (1999). *Feeling power: Emotions and education.* New York: Routledge.

Bush, G. W. (2001). Address to the nation. In *The greatest American speeches.* London: Quercus.

Freire, P. (1970). *Pedagogy of the oppressed.* New York: Herder and Herder.

Gee, J. P. (2004). *Situated language and learning: A critique of traditional schooling.* New York: Routledge.

Kincheloe, J. (2008). Critical pedagogy and the knowledge wars of the twenty-first century. *The International Journal of Critical Pedagogy.*

"Freedom tower." Retrieved June 11, 2008, from http://www.lowermanhattan.info/construction/project_updates/freedom_tower_26204.aspx

Tatum, A. (2008). Toward a more anatomically complete model of literacy instruction: A focus on African American male adolescents and texts. *Harvard Educational Review, 78*(1).

Varela, F. J. (1999). *Ethical know-how: Action, wisdom, and cognition.* Stanford, CA: Stanford University Press.

ANDREW H. CHURCHILL

2. ROCKING MY WORLD

Digging out the splinters

Education as the practice of freedom–as opposed to education as the practice of domination–denies that man is abstract, isolated, independent, and unattached to the world; it also denies that the world exists as a reality apart from the people.   – Freire, 1970, p. 81

ACKNOWLEDGING THE AFFECTIVE

I needed help. It was the second term of my first year of graduate school. I was studying in Montreal where the winter days were often bitterly cold and always short. It would be dark before class started at 5:30 p.m. and frankly that was how I was feeling about my studies–in the dark. I was taking my first course in critical pedagogy. Really it was my first course in critical anything. We talked about epistemology, ontology, deconstruction, hegemony, essentialism, constructivism, positivism, and neoliberalism.[1] Words with too many syllables and even more definitions rolled off professors' and classmates' tongues with the greatest of ease. And each of these words was associated with unfamiliar authors, in unfamiliar times and places–Freire in Brazil, Foucault in France, Gramsci in prison, as well as Horkheimer, Adorno and others at the Frankfurt School. I was lost in the intellectual quagmire of grad school!

In an effort to get on top of the terminology, I bought my first dictionary of terms that winter–three of them actually: *Keywords* (Williams, 1983), *New Keywords* (Bennet et al., 2005) and *A Dictionary of Cultural and Critical Theory* (Payne, 1996).[2] I would look up a word, only to find a clever definition that usually referenced at least four other words that I did not know. I would then look up these other words which would then invariably reference the original word. Breaking into this discourse was hard intellectual work but I was determined to be successful.

At 35 years old, I had quit my job running the admissions office at a private high school in New Hampshire and began a Ph.D. program focused on curriculum design. I left because I was frustrated by the school's attempts to change the culture without addressing the curriculum and my inability to help fix this shortcoming. Having spent most of my time outside the classroom in administrative positions, I decided taking the time to study curriculum would help empower me to be more effective in future endeavours. I began my graduate program with a clear

A.H. Churchill (ed.), Rocking Your World: The Emotional Journey
into Critical Discourses, 11–24.

understanding that curriculum could be designed better. Armed with an MBA, a dozen years of management experience, and a keen recognition that most schools were inefficient, I was ready to join the new generation of pragmatic, solution-oriented, technology-savvy school reformers.

My graduate studies have dramatically changed my thinking. What I have found in exploring curriculum studies is a robust on-going debate between the technocratic, neo-liberal approach that described my thinking before graduate school and the critical discourses that were quickly becoming central to my graduate studies. These discourses included critical theory, feminism, queer theory, critical media literacy, new literacies, and more. They question technocratic, pragmatic, universal approaches and instead analyze how issues of power intersect along axes of gender, race, class, and other variables to perpetuate unequal access to resources and maintain societal hierarchies. These discourses espouse complex intellectual arguments where nuances of language and meaning are debated and re-debated. I found myself endlessly trying to sort through these subtleties and develop my own understandings which, as they emerged in conversations and papers, were almost always critiqued by someone with a more sophisticated grasp of the debates. Understanding these discourses was hard, and I was increasingly uncomfortable. Frankly there were times when I just didn't like it all that much.

I tried to understand why I was struggling and came to the realization that it wasn't so much because of the intellectual challenge but the emotional one. The more I read, the more ill at ease I became. For the most part I could understand what it was authors were telling me, but it often contradicted my understanding of the world and my place within it. The ideas were in conflict with the way I had been assembling my world, and this was emotionally disconcerting. Deconstructing hegemonic discourses was forcing me to explore the ways in which the world operates that people don't normally talk about. It is sort of like Dorothy pulling back the curtain and seeing the wizard, or, as will be discussed later, like the scene from *The Matrix* where Neo takes the red pill and sees the matrix for the first time. It was scary, intriguing, confusing, thrilling, disturbing–feelings that had the capacity to rock my world.

My reaction was to either reject what I was reading and spin into a lethargic depression about my studies, or ride the jolt of excitement and stay up reading voraciously all night, consumed by some exciting new idea. I struggled with these feelings as new ways of conceptualizing problems created an exciting myriad of possibilities for a different future but also created moments of self loathing as I reflected on my past and began to realize my own culpability in social systems of oppression.

These feelings confused the intellectual journey. I was not well equipped to deal with them. It felt like they did not belong in my intellectual explorations and thus got in the way–or did they? Maybe this was what should be happening. Shouldn't they muddy the water? Aren't they the power and soul of critical discourses? And, if so, why weren't more writers speaking to me about these feelings? Why was this component of my education left unexamined?

One evening before class, I asked my professor these questions. It seemed innocuous at the time, but he thought it was important enough that he asked me to bring them to class. Then, he suggested I integrate them into my term paper, and then finally into a book proposal–which is how this project came to be. Along the way, I shared the idea with peers, and many became excited about exploring their own experiences and adding their stories to this collection. So what has emerged is *Rocking Your World*, a book of stories about personal journeys into critical discourses and how these journeys have impacted us not only intellectually but emotionally as well.

These narratives are not offered as a final truth, nor are they commandments for how to go about this journey. They are offered in the spirit of friendship, sharing and empathy. I outlined the hope for these stories in the book prospectus:

> This is what it was like for me. You will create your own journey, but you are not alone. This journey is not an easy one. There are difficulties for each of us who embrace casting a more critical gaze on our world and accept the challenge of renegotiating our knowledge about the world and our identity within it, but it is one that people have travelled before.

Hopefully, the sharing of these stories will help readers gain the courage, passion and drive to understand critical discourses, reconsider knowledge about the world and forge a new identity that de-centres selfhood as one comes to appreciate the complexity of alternate viewpoints and re-sees the world with what I referred to earlier as a more critical gaze.

THE JOURNEY

> As individuals begin to understand th(e) power-related and socially constructed dimension of the world, they sometimes feel like refugees in relation to the hegemonic cosmos to which they can never return. (Kincheloe, 2008, p. 9)

Now that you know how the book project began, the balance of this chapter will explore some personal reflections about how the stories in this book have impacted my own thinking. My thoughts here are not to be consumed as a summary or preview of chapters to follow but more as just one reaction (of the many possible) to reading them.

During the past year I have had the pleasure of working with over a dozen colleagues to assemble these stories. With the reading of each chapter, I have continued to learn and appreciate how critical discourses impact different people in different ways. For instance **Sandra Chang-Kredl** in her chapter, "'My Future Self N' Me,'" details a number of academic discourses that bring greater clarity to the importance of self reflection. As she reviews this literature, she shares the impact of this emerging appreciation of self reflection on her personal and professional life–thus providing a compelling autobiographical illustration of what the authors she is reading are advocating. Sandra's chapter provided for me a testament to the powerful impact the process of self reflection can have and has served as inspiration for me to continue with my own. This impact is taken up again in the final chapter, "A Conversation Amongst the Authors."

Seeing the Matrix

The title of **Elizabeth Meyer**'s piece, "I Am (Not) a Feminist: Unplugging from the heterosexual matrix," triggered for me an important early reflection about the nature of exploring critical discourses. In the movie referenced by her title, *The Matrix* (1999), the two main characters discuss "unplugging." In this scene, Morpheus talks to Neo about his desire to know more:

> Let me tell you why you're here. You're here because you know something. What you know you can't explain–but you feel it. You've felt it your entire life: that there's something wrong with the world. You don't know what it is, but it's there–like a splinter in your mind driving you mad .... Like everyone else, you were born into bondage. Born into a prison that you cannot smell or taste or touch–a prison for your mind.

In effort to further explain the Matrix, Morpheus continues:

> Unfortunately no one can be told what the Matrix is. You have to see it for yourself .... This is your last chance. After this there is no turning back. You take the blue pill, the story ends, you wake up in your bed and believe whatever you want to believe. You take the red pill, you stay in Wonderland and I show you how deep the rabbit hole goes.

This scene offers important insights into the journey of exploring critical discourse. Specifically the phrase "born into a prison that you cannot smell or taste or touch–a prison for your mind" is an elegantly simple and compelling description for what Gramsci labels hegemony (1971). Furthermore Morpheus' observation that Neo is caught in a space of "knowing there's something wrong with the world" and describing this as a "splinter in your mind" captures precisely the feeling that frequently re-occurs during this journey into criticality. In my own experiences, I often find myself stuck in moments where I am not quite able to articulate what I feel is discomforting–I just can't quite get my mind wrapped around it. This to me is perfectly described in Morpheus' analogy–like trying to remove a splinter lodged so deep that no matter how hard you probe, you can't dig it out.

Elizabeth's chapter asks a number of important follow up questions about why more people are not interested in examining their own beliefs–in essence, exploring criticality:

> Why aren't more people pissed off? What about people with privilege who never experience discrimination? Will they forever remain plugged into the Matrix living the manufactured reality that is being pumped into them? How do we get people to unplug when it is so painful? (p. 39)

I believe these questions are central to the following discussions about this journey.

Stubborn Resistance

Brad Porfilio in his chapter, "From Working Class Liberal to Transformative Scholar Practitioner," details the difficulty his university students have in their journeys. Their rejection of the "red pill" when he offers it and the myriad of reasons for this rejection shows the lengths that some students go to avoid engaging in dialogues that force them to reconsider their fundamental assumptions about education.

Brad's piece reminds me of notions in psychology about cognitive dissonance—the disruption that occurs when our beliefs about how and why people behave come in conflict with the order we have created in our own worlds, the associated discomfort of this disruption, and our motivation to relieve this discomfort. We react to this challenge by either rejecting the suppositions put forward (which Brad observes in the majority of his students) or by examining our previously unexamined assumptions. This second alternative is infinitely more complex and difficult but, ultimately, much more important and powerful.

From my own experience, I know that my initial efforts were focused on rejecting or manipulating new ideas in a manner that would synchronize neatly with the order I had created for myself; one that would not challenge my ideas about improving education or my vision of its purpose. For instance, I would shape my emergent understanding of critical discourses to converge with my technocratic ideas about education rather than challenge my core assumptions. It was only after multiple failed attempts to do this that I have begun instead to question fundamental assumptions about education. These questions are less about curricular pedagogy and more about examining basic goals of the process—for instance the role of education in sorting society into a hierarchy of intelligence. I find this work rewarding because it deals with the most fundamental issues of social justice.

Reconciling Personal History

While many of the authors in this book deal explicitly with reconciling issues around personal history, **Anie Desautel**'s piece, "Walking back along the Path," in which she reflects on her experiences as a teacher in the Canadian North, triggered a particularly powerful memory from my own experience in schools. I make meaning of this memory in the context of **Noah De Lissovoy**'s "The Hegemonic Consensus" in which he carefully documents the power of neo-liberal discourses to co-opt progressive spaces. My self-reflection details how a more critical appreciation for education—one that considers how issues of power and privilege intersect with emerging so-called progressive pedagogy to potentially and continually re-inscribe systems of social stratification along lines of gender, race, class and privilege—challenges me to see previous experiences in a different way.

Before graduate school, I worked at what would be considered a progressive (and by some people even radical) private school in the northeast United States. Central to the educational philosophy within the school was a rejection of narrow understandings of intelligence. This was particularly embodied by the explicit embracing of Gardner's theories of multiple intelligences (MI)[3] and the associated rejection of the negative labelling of learning disabilities. This was carried out in a variety of ways and was expressed symbolically by the school's renaming of its academic support centre to "The Center for CreativeIntelligence"[4] and the associated efforts to see individual learning styles as a manifestation of each student's unique talent rather than as an expression of academic shortcoming.

While I still feel this school's model was undoubtedly more progressive (and frankly better) than the paradigmatic models of most schools, I have come to appreciate some of its shortcomings. Particularly troublesome is reconsidering the role that Gardner's theories of MI had vis-à-vis our conceptualization of students on athletic scholarships–many of whom were African American students from urban areas. Many of these students struggled academically.[5] Gardner's conceptualization of intelligence offered us an alternative to labelling these students as "less smart." These students had their own intelligence which Gardner would label "bodily-kinesthetic." It was not that they were not "smart," it was simply that they did not have the linguistic or spatial-mathematical intelligence which was demanded by our curriculum and central for success in the traditional testing done in our classrooms. By constructing our culture in a way that everything we said and did was geared towards celebrating a non-monolithic view of intelligence, we could celebrate everyone's ability regardless of the domain in which it emerged. This provided a perfect solution to ease the angst brought about by the uncomfortable intersection of class, race and academic performance.

But how would this conceptualization play itself out if we were to consider more carefully class, race, privilege or various other social dimensions that critical discourses demand of us. I remember that our highest awards went to students who possessed a combination of Gardner's intelligences (specifically linguistic, mathematical, bodily-kinesthetic, personal and sometimes even musical). In my time at the school, this package of attributes was most often embodied in a White, middle class student. On the rare occasion that an African American student did win one of the highest awards it was because the student's combination of bodily-kinesthetic and personal intelligences was so extraordinary that the lack of exceptional academic achievement normally required for the award could be overlooked. Multiple intelligences thus served to justify the academic failings of marginalized students by crafting a model that continued to keep primal the talent level of the individual without considering a different model of cognition that would question the relationship between the individual and the school's curriculum (and the White middle class adults designing it) as central to any discussion about what it means to have intelligence.

This analysis[6] challenges me to reconsider the progressive ideas about education that I once espoused and forces me to re-evaluate the programs I once championed. In doing so, I have to accept responsibility for the role I myself may have unwittingly played (and at times continue to do so without realizing it) in perpetuating a society divided along lines of race, class, power and a myriad of other socially constructed attributes.

Seeing That Which We Have Not Seen Before

Eloise Tan in her piece, "Critical Pedagogy and the Great White Hope Dilemma," examines the role of positionality (who one is relative to issues of race, class, gender, privilege, etc.) versus ideology (how one sees and what one assumes about the world). In her chapter, Eloise shares her struggle with the negative affective impact caused by the dominance of white male voices in critical pedagogy. In the following quote, she describes her feelings during a research symposium on critical pedagogy where she feels this experience:

> The whiteness of these talks can be deafening; the maleness overpowering. I wonder what it would be like to listen to Paulo Freire and have the room to breathe in a little colour. (p. 151)

Each time I read this, I am reminded of a place in my past dominated by a Whiteness I had never before fully acknowledged. In so doing, I become increasingly aware of how the silent machinations of power often make certain injustices invisible.

This place is a small ski resort in the mountains of Utah. My family lives mostly on the east coast, but this mountain village is so special we have made the trip there on and off for some thirty years. Here, kids learn how to ski for the first time, cousins visit with each other, and grandparents ski with grandchildren. The same Swiss ski instructor guides young and old family members down the tough trails every year. It has become a favourite destination for four generations.

During my last trip there, I remember sitting at the bar at the end of a long day of skiing, enjoying the warmth of the fire and looking out at the ski slopes and mountain ranges basked in the late afternoon sun. As I sat there, I was suddenly struck by the fact that four people occupying one of the adjacent tables were black. At that moment, I realized that in all of my years of coming to this place not once could I remember a non-white group. As I tried to process this information, I could not figure out what was bothering me. I struggled and struggled to identify my unease and was besieged by a myriad of reflections. I thought about the lineage of wealth that allows people to come to a place like this and how for many people in that room the lineage of this wealth is directly or indirectly a result of colonial practices which have included the practice of slavery and the theft of Native American land. But the disturbance of this moment went further: it was the realization that in all my years coming here and all my years believing that this was truly one of the most beautiful and special places in the world, no one had ever acknowledged (let alone talked about or been bothered by) its Whiteness. Why had this conversation never happened?

For me this question was followed by a whole host of uncomfortable feelings that even now I continue to think about. Did I suddenly need to question my happy memories about this place? Should I feel badly for my experience here? Do I need to reject the love I still feel for it? Answering these types of questions becomes part and parcel of this journey into developing criticality because during it we cannot help but ask these critical questions. As Shirley Steinberg reminded me in a recent conversation "criticality happens when one does not stop with just noticing what is there, but also notices what is missing."[7]

Questioning Friends and Family

> White students learning to think critically about issues of race and racism may go home for the holidays and see their parents in a different light. They may recognize the non-progressive thinking, racism, and so on, and it may hurt them that new ways of knowing may create estrangement where there was none. (hooks, 1994, p. 43)

As critical understanding develops, moments such as bell hooks describes above inevitably spill over into our personal lives and relationships. **Andrea Sterzuk** in her piece, "From Buffalo Plains to Wheat Fields," talks about how understanding the colonial history of her prairie hometown in Midwestern Canada impacts her closest relationships. In reading her story, I think about some of the conversations that a more critical understanding has caused me to have with my own family and the unease and trepidation with which I approach these conversations.

Let me start with a disclaimer: I find my family receptive and curious about my studies, and often disarmingly open to listening to the ideas I am trying myself to understand. I count myself lucky in this regard and know that others have less support in their journeys–which makes me appreciate even more the work they do in navigating these choppy waters.

A conversation with my brother early in my new critical thinking process stands out. We were talking about his volunteer work as a board member for a charter school in Boston.[8] The hundreds of volunteer hours he has given has resulted in, not surprisingly, an emotional engagement with this school and its students. I have visited the school and have seen first-hand the focus and commitment of its staff and students. This visit left no doubt in my mind that the school is helping its students achieve success in ways that would otherwise be unattainable. Because of this I admire and support my brother's work.

However, armed with a more critical understanding of the potential impact this work has on the larger conversation about schooling, the role of charter schools in perpetuating certain myths about education now troubles me.[9] In some ways critiquing this work is not unlike my earlier critique of the school where I worked: it has less to do with the micro and the local (that is focusing on the isolated successes of how this school has positively impacted hundreds of students–this success is unmistakable) and more to do with the macro and the meta (that is, examining charter schools in the context of an unjust school funding system which is having a devastating impact on the nation's poorest students). This impact is famously documented in Kozol's book *Savage Inequalities: Children in America's Schools* (1992).

This macro impact of the success of charter schools can be understood as contributing to and perpetuating the myth that the resource gap between high resource, wealthy public schools and low resource, poorer public schools is somehow not to blame for their different student achievement levels. This is proven by the success of charter schools (with supposedly no more resources per pupil than the average) to successfully produce higher achieving students than their traditional counterparts. There is an implicit conclusion that arises from the assumption that the success of charter schools is directly linked to students' willingness to do homework, the school's disciplined academic culture, and the degree of positive involvement of parents: that the failure of the traditional public schools in the same neighbourhoods must be because students are not motivated to succeed, the academic culture does not reinforce discipline, and parents don't care to be involved. This implicit conclusion hides the also important considerations of major resource discrepancies and the curriculum bias of White middle class knowledge. Thus resource discrepancies and curriculum bias are exonerated, replaced with evidence that points to the level of motivation of the community, parents, teachers and students as most important to school success.

The defining moment of this conversation with my brother arose while we were jogging together. Rather than simply state my emerging discomfort with the celebration of charter schools, I couched my thoughts with "what my supervisor might say is …." This provided me a more protected space to put forward these thoughts while minimizing the risk of offending my brother and jeopardizing my relationship. I was relieved when his reaction was to be interested in and open to these ideas. This has since given me more confidence to take these types of risks in other conversations.

As we enter spaces of critical discourses, and as we begin to see issues previously veiled by personal assumptions and societal positionality, we, as Andrea points out in her piece, invariably find ourselves challenging the thinking and the work of those closest to us.

Praxis: Challenging Theory, Challenging Practice

The relationship between theory and practice/practice and theory is central to how critical discourses impact the world, and how the world impacts critical discourses. While many of the chapters in this book can be understood as actively engaging with this concept, two triggered important reflections for me.

In the first, entitled "Challenging Paradigms: Deconstructing and reconstructing my positionality as a non-Indigenious researcher," **Kevin O'Connor** reflects on the challenge of bringing his work in experiential education with Native communities into the academy. One significant aspect of Kevin's piece is how his deep exploration of theory allows him to reject some of the initial limitations the academy attempts to put on his work. This has encouraged me to reflect about the expectations (and restrictions) the academy places on me as a graduate student and emerging scholar.

On a personal level this book project represents an interesting example of just such a struggle. I have been questioned by some professors and graduate colleagues as to why I was spending time writing and editing a book when I had not yet completed my dissertation.[10] Embedded within this line of questioning I imagined the unspoken words, "you are not yet qualified for this type of work and should be spending your time first proving your worth."

My emerging criticality challenges this voice. Critical discourses question the way power silently operates to value or devalue certain knowledge and, in turn, cries out against the devaluing of graduate student voices.[11] This power struggle over knowledge production and the right to do (or not do) this work speaks to the challenge many graduate students have getting their voices heard and their work recognized. I find it heartening that this book has not only provided a place for me to begin developing my own voice but for other graduate students to have their voices heard as well.[12]

While keeping in mind the topic of knowledge production and its rightful producers, I also want to reflect on **Carmen Lavoie**'s "Activism Where I Stand." This chapter is a thoughtful reflection on her path through graduate studies that focuses on her frustration with the disconnect between academic studies and activism. Carmen describes how she has challenged this disconnect and brought academics and activism closer together in her own life. I found myself wondering about my own particular activism and its connection (or disconnect) to my own studies.

I have never considered myself, nor do I think most other people would label me, an activist. I have not participated in many political protests, nor have I done much work with grassroots community organizations. So how does my criticality actively express itself? What avenues do I find in my life that connect my intellectual reflections with the real world and make my criticality matter?

These questions lead me to consider the ways in which I challenge people to think differently about their worlds. Earlier, I talked about conversations with my brother and the dilemma of the public school system in Massachusetts where he lives. Is this activism? Another example is a recent project in which I did research for a task force charged with considering the Internet and its impact on schools. One of the primary recommendations was to try and change media discourse away from demonizing technology, the medium, to a more considered position that also acknowledges the cultural issues that shape adolescent behaviours (QESBA Task Force, 2008). The very day after this report was released, the Montreal *Gazette* ran an editorial entitled "Cyber-bullying root causes must be addressed" (2008) with just this message and credited the work of the Task Force for this reconsidered position. Should this work be considered activism?

I am not sure I know the answer, but I do know I want to believe that we need to broaden definitions of activism to include challenging how people think about their worlds. Regardless, acknowledging how I impact the world beyond the academic walls of the institution in which I study has been important for me, and I credit Carmen for helping me consider more deeply the relationship between activism and academics.

Difficulties of Integration

This conversation about activism leads into some final considerations about the journey into criticality. I want to highlight three authors who reflect upon the challenges of integrating critical thinking into their teaching and scholarship. The first has to do with developing a confidence in one's own voice; the second addresses the institutional and societal barriers to this work, and the third exposes the barriers we create for each other.

Dana Salter's piece, "First Dance," has been seminal in helping me reflect further on just how complicated it is for us to actually integrate the ideas we read into the world outside of the academy. In her chapter, she describes how she helps a colleague find a new voice in his teaching practice which in turn helps her further develop her own. Of particular importance is how they developed this voice in a way that gave homage not only to the ideas they had discovered in their reading but also to their own histories and their own selves.

As I read this chapter, I thought back to a moment in my own practice as a more critical teacher when I began to develop my own critical voice. As a teaching assistant grading undergraduate papers, I remember clumsily trying to find a critical voice. As I began offering my feedback to the students on their reflection papers, I felt ready to challenge their thinking and encourage them to consider issues more critically. But this was challenging for a number of reasons. First, I was confronted with the impression that the students were more interested in their grades than my feedback. Second, I was worried how they would react. What if they disagreed with my comment and sent it to the course professor? What if my course professor then did not agree with it? What if they were right to question me and my comment really was nonsensical?

These doubts crowded my mind. It was hard enough to learn to think more critically myself, but now I had to try and ask others to do the same. This brought my process out into the public. I found myself vetting comments with friends or previewing them with the professor before submitting them to students, in effort to protect myself. Even then, I remember anxiously awaiting the students' respective approvals so I could rest easy. In her chapter Dana aptly describes the process as "tricky, deliberate, often not incorporating the most popular moves" as well as "painful and emotionally draining" (p. 112).

In learning about the experiences of several authors in this book, I have come to appreciate that some people do not always get the kind of support that I have had during my journey into criticality. Specifically I want to reflect on the chapter written by **Priya Parmar**, "The 'Dangers' of Teaching a Critical Pedagogy," in which she shares her experience fighting institutional barriers she has come up against in her work. I found inspirational her courage to fight through a media storm that attempted to silence her critical voice. It also deepened my consideration of how teaching a critical pedagogy can be met with such harsh and vengeful reactions–although I am learning to be less surprised by this kind of backlash.

This backlash reminds me of the phrase "no good deed goes unpunished."[13] Priya's story of teaching a critical pedagogy exemplifies how critical work is often vilified for disrupting the status quo and exemplifies the extent to which the status quo will fight back against this disruption. More importantly, it serves as inspiration for how critical scholars can be successful if they have the fortitude to stand their ground and resist the attempted silencing of their voices!

Unfortunately, critical thinking not only faces rejection from the status quo, but also comes up against significant critiques from within its own community. **Jonathan Langdon** in his chapter, "'Costly Gestures,'" details how critiques also emanate from within critical discourses circles and the divisive force they create. This chapter caused me to reflect ever more deeply about my actions and words and their potential impacts–wanting to avoid participating in the kind of destructive force that he details.

For me, Jonathan's chapter touches the personal as I struggle with how I have critiqued my brother's work with charter schools. How do I navigate the spaces around how I see the world and the power plays that create the need for charter schools and how my brother views the world and his attempts to make it a better place. Appreciating the value and cost of both our beliefs is invaluable. I hope that in my deconstruction of charter schools and questioning the macro impact of their existence, I have not devalued the good work that my brother has done. Jonathan's chapter has helped me better understand the need to be cautious and considerate as I engage in these critiques–especially as they impact such valued relationships. His remarks about graduate student communities serve as a valuable insight that extends beyond the academy:

> Likewise, graduate student communities have much to gain from each other as the process of learning cannot simply be one of naïve uncriticality, where nothing is challenged and no re-articulation of ideas occurs. It is the timbre, the tone, and the manner in which these processes occur that is at stake here. In other words, as graduate students trained in the art of critical analysis, we must strive to achieve the complex balance between collaboration and criticality in order for real sites of mutual learning to emerge. (p. 160)

BEGINNINGS

This book for me is really a beginning and so, appropriately, this chapter does not end with a conclusion. By sharing how each author's contribution has impacted the way I think, behave and feel, I hope that this chapter opens up a myriad of emotional and intellectual spaces for the authors to impact you as well. This is, after all, the goal of *Rocking Your World*.

NOTES

[1] Some of these terms will be explored in more detail later in this chapter. Others will be talked about in detail by other authors.

[2] I recommend buying at least one of these term dictionaries as well as using Wikipedia which has the advantage of hot-linking between terms. I also bought a number of introductory texts. The ones I would most recommend are: *Introduction to Critical Theory: Horkheimer to Habermas* (Held, 1980), *Critical Theory Today: A User Friendly Guide* (Tyson, 1999) and *Critical Pedagogy Primer* (Kincheloe, 2004a).

[3] This theory was first put forth in Gardner's seminal book *Frames of Mind* (1983) in which he details how school success requires primarily only two of the many human intelligences–linguistic and logical-mathematical. His introduction of the idea that people exhibit an array of other intelligences–such as bodily-kinesthetic, musical and personal–has gained widespread acceptance among progressive educators.

[4] This renaming was done in the late 90's at New Hampton School. The name has been since changed back to a more traditional one (The Academic Support Program) although the philosophy remains similar.

[5] In no way should this statement be construed to imply that all African American male athletes struggle academically. However private school hierarchies are such that African American males who had demonstrated abilities to excel in traditional curricula went to more elite schools than the one at which I worked.

[6] I am indebted to Kincheloe's book *Multiple Intelligences Reconsidered* (2004b) for the specifics of this analysis. For those familiar with Gardner's work and interested in exploring how critical thinking intersects with educational practice, I strongly recommend this book as an accessible example.

[7] This conversation happened in a coffee shop in Montreal in response to my sharing of this reflection with Shirley. I have quoted her here because I believe she captures succinctly such an important point.

[8] For those not familiar with charter schools, they are public schools in the United States that "often have greater control of their budgets, greater discretion over hiring and staffing decisions, and greater opportunity to create innovative programs….[and] their practices can inspire and inform other school communities striving to ensure that all of their students, regardless of their race, ZIP code, learning differences, or home language, are successful learners capable of meeting high academic standards." (Charter high schools: Closing the achievement gap, 2008, p. 6) In this particular case South Boston Charter School is in an urban setting and works with a student population with historically low graduation and college matriculation rates relative to more wealthy suburban schools nearby.

[9] This understanding is particularly informed by my reading of Ellen Brantlinger's book *Dividing Classes: How the middle class negotiates and rationalizes school privilege* (2003). I highly recommend this book, along with Kozol's book *Savage Inequalities* (1992), to anyone wanting to learn more about the justification of unequal funding in American schools.

[10] Fortunately for me, the majority of my professors at McGill have expressed a different attitude. They have embraced the idea that I would be doing public scholarly work even in the midst of learning how such work should be done. They also reject the idea that my voice is not yet of value. For this I am tremendously grateful–there is enough self doubt from graduate students themselves without the academy adding to the cacophony of our own critical voices.

[11] Critical discourses also cry out against the devaluing of other marginalized discourses. Specifically, please see chapters in this volume by Priya Parmar, Brad Porfilio, and Noah De Lissovoy to see examples of how the academy actively devalues their critical scholarship even though they are credentialed in their status as professors.

[12] Given the topic at hand (the journey *into* critical discourse) it certainly seems an appropriate venue; yet, it would hardly be surprising if such a book were written by established scholars who had long ago learned the way.

[13] I owe this phrase to the headmaster of the school where I worked before beginning my graduate studies, Dr. Jeffrey Beedy. He would often remind our Leadership Team that even though a decision seemed right, it would not necessarily be popular. For example, whenever we chose not to expel a student because of extenuating circumstances that we believed warranted further consideration, we would inevitably be accused of favouritism.

REFERENCES

Bennett, T., Grossberg, L., Morris, M., & Williams, R. (2005). *New keywords: A revised vocabulary of culture and society.* Malden, MA: Blackwell Pub.

Brantlinger, E. (2003). *Dividing classes: How the middle class negotiates and rationalizes school advantage.* London: RoutledgeFalmer.

Charter high schools: Closing the achievement gap. (2008). Retrieved June 3, 2008, from http://www.ed.gov/admins/comm/choice/charterhs/report.pdf

Cyber-bullying root causes must be addressed. (2008, June 4). Montreal Gazette.

Freire, P. (1970). *Pedagogy of the oppressed.* New York: Herder and Herder.

Gardner, H. (1983). *Frames of mind: The theory of multiple intelligences.* New York: Basic Books.

Gramsci, A., Hoare, Q., & Nowell-Smith, G. (1971). *Selections from the prison notebooks of Antonio Gramsci* (1st ed.). New York: International Publishers.

Held, D. (1980). *Introduction to critical theory: Horkheimer to Habermas.* Berkeley: University of California Press.

Hooks, B. (1994). *Teaching to transgress: Education as the practice of freedom.* New York: Routledge.

Kincheloe, J. (2008). Critical pedagogy and the knowledge wars of the twenty-first century. *The International Journal of Critical Pedagogy.*

Kincheloe, J. L. (2004a). *Critical pedagogy primer.* New York: P. Lang.

Kincheloe, J. L. (2004b). *Multiple intelligences reconsidered.* New York: P. Lang.

Kozol, J. (1992). *Savage inequalities: Children in America's schools* (1st ed.). New York: HarperPerennial.

Payne, M. (Ed.). (1996). *A dictionary of cultural and critical theory.* Cornwall, UK: Blackwell Publishing Ltd.

QESBA Task Force. (2008). Towards empowerment, respect, and accountability: Report and recommendations on the impact of the Internet and related technologies on English public schools in Quebec. Retrieved June 8, from http://www.qesba.qc.ca/en/index.shtml

Tyson, L. (1999). *Critical theory today: A user-friendly guide.* New York: Garland Pub.

Williams, R. (1983). *Keywords: A vocabulary of culture and society* (Rev. ed.). London: Fontana.

Part II: **Exploring our past, negotiating our future**

ANDREA STERZUK

3. FROM BUFFALO PLAINS TO WHEAT FIELDS

Critical thinking in the Canadian prairies

BEGINNING AT THE BEGINNING

I grew up in a small town in the Canadian prairies. My father was a high school teacher, and my mother worked for a local business. While both my parents were born in Canada, their parents were White settler immigrants from Western and Eastern Europe. My parents were raised on farms close to small rural communities and chose a similar upbringing for my siblings and me. My brothers, sister, and I lived with my parents in a large house on the edge of our town. From my family's vegetable garden, I could look out across farmers' fields to where one of two railway lines entered my town. This railway line intersected with the other national railway on the south end of town; trains passing over this intersection produced a strange clickety-clack noise that frightened me when it woke me up in the night. This second railway ran alongside the string of grain elevators that divided my town in two. In the summer months, trains using this railway often prevented children from reaching the swimming pool located on the other side of the tracks. Unbeknownst to our parents, this obstacle often drove us to the dangerous pursuit of dragging our bicycles under railway cars that were being filled at the grain elevators. Grain elevators like the ones that figure so prominently in my childhood memories have now mostly disappeared from big sky country. Throughout my childhood days, however, they were a comfortable presence and as familiar to small town residents as the railways that connect one town to the next.

Just as I have used grain elevators and railways in these introductory anecdotes describing my small town childhood, this imagery is also used to represent the Canadian prairies on flags, coat of arms, license plates, and souvenirs. Viewed from a different angle, however, these agricultural symbols are also representative of another facet of Canadian history: colonialism.[1] As is the case in any colonial story, land settlement and development by newcomers in the Canadian prairies occurred at an enormous expense to Indigenous peoples living there. The arrival of the railway, and the agricultural expansion it allowed, is intertwined with the subjugation of Indigenous peoples. Indeed, the public execution of Louis Riel, Métis resistance leader, and the completion of the Canadian Pacific Railway coincided in the same month in 1885 (Bumsted, 2000). In the Canadian prairies, First Peoples were stripped of land as imperial institutions of domination such as the Royal Northwest Mounted Police were established. First Nations were confined to reserves, and White settlers acquired their seized land. Subsequently, First

A.H. Churchill (ed.), Rocking Your World: The Emotional Journey into Critical Discourses, 27–33.

Nations children were processed through a brutal machine of assimilation: the residential school system.[2] All of these acts shared the common goal of maintaining control and power of land and resources, land that has been farmed and settled by my family and other settlers in the Canadian prairies.

How have I come to reconcile the comforting symbols of my childhood with the role they play in the subjugation of Indigenous peoples? Developing critical consciousness has not been a simple process, and this journey is not one that is unique to me. I did not grow up understanding or thinking about colonialism, the power relations at play in the Canadian prairies, and the privileged position afforded to me as a White settler. Colonialism, and my complicit[3] role in it, is something that I have come to understand through conversations with friends, studies, research, jobs, observation, and by listening to those who are wiser. Changing my ways of viewing history, education, and social justice has taken time, personal investment, a reshaping of my own identity, and has affected my personal relationships and connections to my home province. These experiences have not always been easy but I am glad to have had them. Yet, like the others who share their stories in this book, I wonder how my journey into critical awareness might have been different if someone along the way had told me that things were most likely going to get a little messy or emotional, that this process is unavoidably bumpy. I choose to share my story because I hope that in doing so, it might help others make sense of their own experiences and understandings of critical theory and practice.

MY ENTRY INTO CRITICAL AWARENESS

I trained as a teacher in my home province and then taught French in schools in Western and Northern Canada before returning to university to begin my graduate studies and research in second language education. Looking back, my early teaching experiences might have been when I first started to become consciously aware of power imbalances in Canadian schools and to consider that it might be my responsibility as a teacher to interact purposively with that imbalance. I can remember hearing teachers talk about language and literacy deficits and the need for "early intervention" among certain groups of students, mainly Indigenous students, and feeling uncomfortable with the nature of these conversations. While I think I began to be aware of inequity in education during this time, I do not think I took action in any real way other than through my thoughts and observations.

After teaching and working in Western Canada, I made the move east to begin my graduate studies in education. I enrolled in a masters program in second language education but had no clear plan regarding my research goals. When I began my graduate courses, my observations from working as an elementary school teacher, coupled with my childhood experiences growing up in the Canadian prairies, led me to develop my interest in the experiences of Indigenous English-speaking children[4] in settler English classrooms. Initially, however, I thought of my research as descriptive; I would simply act as an observer, take note of the experiences of the students and record these findings in my study. My responsibility or role as a researcher would end there. This approach to research was what I found in the linguistic literature that I was using as my literature framework and, as a beginning researcher, I chose to follow this model.

It was while I was collecting data for my M.A. study that I began to realize that how I described my research in theoretical terms didn't actually match up with my goals as a researcher. I believe that this conflict arose from my observations of procedures and practices that discriminated against Indigenous English-speaking students and my lack of words and theory to make sense of what I was witnessing. Additionally, I began to feel a sense of urgency to create change and to use my research as a means of countering the inequity that I observed in the school where I was conducting my research. Yet, this desire to create change or to talk about injustices wasn't present in much of the sociolinguistics literature that I had been reading. I needed to know more about power, social justice, and inequity in education but didn't yet have words to describe what it was that I needed to learn.

This impasse began to be resolved during a qualitative research methods course that I took during my first semester of my Ph.D. studies. During a classroom discussion, a fellow student talked about critical pedagogy and research. I wasn't familiar with the authors she mentioned so, during a class break, I asked her for more information. This brief exchange was the starting point for me to begin to understand my research in a new way. My classmate provided me with the references for one or two articles. Reading these first articles, and others that I located once I knew what to look for, is what pushed me in the direction of critical research. While I have come to understand that I was intuitively addressing issues of power and institutional racism[5] in my early writing, it wasn't until I was exposed to critical theory that I began to have the words to address what I observed in my research.

This initial explosion of reading was followed by my enrolment in a course about critical issues in second language education which further exposed me to issues of power as they relate to minority language education. Yet, as my understanding of my research became more nuanced, the inner conflict I was experiencing grew as I attempted to reconcile my White settler identity with my research, new ideas, and changing beliefs. If this internal conflict had remained on the inside, I might have felt less shaken by the myriad of feelings that I was experiencing. Confronting the colonial history of my home province led me, however, into confrontations with family and friends. The prairie west's history is characterized by a hegemonic narrative of pioneer grit, and my new ideas disrupted this popular perception of prairie history. Looking back, it does not seem surprising, then, that my developing critical consciousness was met with resistance by others from my home province. Yet, at the time, I was ill prepared for this rocky period of my research and life.

RENEGOTIATING ME

As a child, I can remember being given new toys and playing obsessively with them for weeks on end. I think the same sort of behaviour occurs when I grapple with a new idea or concept in my academic life. Certainly, when I began to navigate issues of power in my research and writing, these ideas didn't remain within the margins of the books that I was reading. Instead, my emerging critical consciousness spilled over into my relationships and conversations with friends and family. In fact, it didn't just spill a little; it flooded my entire life.

The experiences that I am describing in this chapter are personal and, as I write, I am aware that while my stories are mine to share, it is not, however, my right to share the stories of others. As such, I choose not to describe explicitly the conflicts I experienced when my critical consciousness began to emerge. Rather, I will tell my story by describing my feelings when I began to realize that my journey was, however temporarily, creating distance between my loved ones and me. I call this distance temporary because it seems to me that there is a way to reconcile a change in one's identity and maintain or renovate personal relationships. Before further describing my experience with renegotiating self and my relationships it seems important to briefly describe how this distance was first created.

When I began to consider my complicit role in the colonialism that shapes my home province, I dealt with these ideas by entering into conversation with friends and family. This may seem, at first, like an odd choice. Why would I discuss potentially controversial topics with those who would seem most likely to be resistant to my changing ideas? Initially, I did not want to enter into academic conversations about institutional racism and colonialism with outsiders to my province. I believe that I was, in some way, attempting to respect the unwritten rule of my home province that dictates that discussions of privilege and power along race lines are not acceptable. Unfortunately, while I was engaging with my developing critical awareness that was fuelled by my reading, research, and university discussions, my friends and family were not necessarily travelling with me on the same journey. As such, for a number of years, conversations about what I was studying sometimes escalated into arguments ending in tears and angry words.

Inevitably, I began to choose carefully the individuals with whom I would talk about my developing ideas. Consciously choosing not to discuss the ideas and activities that filled up the majority of my waking hours created a distance between my loved ones and me. With so many topics of discussion being off limits, there were many facets of my identity that I could not access when I was in my home province or in long distance phone conversations. For a long time, I felt like a false version of myself in exchanges with family and friends; this created sadness and frustration for both them and me. Additionally, I was not entirely aware of why I was sometimes limiting my contact with them and, therefore, was unable to explain to them why I was guarded or absent. While I now understand this space as having been necessary for me in order to become comfortable with my critical consciousness, it seems that I created anger and confusion by negotiating this necessary distance. Fortunately, this need for space did not last forever. I am now secure enough in my ideas around privilege and power to be able to talk about them, not only in my academic work, but also with friends and family. This emerging sense of confidence in my critical awareness allows me to engage more fully in existing and new personal relationships.

EMERGING BUT STILL LEARNING

I do not understand critical awareness to be a goal or a product. Rather, I see the development of this consciousness as a process. As such, I still have thinking, reading, living, and talking to do so that I can continue to grow in my ideas. My understanding of this journey is that it does not occur inside classroom walls or between the covers of books and academic journals. In order to become comfortable with these new ideas and, subsequently, myself, I have found it necessary to engage in the world around me and to live out loud my new critical consciousness. In this manner, my ideas do not become static, and I can continue to be influenced by those who are also on this path towards understanding and interacting with issues of power.

I have recently moved back to the prairie provinces and am aware that this re-entry into my childhood world is bound to stir up emotions. Drawing on the confidence that grew out of my previous experiences with the emotional aspects of critical awareness, I feel better equipped to deal with the inevitable resistance that I will meet in this next chapter of my life. I do not mean to say that conflict or hostility is any less jarring each time it is lived. It is, however, comforting to know that I further develop my ideas and confidence each time that I step out into life with my thoughts and words.

As I have become more comfortable with my critical consciousness, so have my loved ones. I do not know if they are also moving towards a new awareness; I no longer push them to accept my ideas or beliefs. What has changed is that things are less bumpy between us when I discuss my work. My friends and family have accepted the changing nature of my identity and seem comfortable with my ideas, opinions, and strong will. I am thankful that we have negotiated a new way of interacting with one another and that the distance between us is no longer as vast as the prairies landscape that continues to link us. It is said, however, that change is the only constant. I am sure that there will continue to be periods of frustration when my academic and personal worlds collide with conflicting ideas. The difference between now and when I began to explore criticality is that I know that new awareness comes from those moments of conflict and that I emerge transformed from them as well.

BRACE YOURSELF

We all have different starting points in developing critical awareness. Some people are born understanding the need for social justice because their position in the world forces them, every day, to collide with inequity. Others can spend their entire lives blind to or ignoring these issues because their privilege allows them to operate comfortably in the world. Given that we all have different starting points, no one's journey towards criticality is the same and, therefore, there is no map that can be handed to assist someone who is moving towards developing critical awareness. I do believe, however, that we can learn from the stories of others, not just in developing critical awareness but in all facets of our lives. This belief in learning from stories is why I am thankful to be able to contribute to the stories shared in this volume of work. If even one person is able to take something from my story and apply it to their own process then the writing and sharing of my story has achieved the goal of contributing to change.

Given the unique nature of developing critical awareness, I have no words of wisdom to offer, but I can perhaps summarize some of the key lessons I have learned over the past few years. First of all, as the above title indicates, it is probably wise to brace yourself for the inevitable conflict and resulting emotions that will arise as you grapple with your critical awareness. I do not know why or when you will encounter these types of situations but I feel sure that if you are engaging in critical thought and conversation that you will have moments of emotional explosions, be they internal or in exchanges with those individuals with whom you surround yourself. My own experiences taught me that these uncomfortable moments are okay and that there is actually important growth that occurs. Brace yourself but do not attempt to avoid conflict because this is where the most powerful learning is likely to occur.

I have also learned that change cannot occur simply by reading and then willing myself to see things differently. This type of change is superficial at best and is easily cast off in the first uncomfortable social encounter when one's changing ideas do not match up with the ideas of others. For myself, it was important to travel, to talk to new people, to listen to others, to look inside myself and examine my own complicit role in colonialism and, probably most importantly, to learn to not be afraid to ask questions and look foolish. Admitting uncertainty or confusion to others often led to moments of understanding and allowed me to move along my process of developing critical awareness.

Finally, I think it is probably important to talk about the amount of time that it has taken for me to move towards this new way of understanding the world. My critical consciousness did not develop overnight but over the course of roughly ten years. The changes that occurred in my thinking affected my personal life. Had they occurred rapidly, I do not know if my personal relationships or my own sense of self could have remained intact. I am thankful, therefore, that this sort of work takes long-term investment. I think the importance of time and patience is another valuable lesson that I am learning in this process. Things may not seem instantly comfortable when I engage with a new idea but, with time, I relax into the new concept, and the uncomfortable feelings that I initially experience lessen or disappear.

Wherever you are on your journey to developing critical awareness, it's helpful to remember that there are others who are engaging with the same ideas as you. You can seek out allies in the pages of a book, in classrooms and on the streets around you. It's important to find support for yourself as you move along your process. Developing critical awareness is valuable work and doesn't simply contribute to your own life but can have an effect on the world around you. Whatever stage you are at and however you choose to contribute to this ongoing conversation, know that there are others experiencing these things too.

NOTES

[1] Colonialism in the Saskatchewan context refers to both the displacement and subjugation of Indigenous peoples by Settlers as well as the set of beliefs that is used to legitimize colonial systems. For further information on colonialism see Said (1978) and Smith (1999).

[2] Anglican, Catholic, Presbyterian, and United Churches operated residential schools in Canada for over 100 years. Thousands of Indigenous students were subjected to neglect and abuse in a system which strove to sever family relationships and "civilize" Indigenous children. For more information about the Canadian residential school system, see Milloy (1999).

[3] I describe myself as complicit in colonialism because, as a White settler, I benefit from the privilege afforded to me by the institutions in my province.

[4] The term *Indigenous English* refers to a variety of English (or a spectrum of English language varieties) that differs systematically from the Saskatchewan settler variety (varieties) in terms of lexical, morphological, syntactic, and phonological differences. Indigenous English-speaking students experience academic difficulties and discrimination in schools. For more information about Indigenous English see Sterzuk (2008).

[5] Institutional racism refers to policies and procedures, accepted as common practice, which discriminate against members of social groups which have been historically marginalized. For further reading about institutional racism in schools, see Delpit (1988).

REFERENCES

Bumsted, J. M. (2001). *Louis Riel v. Canada: The making of a rebel.* Winnipeg, MB: Great Plains Publications.

Delpit, L. (1988). The silenced dialogue: Power and pedagogy in educating other people's children. *Harvard Education Review, 58*(3), 280–298.

Milloy, J. (1999). *A national crime. The Canadian government and the residential school system 1879 to 1986.* Winnipeg: The University of Manitoba Press.

Smith, L. (1999). *Decolonizing methodologies: Research and indigenous peoples.* New York: St. Martin's Press, LLC.

Said, E. (1978). *Orientalism.* New York: Vintage.

Sterzuk, A. (2008). Whose English counts? Indigenous English in Saskatchewan schools. *McGill Journal of Education, 43*(1), 9–19.

ELIZABETH J. MEYER

4. I AM (NOT) A FEMINIST

Unplugging from the heterosexual matrix[1]

THE QUESTION

"This is a very male-oriented school, and we've had problems in the past with teachers who identify as feminists. Would you describe yourself in this way? How do you see yourself working in a male-oriented environment?"

I am not a feminist. Or so I thought when I was interviewed for my first teaching job in the winter of 1993. During my day long visit to a private boarding school in the mountains of upstate New York, I was asked these questions in one of my interviews. I was surprised by the questions, and I didn't know what the right answer would be. I had never really thought about it. The dean who posed these questions filled my puzzled silence by stating that she was a working mother who believed in equality, but did not identify as a feminist.

Following her cue, I echoed back that I was not a feminist and talked about my ability to work in a male-dominated environment since I grew up with two older brothers. She nodded in approval and went on to explain that they had difficulties in the past with feminist teachers who had created problems in the school community.

It seemed like an odd thing to discuss in a job interview, but I didn't think much more about it. I was 22, didn't have a teaching certificate and was anxious to land my first real job out of college.

This was one of many moments that played a role in my development of a critical consciousness. The following chapter outlines the key moments on my personal journey and my intellectual awakening. In crafting this chapter, I reflect on my privileged upbringing as well as the conflicts I endured during my teaching and graduate school experiences. The emotional crisis moments that occurred along this journey helped me develop a deeper understanding of critical theory that went beyond the intellectual. By sharing these moments here, I hope to help others develop a new understanding of the world they live in.

THE MATRIX

Growing up I always loved school and had done well there. I changed schools many times due to my father's job in the U.S. Air Force, so I was constantly the new kid who had to step back and find a way to fit in at the beginning of school every other year. I became quite a chameleon who was good at changing my clothes, speech patterns, and after school interests in order to blend in to my new

A.H. Churchill (ed.), Rocking Your World: The Emotional Journey into Critical Discourses, 35–44.

community. As a middle class white girl from a nuclear family with two educated parents, two cars, and 2.2 kids, I was pretty successful at blending in at any school I attended. I was a Campfire Girl in Maryland, a second baseman on my Little League team in Ohio, head cheerleader in Texas, an actress-singer-dancer at prep school in Connecticut, and a sorority girl at college in Louisiana. I got good grades. I joined clubs. Boys liked me. I was an all-American girl. Aside from a few bumps along the road, life was going to be a smooth ride–except something changed after my second year of college. I fell in love.

This love radically changed me and how I experienced the world. Marie[2] was a strong, outdoorsy, white, working class woman I met while working at a summer camp in New Hampshire. She challenged my thinking and views of the world in many ways. Initially, she hated me because I was a part of the clique of counselors who had spent many summers at that camp. We were loud, had endless inside jokes, and had deep connections with many of the families whose daughters summered there. We ran the place.

Marie was new and kept to herself. She lived nearby, but was from a different world. After a series of staff scheduling overlaps–life guarding, days off, and nights by the patrol fire–we eventually became friends. Over the course of two months, I had become fascinated with her outdoor skills and was touched by her painful life experiences and emotional strengths as I learned more about Marie and her world. She was a survivor of child sexual abuse. She was a member of the canine search and rescue team. She had been supporting herself since she was 17. Her life was so different from mine that I was forced to see the world in a new way. I admired her, respected her, and had fallen completely in love with her. I was also unbelievably freaked out about what that meant. I was terrified of being 'gay.' I started to see how privileged my life was when I saw how my life would change if I lost one aspect of it: my heterosexual privilege.

It took four months of exchanging long letters across the ocean while I was studying in France (this was in 1991 before email) for us to share our feelings with each other. We had vowed not to date anyone while we were apart, but didn't share a first kiss until 6 months later: New Year's Eve. We were together for almost a year before I could tell my family. In coming out to them, I was slowly coming out to myself, but I never used the words "gay," "lesbian," or "bisexual." I was simply in love with Marie.

I finished college a semester early to be with her. I was horrified with my life as a southern sorority girl and couldn't play the part anymore. I moved in with Marie in December of 1992 and got a job teaching skiing at a nearby resort in New Hampshire. We were finally together for real. Life was good–for a moment. It turned out we weren't ready for the realities and pressures of living in a small mountain town as a closeted same-sex couple. The relationship ended, and I moved out. I had not formulated an identity for myself as a lesbian, so I went back to dating men. I believed that Marie was an exception and, when that relationship was over, I returned to my expected heterosexuality.

I was looking to start a career, and I wanted to find a job at a boarding school similar to the one I had attended. What do you do with a BA in French? I figured I would try out teaching until I decided what I really wanted to do with my life. I found a placement agency that sent me to the mountains of upstate New York for the interview I mentioned at the beginning of my story. I got the job.

THE GATEKEEPERS

During my first few months working at Winter Mountain School,[3] I quickly learned why feminist teachers had "caused problems" there in the past. This was a small school of around 120 students that was 65% male. The school had three boys' hockey teams but none for girls. There were strong female athletes at the school, but most of them excelled in individual sports and had their own private coaches. The hockey culture dominated everything at the school, and although I am a huge hockey fan, I felt how the macho hockey ethos (which I now name as hegemonic masculinity[4]) silenced and marginalized other teachers and students. Ruby was one of them.

Ruby was a senior who had attended Winter Mountain for four years and was a leader in her class. I didn't have her in any of my classes, but it was a small school and she began seeking me out to talk. She loved to tell me about her recent summer experience on a wilderness expedition and the amazing friend she made over the summer. She told me about their long late-night conversations on the phone and how she missed her so much it hurt. She talked endlessly about her plans to visit her on the next vacation. I understood. It made me miss Marie. Her dorm-mates were starting to joke about her late night phone calls, and the boys were starting to harass her. They called her "rug-muncher," "muff-diver," "dyke." I did what I could to offer support, but I felt pretty helpless to change the negative repercussions she was feeling for falling in love with a girl.

One day, my boyfriend (and assistant coach for the varsity hockey team), John Spear,[5] showed me a copy of a newsletter that had arrived at the school library called *Speaking Out*. He and I had had many conversations about my relationship with Marie, and he was incredibly open and supportive. The newsletter was published by and for gay and lesbian teachers. I was intrigued. I was slowly developing a feminist consciousness in opposition to the culture of this über-macho school and wanted to do something for myself and for Ruby. John and I both decided to write articles for the next newsletter about how to support gay and lesbian students in the school. I wrote about how I shared with my students Melissa Etheridge's new album *Yes I am* and Rita Mae Brown novels such as *Venus Envy* and *Rubyfruit Jungle*. I also wrote about the recent play I directed that featured a lesbian and bisexual character due to my regendering[6] of roles. I framed the piece by reflecting on my hopes as a teacher: "I graduated from high school fairly ignorant of [gay] issues and was extremely homophobic. I'm hoping that as a teacher in a similar environment, I can save a few students from fumbling through the same frightening dark haze that obscured my soul for so many years" (Meyer, 1994). The article wasn't radical, but it was offering support by trying to reduce the feelings of isolation and invisibility that both Ruby and I felt. In a small town, before the internet, these representations were important to us both. It was what I could offer.

I began to take more risks as the school year went on, and I felt more confident in my position there. I had my contract renewed, and I was looking forward to returning the following year. That April, John and I attended a conference in Boston organized by the Gay, Lesbian, and Straight Teachers Network (GLSTN, now known as the Gay, Lesbian, and Straight Education Network, or GLSEN). This conference inspired me and filled me with ideas and opportunities for action. I was developing a more active political consciousness. I also was starting to recognize the potential I had as a teacher. I began to brainstorm ways that I could introduce some new ideas at Winter Mountain. Just a few weeks before graduation, Ruby was kicked out of school and sent home because a friend accused her of using her calling card without her permission. It was the final straw in a series of unfortunate events and she was forced to go home.

After Ruby's departure, the head of school ambushed me by calling me to his office on a Sunday afternoon in May when the school was deserted. I left that meeting shaking and confused. I had been fired. I was told I was losing my job over that newsletter article in which I had named the school where I worked, and had come out as bisexual. This had infuriated the headmaster. There were two weeks left in the school year, and I had to find a new place to live, a new job, and try to make sense out of what had just happened. I was furious. I was filled with self-righteousness. This is America. I'm going to sue. I wrote letters to GLSTN, the American Civil Liberties Union, The National Organization of Women, and Lambda Legal Defense Fund. I filed a complaint with the state labor board. I called lawyers in my family, cried to my parents and wrote letters to local newspapers about what had happened.

There was no massive call to action. No one rallied around a first year bisexual teacher losing her job.

THE REAL WORLD

That was the summer of 1994. It was also the summer of the 25th anniversary of the Stonewall Riots. The Gay Games were being celebrated at the same time in New York City. I followed my hurt and my anger to Manhattan and came storming out of the closet by joining the Lesbian Avengers. They met weekly on the top floor of The Gay, Lesbian, Bisexual and Transgender Community Centre. I had tried out several different community organizations that used the centre to meet, but I knew the minute I walked into that room I had found the group I was looking for. I was blown away by the strength and passion and knowledge of the women in this group. I learned about direct action campaigns: grassroots activism and the gay and lesbian community. I heard about frustrations between gays and lesbians, the division between ACT-UP and the Avengers, anger between white lesbians and lesbians of colour, misunderstandings between lesbians and transgender women, as well as the impacts of class divisions and linguistic barriers.

Injustice was more common than I thought. I had been carefully taught my entire life to believe in the myth of meritocracy[7]–that this country is one of endless opportunity and that if you lose your job or can't find housing or don't finish school, it is your individual failure. Did this mean I had failed? This was my crisis moment.

The world that I had been brought up in had disappeared. I was being forcibly ripped from my comfortable cocoon, and I couldn't crawl back in. Initially I fought hard to get back in. I liked the safety and the warmth of these walls, the glow of these lamps, the way the world looked from here. It was what I knew. I didn't want to lose that. I didn't want to know differently. But this crisis meant that I could no longer imagine that life was fair and that bad things only happened to bad people. So I finished the job myself: I fled my cocoon and plunged into the real world. As Ani Difranco sings, "some guy designed the room I'm standing in/another built it with his own tools/who says I like right angles?/these are not my laws/these are not my rules" (1992).

My middle class white girl woes were surprising only to me. My privilege had carefully protected me from this knowledge and kept these social realities invisible to me. My NYC Lesbian Avenger friends seemed to shake their heads and chuckle at my naïveté–was I the only one who had completely bought this "America, the beautiful" shit, hook, line, and sinker? I felt betrayed, duped, misled. What was all that crap about "the land of the free" and "all men are created equal?" Why aren't more people pissed off? Why did this have to happen *to* me for me to see what was always there? What about people with privilege who never experience overt discrimination? Will they forever remain plugged into the Matrix living the manufactured reality that is being pumped into them? Or is there a way to raise their consciousness? How do we get people to unplug when it is so painful?

I spent a year illegally wheatpasting city signposts, marching in the streets, participating in kiss-ins, and demonstrating in front of homophobic businesses in New York. I wore black leather and pierced my eyebrow. Was anybody listening? Did all of this public fury ever result in any long term change? I didn't know. I only knew that I had to know more, and this activist shit was draining me. I was sick of screaming myself hoarse on the streets, so I decided to "learn the code"[8] and work from within: I applied to graduate school.

TRAINING BEGINS

I fled the city and my activist angst and returned to the mountains for temporary relief. First, I taught wilderness medicine in Idaho, and then led adventure trips in Maine before landing in Boulder, Colorado to start a Master's degree in Social, Multicultural and Bilingual Foundations of Education. I was in my first semester of graduate school taking the obtusely titled course "Disciplined Inquiry" with Professor Margaret LeCompte when I first encountered the writings of Henry Giroux.

I had been suffering through my first semester of coursework dutifully digesting all the theory that was being thrown at me when I read Giroux's "Critical Theory and the Politics of Culture and Voice: Rethinking the discourse of educational research" (1986). Something changed when I read that article; it resonated with me. This was a scholar whose ideas got at what I had been struggling with. In my final standpoint paper for the course, I wrote:

> Henry Giroux's article on "Critical Theory and the Politics of Culture and Voice" was very exciting for me to read. It was the first article that I completely identified with and spoke to many of the ideas I had begun to formulate on my own. Acknowledging the fact that schools reinforce the oppression of society and the need to undo these structures was very reassuring to hear …. In short, I see myself as a post modern, critical theorist, lesbian feminist activist. How this came out of a traditional Air Force upbringing is still a puzzle to my family. I have experienced privilege in my life as well as discrimination. The combination of these forces is what drives me to understand and deconstruct the damaging structures of our culture. By virtue of my experience in the schools, I feel that education is one of the most powerful ways to reach people. (Meyer, 1995b, 8-9)

This class offered me the language and a body of work from which my emerging ideas could grow. It also forced me to go back and reflect on a course I had taken in my last semester of college for my B.A. in French: "Concepts of Literary Criticism." I was finally able to make some sense out of the theories of Jacques Derrida (1967/1986), Jacques Lacan (1957/1986), and Michel Foucault (1971/1986) that had baffled me back then by connecting them to Giroux's discussion of Bakhtin. I wrote "The common thread these writers develop is the idea of language as power …. The word is more powerful than the symbol or idea that it represents, so by controlling language, one can control the way people think and define the world around them" (Meyer, 1995b, p. 8).

I was grateful for the introduction to Giroux and other theorists such as Ann Fausto-Sterling (1981) and Evelyn Fox Keller (1978) who enriched my ideas about gender and feminist theory. I remember revisiting the feminist question with this class. One night when we were talking about issues of gender equity, I was getting frustrated with many of the students' comments and posed a question that had been posed to me in that first teaching interview: are a you feminist? In a class of 30 graduate students—predominantly female—only about five people (including the professor) raised their hands. I was so frustrated. Why didn't people get it? I got it. Partly. Mostly. Why can't they?

RADICAL THEORIES OF EDUCATION

The next semester I enrolled in another obtusely titled course "Radical Theories of Education" with Professor Dan Liston. I didn't know what we were going to study, but a classmate encouraged me to take it, so I signed up. It was great. I was so excited by the treatment of the topics of class, race, ethnicity, and gender that were presented on the syllabus. Did this make me radical? I wasn't sure. It seemed like a scary word, and I wasn't really sure what it meant. This was where I first encountered the work of Paulo Freire. I wrote about his discussion of banking versus problem posing education and praxis:

> One of the strongest points in *Pedagogy of the Oppressed* is Freire's discussion of these two opposite forms of education [banking and problem posing], and how productive problem posing education can be to achieving a truly liberated society. The concept of praxis, and stimulating creativity and reflection are very exciting ideas in the development of human beings. It can help reduce feelings of alienation by encouraging people to "transcend themselves, [and to] move forward and look ahead" (1970/1993, 65). (Meyer, 1996, p. 6)

I appreciated the theories studied and thrived on the class discussion, but was left wondering how all of these theories might talk about sexual orientation. Why did we never discuss homophobia? We were constantly grappling with racism, sexism, and classism, but the only time homophobia came up was if I made the connection, or Angela, the other lesbian in the class, asked the question. We read Michael Apple (1990), bell hooks (1994), Sandra Bartky (1990), Jonathan Kozol (1991) and talked about oppression, inequality, and systemic problems in capitalist schools. In this moment, I couldn't help but ask myself: why are these theories radical? What is it about equality, human rights, and valuing individual differences that is radical? Is radical a state of mind or a level of action? Can it be one without the other?

I wrote my Master's thesis on a philosophical topic hoping to force issues of sexual orientation into the academic discourse. My paper was titled "Equal Educational Opportunity for Sexual Minority Youth" (1997) and built on democratic theories of education[9] advanced by Amy Gutman (1987) and Ken Howe (1997). I had to cobble together an argument for inclusion of queer issues because very little information existed in academic scholarship on sexual orientation issues in education. I built on work by Eric Rofes (1989), James Sears (1992), Richard Friend (1993), and Art Lipkin (1995) and writings in popular media by Dan Woog (1995) and Kevin Jennings (1994) to support my arguments.

Unfortunately, ten years later, these ideas are still considered radical. Although my scholarship has evolved from a framework of gay and lesbian identity and experience to one informed by queer theory (see Jagose, 1996; Meyer, 2006, 2007; Sullivan, 2003), the realities in schools and classrooms haven't changed significantly. We still have to fight to include issues related to sexual orientation and gender identity in education courses and texts. The actions taken by the National Council for Accreditation of Teacher Education in 2006 to remove "social justice" and "sexual orientation" from their accreditation standards, and research on the under and misrepresentation of gay, lesbian, bisexual, and transgender issues in Foundations of Education texts are evidence of this ongoing struggle (Jennings & MacGillivray, 2007). My scholarship, as informed by my understandings of critical theory, hopes to contribute to meaningful social change.

FOLLOW THE WHITE RABBIT

In August of 1999, I got a phone call from Ruby. She'd had a rough patch after leaving Winter Mountain, but was proud to tell me that she was finishing college and had found a job in NYC. She told me how she really appreciated everything I had done that year and apologized for not helping me more in my legal case against the school. She told me about her girlfriend and said that I had saved her life that year. It was so rewarding to reconnect with her and know that she was well. Although I look back and feel that my actions then weren't "radical," they had impacted someone else's life for the better. For educators, even small acts of resistance can be radical.

I am a feminist. I am a radical queer scholar activist educator who is aware of the political nature of these labels. I know they scare some people. I know I might not get jobs because of what I am writing here, but I also know that I can't work where I'm not allowed to act responsibly in the face of oppression. We need to name things. We need to interrupt sexist, racist, and homophobic incidents when they occur. If we get mired down in the liberal humanist discourse of generic kindness and the "can't we all just get along" attitude, we will never be able to take apart and make visible the deeper structures that allow inequalities to persist. Just as Peggy McIntosh's work as a feminist trying to expose male privilege helped her learn to see white privilege (1988/2004), it was my loss of heterosexual privilege that forced me to swallow the red pill and build a new understanding of the world. This is the language and the strength that critical theory has given me. I am still in the process of learning to renegotiate the world and my place in it. I hope the story of my queer journey may help others to "unplug" and work against oppression in all its forms. Follow the white rabbit (Carroll, 1865; Wachowski & Wachowski, 1999).

NOTES

[1] See (Butler, 1990) for more on the concept of the Heterosexual Matrix.

[2] When first names only are used, a pseudonym has been provided. When last names are provided, they refer to the actual individual whose public scholarship or activism is relevant to the experiences shared here.

[3] Not the actual name of the school.

[4] The concept of hegemonic masculinity is taken from (Connell, 1995). He proposes that there are four main categories of masculinity: hegemonic, subordinate, complicit, and marginalized. Hegemonic masculinity is a form of culturally dominant masculinity that can shift and change depending on the relations involved. In North America, it often includes such characteristics as athleticism, hyper-heterosexuality, violence, and dominance. Please see (Woog, 1998) for more information on hockey and homophobia.

[5] John went on to become a key staff person in the Gay, Lesbian, and Straight Education Network and a national figure in its projects aimed at creating safer schools for all.

[6] I recast one of the male parts with a female actor due to the limited number of males interested in auditioning for the play and the amount of females interested in participating. This change made one character lesbian, and another bisexual.

7   A meritocracy is a society in which each individual earns his/her status due to his/her own efforts, without a connection to one's family or status at birth. This myth of meritocracy allows the financially successful in a democratic capitalist society to believe that they earned their place on the economic ladder on their own merit. It also perpetuates the elusive American dream: with hard work and initiative anyone can succeed. This myth allows those living in poverty to be blamed for their circumstances and allows society to ignore the impact of systemic factors such as sexism, racism, and classism on one's economic status.

8   This refers to Neo's learning how to maximize his impact on the world inside The Matrix by mastering the code (Wachowski & Wachowski, 1999).

9   Democratic theories of education argue for more equitable access to and outcomes from educational opportunities. These theories explore barriers and facilitators to academic success in public schools and argue for educational reforms that would more effectively "level the playing field" for all students in public schools.

REFERENCES

Apple, M. (1990). *Ideology and the curriculum.* New York: Routledge.

Bartky, S. (1990). *Femininity and domination: Studies in the phenomenology of oppression.* New York and London: Routledge.

Britzman, D. (2000). Precocious education. In S. Talburt & S. Steinberg (Eds.), *Thinking queer: Sexuality, culture, and education* (pp. 33–60). New York: Peter Lang.

Butler, J. (1990). *Gender trouble.* New York: Routledge Falmer.

Carroll, L. (1865). *Alice's adventures in wonderland.*

Connell, R. W. (1995). *Masculinities.* Sydney: Allen and Unwin.

Derrida, J. ([1967] 1986). Of grammatology. In H. Adams & L. Searle (Eds.), *Critical theory since 1965* (pp. 94–119). Tallahassee: University Presses of Florida.

Difranco, A. (1992). I'm no heroine. On *Imperfectly* [CD]. Buffalo, NY: Righteous Babe Records.

Fausto-Sterling, A. (1981). The myth of neutrality: Race, sex, and class in science. *Radical Teacher, 19,* 207–216.

Foucault, M. ([1971] 1986). The discourse on language. In H. Adams & L. Searle (Eds.), *Critical theory since 1965* (pp. 148–162). Tallahassee: University Presses of Florida.

Freire, P. (1970/1993). *Pedagogy of the oppressed.* New York: Continuum.

Friend, R. (1993). Choices, not closets: Heterosexism and homophobia in schools. In L. Weis & M. Fine (Eds.), *Beyond silenced voices: Class, race, and gender in United States schools* (pp. 209–235). Albany: State University of New York Press.

Giroux, H. (1986). Critical theory and the politics of culture and voice: Rethinking the discourse of educational research. *Journal of Thought, 21*(3), 84–105.

Gutman, A. (1987). *Democratic education.* Princeton, NJ: Princeton University Press.

Hooks, B. (1994). Love as the practice of freedom. In *Outlaw culture* (pp. 243–250). New York: Routledge.

Howe, K. (1997). *Understanding equal educational opportunity: Social justice and democracy in schooling.* New York: Teacher's College Press.

Jagose, A. (1996). *Queer theory: An introduction.* New York: New York University Press.

Jennings, K. (Ed.). (1994). *One teacher in 10.* Boston: Alyson Publications, Inc.

Jennings, T., & MacGillivray, I. (2007, April). *A content analysis exploring queer topics in foundations of education textbooks.* Paper presented at the annual meeting of the American Educational Research Association, Chicago, IL.

Keller, E. F. (1978). Gender and science. *Psychoanalysis and Contemporary Thought, 1*(3).

Kozol, J. (1991). *Savage inequalities.* New York: Crown.

Lacan, J. ([1957] 1986). The agency of the letter in the unconscious or reason since Freud. In H. Adams & L. Searle (Eds.), *Critical theory since 1965* (pp. 738–756). Tallahassee: University Presses of Florida.

Lipkin, A. (1995). The case for a gay and lesbian curriculum. In G. Unks (Ed.), *The gay teen* (pp. 31–52). New York: Routledge.

McIntosh, P. (1988/2004). White privilege and male privilege: A personal account of coming to see correspondence through work in women's studies. In J. F. Healey & E. O'Brien (Eds.), *Race, ethnicity, and gender* (pp. 295–301). London: Pine Forge Press.

Meyer, E. (1994). A comprehensive approach. In A. L. Chase, (Ed.), *Speaking out: A forum for sexual minority issues in the boarding school community, 2*(4), 10–11. San Francisco, CA: Independent Press.

Meyer, E. (1995a). Disciplined inquiry - Homework #2 (p. 9). Boulder, CO: University of Colorado.

Meyer, E. (1995b). Standpoint paper (p. 10). Boulder, CO: University of Colorado.

Meyer, E. (1996). Marxist analyses of schooling (p. 7). Boulder, CO: University of Colorado.

Meyer, E. (1997). *Equal educational opportunity for sexual minority youth.* Unpublished Masters Thesis, University of Colorado, Boulder.

Meyer, E. (2006). Gendered harassment in North America: School-based interventions for reducing homophobia and heterosexism. In C. Mitchell & F. Leach (Eds.), *Combating gender violence in and around schools* (pp. 43–50). UK: Trentham Books.

Meyer, E. (2007). But I'm not gay: What straight teachers need to know about queer theory. In N. Rodriguez & W. F. Pinar (Eds.), *Queering straight teachers* (pp. 1–17). New York: Peter Lang.

Rofes, E. (1989). Opening up the classroom closet: Responding to the educational needs of gay and lesbian youth. *Harvard Educational Review, 59,* 444–453.

Sears, J. (1991). Educators, homosexuality, and homosexual students: Are personal feelings related to professional beliefs? *Journal of Homosexuality, 22*(3–4), 29–79.

Sullivan, N. (2003). *A critical introduction to queer theory.* New York: New York University Press.

Wachowski, L., & Wachowski, A. (Writer) (1999). *The matrix* [Film]. USA: Warner Bros. Pictures.

Woog, D. (1995). *School's out: The impact of gay and lesbian issues on America's schools.* Boston: Alyson Publications.

Woog, D. (1998). *Jocks: True stories of America's gay male athletes.* Los Angeles: Alyson.

SANDRA CHANG-KREDL

5. "MY FUTURE SELF N' ME"

Currere and childhood fiction in education

"MY FUTURE SELF N' ME"

One episode of the animated television series South Park, "My Future Self n' Me" (originally aired December 4, 2002), resonates with my own memories of childhood.

In this episode, eight-year-old Stan's parents hire an actor from a company called Motivation Corp. to appear as Stan's future self in what is presented to Stan as a time warp. The actor plays a sloppily-dressed, paunch-bellied, unemployed, drug-addicted 32-year-old (with beer and cigarette constantly in tow) juxtaposed next to a pure, sharp-minded, and untainted Stan as child. Stan's parents use "Future Stan" (depicted as Loser Stan) as leverage to convince Stan that the only way to avoid this future is to study hard in school and to stay clear of drugs and alcohol.

Although presented in inflated cartoon style, Stan's predicament is not that far from many children's experiences (my own included) of being warned, "If you don't listen to us, you'll end up: a) in a bad job, b) unhealthy, c) a drug addict, d) generally unsuccessful"–or, in Future Stan's case, all of the above. After all, already being an adult is the angle that parents and teachers have over children.

FICTION AND MEMORIES

Many aspects of childhood can only be understood in its afterlife. But memories are, as Erica Rand (1995) describes, "notoriously unreliable" (p. 94). Adults tend to interpret their childhood memories in order to explain their present as a logical outgrowth in a "mixture of history and myth" (Rand, p. 114). However, accuracy– in this case, of childhood events–isn't always what matters. It's the transformations of childhood experiences into adult memories, and the complex relationship between the child self and the adult self that counts.

Fictional stories can be used as focal points through which to investigate one's memories and assumptions (Sumara and Davis, 1998; Gough, 1998). Goodson (1998) writes that "[a] story is never just a story"–stories are statements about beliefs and values and as such, they carry social and political messages (p. 12). They "inform the particular details of a life" (Strong-Wilson, 2008, p. 34). Stories also allow us to appreciate that our individual subjects are, in many ways, also collective subjects.

A.H. Churchill (ed.), Rocking Your World: The Emotional Journey into Critical Discourses, 45–52.

As a child, my daily life involved a regular dose of anxiety, not because of tangible threats such as war or physical suffering, but through an elusive sense that any wrong move carried the potential to thwart my future life. It may be that I was hardwired psychologically for gratuitous anxiety, or it may be that my experiences carried similarities to eight-year-old Stan's. The feeling that Stan had when his parents explained to him that "Loser Stan" could be his future self is one that I could connect to: as a child, I used to pick out random adults on the street and feel that jolt of fear that this could possibly be my future identity. It may have been the lower status job that the adult had, or the way the adult looked or dressed–either way, I defined that person based on cursory, external reference points. What happened was that I had absorbed the future-directed idea passed down to me that childhood was, first and foremost, a preparation for adulthood. And as a child, I understood adulthood through its most superficial features–the features that, as an adult, I would recognize as a person's "ascribed status or place in an established order," namely career, class status, and the like (Goodson, 1998, p. 4).

CURRERE: STORYING AN IDENTITY

Curriculum theorist William Pinar (2004) asks teachers and teacher educators to become "temporal," to live "simultaneously in the past, present, and future" (p. 4). Pinar developed the curriculum approach called *currere* ("the running, or lived experience, of the course"), which is an autobiographical method emphasizing "the significance of subjectivity" in the study and process of education (2004, p. 2).

I'll admit that I've always felt skeptical about autobiography as a method of research. Attempts at this work would leave me feeling exposed, vulnerable, and displayed, as well as seeming methodologically less than rigorous. But Andrew invited me to write a chapter in this book–a book of personal stories about what happens to us as we develop a more critical gaze. This persuaded me to return to *currere*, a concept which I had read about in my curriculum studies courses and, likely because I was approaching the concept with a purpose, I was won over this time around by the arguments presented by Pinar (2004), Grumet (1991), and many others (see Pinar's edited collection, 1998) who press for the use of self-study in developing critical thinking and practice in education.

The most compelling argument for me is that self-understanding and social change are necessarily dual processes. Pinar (2004) writes that "[t]he significance of subjectivity is not as a solipsistic retreat from the public sphere ... [t]he significance of subjectivity is that it is inseparable from the social" (p. 4). In other words, the autobiographical is the political: "complementary projects of self-mobilization for social reconstruction" (Pinar, p. 4).

For young people, the threat of future failure is a powerful motivating factor in schools: if you don't prove yourself in elementary school, you won't get into one of the "better" high schools, the "better" universities, the "better" tracks, the "better" neighbourhoods, etc. In this chapter, I examine how my childhood memories play themselves out in my adult years. As Faulkner (1951) famously wrote: "The past is never dead. It's not even past."

GROWING UP (OR BACK OR DOWN) AS A TEACHER

When I graduated with a Bachelor's degree in Education, I hurried to find a teaching position. The prospects weren't good in my province for elementary school positions so I decided to see what was available in early childhood settings– just for a short stint before moving on. I secured a teaching position at a daycare in an unfamiliar part of town. The experience was less than encouraging: children were herded in front of the television to watch episodes of Barney, then fed, diapered, put to bed, and cleaned up strategically right before pick-up. Understaffed, the director's brother would quiet the children down with his booming voice. As soon as the director discovered that I had a good hand at recreating cartoon figures, she pulled me out of the children's area and had me draw Sesame Street characters for the window display as promotion. I left after two months.

Then I took on a position at the daycare ("Centre de la Petite Enfance") in Concordia University's downtown campus, an early childhood setting that served faculty, staff, and students of the university community. The director hired exclusively teachers with Bachelor's degrees in Education. Affiliated with the university's Early Childhood Education program, Education students were placed in the centre for their teaching internships. I loved my job in this privileged, middle-class setting and happily dedicated four years to teaching three- and four-year-olds while getting started on a master's degree.

From there, I moved to a director position at Concordia's Loyola campus daycare, an equally advantaged setting, where my work focused on supervising teachers and strengthening a community of children, parents, and staff. Again, I was completely immersed and dedicated to my daily work.

Subsequently, I came to McGill to pursue my doctoral degree in Education. My experience of McGill is that having taught in high schools is well-received; having taught in elementary schools is received too; but let it slip that I was a daycare teacher and I'm greeted with patronizing nods of "oh, you were a daycare 'teacher'" as my audience conjured up images of spit-up, diapers, picture books, parks, crayons, stay-at-home moms, and ethnic nannies–you get the picture. Suddenly, time warp style, I was launched back into being an insecure eight-year-old seeing my current self (the daycare teacher/director) as my future Loser Self. Only in writing this chapter do I recognize, like a kick in the teeth, how I've adapted to my perception of McGill's culture by hiding my past, even managing to rig up my dissertation to conceal any links with the preschool years.

EXCAVATION

There are gaps in my story. On the one hand, I was content in my practice as a teacher and supervisor engaged in making a positive difference in children's, teachers', and parents' lives. On the other hand, I was anxiously motivated by my "ascribed status or place in an established order" (Goodson, 1998, p. 4)–as a child worried about my future career and as a doctoral student concerned about gaining legitimacy and respect in my discipline.

Referring again to the unreliability of memory, the stories we tell about ourselves change over time. The autobiography in *currere* is a person's account of "a particular point in time" but this account isn't fixed (Goodson, 1998, p. 11). Indeed, Grumet (1991) warns against writers reifying their autobiographical writings because "[w]hat is returned in the process of excavation is hardly the original experience" (p. 122). As I wrote earlier, it isn't the accuracy of my memories that matters; it's the pieces I try to fit together between childhood and adulthood that matter. It isn't through the autobiography that critical work happens; it's through the excavation of the autobiography, or what we do with the stories, that critical work happens (Grumet, 1991; Strong-Wilson, 2008). In these "spaces where the pieces [of my story] don't quite meet" (Grumet, p. 122), I need to pause and reflect on how I can readjust my memories in order to make sense of my present and imagine the future.

Memories are messy affairs: they get mixed up with messages from socially-prescribed value systems (status through class, gender, and race), from cultural representations surrounding us (including television, advertisements, and the internet), and from our close relationships with family, school, and friends. Part of the effectiveness of Pinar's method is in identifying and addressing the significance of subjectivity in one's memory work. What I recollect from my McGill experiences in response to my daycare experiences is a combination of (1) actual words people spoke to me and, perhaps more so, (2) my own projections of what I inferred they were thinking.

First, the attitudes which I gleaned directly from comments like "You're too qualified to work in daycare" and from unmistakably condescending looks, feed into a historical, political, and cultural context in which early childhood education is regarded as a "low-status exercise" (Steinberg & Kincheloe, 2004, p. 18). In academia, childhood has been regarded as a banal and transparent phase of life, without concealed ideological meanings worth digging up, and without the political agency of youth cultures. And in professional circles, the values of early childhood education assume that childhood settings should offer the atmosphere of exploration, language, and play, and to a large extent, and that women have no commitments in life beyond responding sensitively to children–values that are "grounded in notions of privilege and middle-class values" (Canella, 1998, p. 167).

Second, the attitudes that originate from my own discomfort and ambivalence in working as a daycare teacher (not truly separable from the more systemic attitude) warrant interrogating my complicity in perpetuating the devaluation of early childhood education. Returning to my identification with Future Stan, my upbringing had me set up to worry about my station in life. How was this message of Future Sandra imparted to me? Why was it given to me? How does it continue to colour my life? Anxiety has an important function in a being's life. It acts as a "signal of danger" (Freud, 1926), a signal that we need to protect ourselves from potential harms. I'll speculate that the harm signalled to me as a child was the threat of failure, of not living up to my potential or my predestined station in life– an effective motivating force. Parents and schools exploit such threats to rationalize the tedium of the typical school experience. Universities, too, thrive on students and faculty fearing they will fail to earn the best grades, fail to procure grants and publications, and fail to win prizes.

A critical disposition forces us to accept that the boundaries that we've believed to be essential are in fact negotiable. In my case, I'm forced to accept that I've been complicit in sustaining a value system that disenfranchises groups of children and their teachers through my ambivalent internalization of this belief system.

ON MOVING FROM THE PERSONAL TO THE PUBLIC

How do I "'relocate' personal experiences into public significance" (Strong-Wilson, 2008, p. 13)? How do I bring the past into the present in order to make a difference? As Boler (1999) cautions, self-reflection can easily "result in no measurable change or good to others or oneself" (p. 178). Knowing thyself isn't the golden key to thinking critically. Further, Grumet (1991) writes that "[w]e fail to distinguish the world we received as children from the one we are responsible to create as adults" (p. 79-80).

When I teach Education students about critical theory, I pose the Marshall McLuhan question: "Who discovered water?" and then I offer the old punch line that it probably wasn't a fish. Thinking critically has to do with removing oneself from one's fishbowl and identifying its contents, and in analysing its contents, "the attempt to understand culture has to include the way it shapes the critic's own consciousness" (Lasch, 1978, p. 16). In other words, cultural politics requires a "politics of the individual" (Lasch, 1978, p. 16). But, ontological and epistemological arguments aside, being critical isn't about having knowledge about criticality. Understanding that one's identity isn't necessarily about societal status isn't the difficult part; living it is.

That's where my contradictions or interstices lie: I can teach about critical theory and toss in fishbowl analogies, all the while unable to recognize how I refuted my own formative experiences as an early childhood teacher because they didn't rank high in the status range–as if it was possible to disown my own experiences, as if the past wouldn't continually hover over me.

Future Stan may have been a manipulative parenting ploy, but the idea of one's identity moving over time is helpful in understanding our conceptualizations of childhood. Metaphors of childhood impart powerful social messages about what to believe and value in children (Cooper, 2006) and, as I've tried to show, adults construct ideas about childhood through residues from their own childhoods and through well-established cultural images (see Jenkins, 1998). Constructed images of childhood frame our consciousness as teachers; any description of children "limits the possibilities that we as educators provide for them" (Canella, 1998, p. 158).

CHILDHOOD AND ADULTHOOD

We function as if there is a clearly demarcated threshold between two separate time-spaces called childhood and adulthood. Developmental stage theorists, such as Piaget (1965) and Kohlberg (1981) perpetuate the narrative of sequential and hierarchical development. But Rose (1984) argues that there is "no childhood which is simply over and done with ... neither childhood nor meaning can be pinned down–they shift, and our own identity with them" (p. 17-18). Time, by definition, is linear–it moves chronologically forward. But in another sense, time is more fluid than this: there are no barriers; everything washes into everything else. Perhaps our childhood(s) and adulthood(s) flow imperceptibly together and apart in the same dirty fishbowl.

Powrie (2005) defines heterospection as a "coinage which attempts to bring together issues of time and space" (p. 341). Referring specifically to films with child protagonists, heterospection describes the situation of the adult spectator viewing the child protagonist on screen as "a combination of dislocation in time and space" (p. 350), where adults relocate themselves into some past place amidst images of childhood: "being-adult while also being-child" (p. 350).

Galbraith (2001), like Pinar, examines how adults can return to and evaluate their own childhoods as part of a larger project to support actual children today without the oppressive forces we carry from our own burden of childhood experiences. By unearthing assumptions in our thinking about childhood, we can ask new questions: What other ways are there to conceptualize childhood (and adulthood)? How are our own childhoods implicated in our decisions to work with children?

WHERE TO, STAN?

As Andrew stated in chapter 2, this is a book about "renegotiating [one's] knowledge about the world and [one's] identity within it" (p. 13). In re-imagining future possibilities for my teacher identity, I'm drawn to Goodson's (1998) claim that identity is not about an ascribed status; rather, "identity is an ongoing project, most commonly an ongoing narrative project" (p. 4). Sumara and Davis (1998) speak of "unskinning" or "unfolding" boundaries as a means of renegotiating one's identity. Boundaries serve a function in understanding the world, but they are always without "clearly demarcated edges" (p. 83).

Pinar (2004) argues that too many of us in the field of Education are lost, asleep, and "too few seem to realize they are even asleep" (p. 3) (see Huebner, 1999; Silverman, 2000). In shaking us out of our complacency and comfort in maintaining the status quo, *currere* encourages teachers and teacher educators to "construct their own understandings of what it means to teach, to study, to become 'educated'" (Pinar, 2004, p. 2). Pinar asks that we take a regressive step, to re-enter the past, "to capture it as it was, and as it hovers over the present" (1976, p. 55).

If we don't take the time to reflect then we will continue to perpetuate ways of teaching that are romanticized but desperate and defensive rather than acknowledge the ambivalences and needs of early childhood teachers (Boldt et al., 2006).

Let me return to the South Park episode for a moment. It's difficult for me to separate my own story from stories I've read or watched. Indeed, writing my personal narrative for this chapter required prompting from a cartoon sequence of an eight-year-old boy confronting his supposed future self and uncovering the manipulative agenda imposed by the adults around him. When faced with the complementary projects of striving to understand oneself and of striving to act for social change (Pinar, 2004, p. 4), I respond by citing Rose (1984): "the only way out is … to go back (or down) in place and time" (p. 43).

Stan: Thanks for staying after school and tutoring me Butters.

Butters: Sure thing, Stan. But how come you care about school work all of a sudden?

Stan: I told you, I can't stand my future self. I have to do whatever I can to not become a loser like him.

Butters: Well, studying is the golden key to the imposing door of success.

Stan: I just can't stand having my future self around all the time. It's driving me crazy. Maybe if I get smarter I won't become him and I won't have to share my room.

"My Future Self n' Me," *South Park*

REFERENCES

Boldt, G. M., Salvio, P. M., & Taubman, P. M. (2006). Introduction. In G. M. Boldt & P. M. Salvio (Eds.), *Love's return: Psychoanalytic essays on childhood, teaching, and learning* (pp. 1–8). New York: Taylor & Francis Group.

Cannella, G. S. (1998). Early childhood education: A call for the construction of revolutionary images. In W. F. Pinar (Ed.), *Curriculum: Toward new identities* (pp. 157-185). New York: Garland Publishing.

Cooper, K. (2006). Beyond the binary: The cyclical nature of identity in education. *Journal of Curriculum Theorizing, 22*(3), 119–131.

Faulkner, W. (1951). *Requiem for a nun.* New York: Random House.

Galbraith, M. (2001). Hear my cry: A manifesto for an emancipatory childhood studies approach to children's literature. *The Lion and the Unicorn, 25*(2), 187–205.

Goodson, I. F. (1998). Storying the self: Life politics and the study of the teacher's life and work. In W. F. Pinar (Ed.), *Curriculum: Toward new identities* (pp. 3–20). New York: Garland Publishing.

Gough, N. (1998). Reflections and diffractions: Functions of fiction in curriculum inquiry. In W. F. Pinar (Ed.), *Curriculum: Toward new identities* (pp. 93–128). New York: Garland Publishing.

Grumet, M. (1991). Curriculum and the art of daily life. In G. Willis & W. H. Schubert (Eds.), *Reflections from the heart of educational inquiry: Understanding curriculum and teaching through the arts* (pp. 74–89). New York: State University of New York Press.

Jenkins, H. (1998). The innocent child and other modern myths. In *The children's culture reader.* New York: New York University Press.

Kamler, B. (2001). *Relocating the personal: A critical writing pedagogy.* Albany, NY: State University of New York Press.

Kohlberg, L. (1981). *The philosophy of moral development: Moral stages and the idea of justice.* San Francisco: Harper & Row.

Parker, T., & Stone, M. (Executive Producers). (2002, December 4). *South Park's "My future self n' me"* [Television broadcast]. New York: Comedy Central.

Piaget, J. (1965). *The moral judgement of the child.* New York: Free Press.

Powrie, P. (2005). Unfamiliar places: 'Heterospection' and recent French films on children. *Screen, 46*(3), 341–352.

Pinar, W. (1994). The method of *currere.* In W. Pinar (Ed.), *Autobiography, politics and sexuality: Essays in curriculum theory 1972–1992* (Vol. 9, pp. 19–27). New York: Peter Lang.

SANDRA CHANG-KREDL

Pitt, A. (2006). Mother love's education. In G. M. Boldt & P. M. Salvios (Eds.), *Love's return: Psychoanalytic essays on childhood, teaching, and learning* (pp. 65–86). New York: Taylor & Francis Group.

Rose, J. (1984). *The case of Peter Pan or the impossibility of children's culture*. London: Macmillan.

Steinberg, S., & Kincheloe, J. (Eds.). (2004). *Kinderculture: The corporate construction of childhood*. Boulder, CO: Westview Press.

Sumara, D. J., & Davis, B. (1998). In W. F. Pinar (Ed.), *Curriculum: Toward new identities* (pp. 93–128). New York: Garland Publishing.

Strong-Wilson, T. (2008). *Bringing memory forward: Storied remembrance in social justice education with teachers*. New York: Peter Lang.

Taubman, P. (2006). I love them to death. In G. M. Boldt & P. M. Salvios (Eds.), *Love's return: Psychoanalytic essays on childhood, teaching, and learning* (pp. 19–32). New York: Taylor & Francis Group.

ANIE DESAUTELS

6. WALKING BACK ALONG THE PATH

Using a self study of writing to appreciate the development of critical consciousness

INTRODUCTION

When I accepted a teaching job in the little Inuit village of Nunavik in the extreme North of Québec (Canada), I was already tired. I had been teaching in Asia for nearly six years and I suffered from an inexplicable heaviness of my whole being. I naïvely thought that maybe moving from a tropical climate to a land of snow would be invigorating and would chase away that strong feeling of stagnation. Children were beginning to appear all the same. Seeking solutions to problems did not spark my creative mind anymore. Even if I had read the latest revolutionary pedagogical discovery on multicultural education, my enthusiasm would not have ignited as it once did. Moreover, I worried that my teaching no longer benefited my students. Analogously, authors like Leah C. Fowler and Carola Conle described how in their career they had reached this stagnating stage where they seemed to "function very much on the surface only" (Conle, 1999, p. 9), where they were "no longer present in [their] teaching, so learning attenuated" (Fowler, 2006, p. 13). Anastasia Kamanos Gamelin referred to a similar experience as "contained desolation" (2005, p. 186).

The new challenges of my teaching position in the North motivated me for awhile but soon enough the motivation bubble deflated. I began to reconsider graduate studies, a project that I had previously abandoned. The goal of my university enrolment would be to revitalize my practice that had become dull and repetitive. The following year, after convincing my partner to move to Montréal and persuading a close friend and professor at McGill University to be my supervisor, the Master's degree phase of my career unfolded.

In this chapter, I propose to revisit the various texts I produced to fulfill graduate course requirements such as midterm and final papers. Through an analysis of texts I wrote during the academic year 2005-2006, it is possible to follow my progression towards a better understanding of critical theory. I search my texts for the emotions they illustrate or hide; I question bold affirmations; I try to understand the purpose of each piece. Juxtaposing these texts helps me to identify signs of a slow recovery from *contained desolation* and to understand how critical theory now impacts my ideas about education.

The interpretative methodology used here is inspired by my work in narrative inquiry[1] and the method of *currere*.[2] My task consists of a long process of writing,

A.H. Churchill (ed.), Rocking Your World: The Emotional Journey into Critical Discourses, 53–65.

rewriting and interpreting personal narratives of my teaching experiences with the intent of developing a "more generative and mindful pedagogy" (Fowler, 2006, p. 15). Required coursework and narrative writing differ, of course. The former rarely takes the form of complex narrative inquiry as suggested by Fowler (2006), in which the student writes several drafts of an analysis of recalled daily life events, always looking for deeper meanings. But revisiting, through an interpretative lens, a series of pieces written during a specific period (graduate studies) can provide insight regarding the development of a critical collective consciousness. The topics I chose, the positions I took, and the personal experiences I wove into my reflection texts, reviewed as a whole, are rich in meaning, especially while reflecting on the influence of critical theory on my life and how I participate in raising critical awareness. When I embarked on my journey into graduate studies, I wished to move beyond the listlessness of a forgetful living (Conle, 1999). Encountering critical pedagogy, curriculum theory and feminism through texts of inspiring authors such as Paulo Freire, William F. Pinar and Madeleine Grumet, I follow a path of ongoing introspection, seeking mindfulness. For this essay, I walk back along the path of work undertaken the previous year and understand how criticality rocked my world.

CONTEXT

As a full-time student, I decided to complete my course work during the first year and to write my thesis once I had returned to Nunavik after two semesters. I had chosen curriculum studies as my specialization and I selected related courses along with a mandatory methodology class.[3] Each professor had their own pedagogy, but in general they required one classroom presentation and one or two essays. Some asked for weekly reflections on the prescribed readings. One collected a portfolio of our best work at the end of the semester.

Upon the completion of my course work and my subsequent return to the North, I engaged in a narrative inquiry of my experience as a primary school teacher in an Inuit school, that I intend to present as my Master's thesis. I took with me all the documentation I had gathered the previous year. I found my course work nicely filed with my class notes according to course name. Since every piece was dated, I could easily determine a chronological order of production, though, the date of a given piece did not matter as much as the concurrence of my courses. Ideas discussed in one class appeared in an essay for another class, course pack references from one professor found their way into a presentation for another professor. The readings I did and the discussions I had with my peers and professors greatly influenced what came out in my class work. Unfortunately, although it would be interesting, it is beyond the scope of this essay to do a detailed comparative analysis of how the thoughts of other authors slither into my argumentation. I shall, however, refer to certain readings when necessary. These were either required readings by my professors or references I needed for my essays and presentations.

Although I tend to view my graduate education globally in terms of what I get out of the experience as a whole, there is a clear progression of my critical views from the moment I began my studies up to the presentation of a final project in my last class. Studying my texts, I am able to identify three phases: distance and denial of responsibility; passionate criticism of myself; and a quest for a balanced and thoughtful criticality. These categories are not clear sequential blocks with a beginning and an end. Rather, they are like three currents of emotional struggle, one blending into another for a time, but then gradually evolving into something else.

DISTANCE AND DENIAL OF RESPONSIBILITY

The very first requested text was a weekly critical reflection on course readings. My fingers stumbled clumsily on my keyboard; I was unsure about what was expected from me. By the second and the third texts, though, I had developed a systematic method of writing: I used topic sentences of the article or the chapter to summarize the text; then, I related it to my experience in some way; and I ended with some questions (my professor insisted that we end our texts with a *critical* question–I did not know what she meant but she seemed to like my work). This writing process fostered a superficial kind of reflection. As illustrated in this excerpt, typical of these assignments, I rarely questioned myself or my practice:

> It is possible to train new teachers; but, how to encourage more traditional ones to change what they have been doing for 20 years? How about directors and the demanding school board? And let's not forget the significant resistance to change coming from the parents. They went to school in the *good old days*, how can we convince them that teachers are not lazy public servants always demanding more money for less work, i.e. less red pen marking? How can we push the education milieu to embrace change?

I inquired about how to change the others. I am not a new teacher; I have not been teaching for two decades, nor am I an administrator or a parent. I could disingenuously conclude from that reflection piece that I am the victim of those who refuse to change and of the educational milieu, never questioning my own behaviour in reaction to change.

When I begun my graduate studies, I wished to research *on* [*sic*] a Burmese tribe, the Karen, living in a refugee camp where I had worked. My supervisor handed me a book from Linda Tuhiwai Smith titled *Decolonizing Methodologies* (1999). I believe that it is the first critical text that tickled me in my sleepwalking state of mind. As a result, in one of my classes I chose that book for a presentation and I wrote a midterm paper on the subject. Since my thesis project was still being developed, in the paper, I summarized Tuhiwai Smith's volume along with similar articles and I agreed that I should follow the author's recommendations. At the end of each section, I tried to link the reported information to my Karen project. But as I moved forward in the essay, I drew fewer and fewer parallels with my project. The last section ended on a single impersonal sentence in which I was completely absent: "Doing research with indigenous groups is complex and requires reflection for any non-indigenous researchers." Tuhiwai Smith is severely critical of research done with indigenous groups. She discussed ethical issues in research, values and culture and colonialism. Yet, I am unable in the midterm paper to explain in which way this concerns me directly. I simply agreed with the author having difficulty understanding the immense engagement that my project would require.[4] The need for reflection alluded to in this quote is a recurrent argument that will be discussed later.

In the first semester, I submitted three final papers all very alike in their denial of personal responsibility. One was a severe criticism of the Québec Policy Statement on Educational Integration and Intercultural Education (Ministère de l'Éducation, 1998). At the time, as a research assistant, I was working on a research project related to that policy, and I thought that the professors involved could use an analysis of the implementation plan. I concluded that this important policy was nothing but a facade; it was never really meant to be implemented thoroughly. Quite exhaustive and meticulous, that essay is of traditional structure, using discourse analysis. I tried to avoid any explicit expression of my opinion. Just as I did in my short reflection pieces, I disapproved of the educational system, in this case at the policy level, without investigating the impact in my classroom and on my practice of such a system.

Another final essay that semester appears to be more personal because I reviewed some aspects of my previous teaching experience in an Inuit school. Reflecting on several pedagogical problems I had experienced, I tried to understand them. There, I made an effort to portray sound pedagogical skills fulfilling stereotypical expectations of what a *good* teacher should do. I even wrote that I taught the "principles of democracy" (but never did). As the analysis of my teaching difficulties progressed in the essay, I increasingly blamed my students. One key cause of my troubles was apparently my pupils' lack of proficiency in their mother tongue. They had been schooled in their language from kindergarten to grade 3 and had received sporadic lessons during the following years by what I judged were incompetent Inuit teachers. I so deeply believed that the source of all struggles was a language proficiency problem that I even supported my point with a fictitious story about a student not being able to translate a simple text. I almost never questioned my pedagogy and my teaching views in that essay. I preferred sentences such as: "Rarely had I encountered such resistance to any form of literacy tasks. Even my interactive writing activities that had once been so popular in my other classes were a total failure in [that school]." I affirmed my competency as a teacher, refraining from challenging how I engaged pedagogically with my students.

The conclusion of that essay strongly expressed my denial of responsibility. The program provided by the school board, I claimed, was inappropriate: students did not master their mother tongue and had low self-esteem; they had no creativity because they learned by listening and watching; and the Inuit teachers were not *properly* trained. I barely discussed issues of culture and values and I certainly did not question my position as a non-Inuk. For my final comment I used a quote from

Annahatak (1994), an Inuit scholar: "My biggest concern is trying to find appropriate schooling to revive students' initiative in learning and living" (p. 16). I added: "I guess one day I will have to go back because now I know that there is more to this land than rocks and more rocks, and snow and more snow. There are children who struggle to understand the current changes in their society." I did not seem ready to see that I had been involved in those changes, that my presence as a non-Inuk had been part of the problem and of the solution, that my supposedly so wonderful teaching methodology might have been inappropriate, and so on.

My first reaction to critical theory was to distance myself from educational problems and to deny that I had a certain responsibility for the difficulties I was condemning. I blamed my students (who were lacking this or that), my colleagues (who were refusing to change, being too old-school or immature), school administrations and governments (who were incapable of understanding my needs, who were being too bureaucratic, too greedy, too fond of useless policies). This first phase in my encounter with critical theory is characterized by the acknowledgement of various discrimination and inequity issues, but a refusal to, at least publicly through coursework, investigate my role in educational problems. As I learned more about topics like curriculum theory, gender issues, endangered cultures and critical pedagogy, a second movement emerged from my texts: I began to acknowledge critical issues around me.

PASSIONATE CRITICISM OF MYSELF

The second phase I noticed in my coursework encompasses presentation and papers suggesting a contrasting view in comparison with the one I just described. Indeed, my standpoint had shifted; I was no longer distant and in denial. I began to continuously blame myself for the misery of the world. Paulo Freire's *Pedagogy of the Oppressed* (2000) brought upon emotions of guilt and shame. I am White, heterosexual, not poor and not disadvantaged in any way; I am, therefore, necessarily oppressing someone, somewhere, in some way. This translated into an overly passionate discourse about any type of discrimination. It was as if I was trying to compensate for my painful culpability by loudly denouncing any injustices, inequities, derogatory comments, racism, homophobia, etc.

Classroom presentations were about Henry Giroux's (1990) critical view on textual authority and about endangered indigenous languages. I also challenged one of my professors who revered Paulo Freire with a presentation of a critical perspective on the *Pedagogy of the Oppressed* elaborated by an Indigenous author (Rasmussen, 2001). I saw criticality even within criticality. There was an urge to show all available witnesses that I was passionately fighting for social justice, if not in action, in words at least.

The work I then produced exposed the discovery of my personal stories as a source of knowledge. I was introduced to various aspects of interpretive inquiry, the method of *currere* (Pinar, 1994) and to Madeleine Grumet's work (1988, 1991). Suddenly, I realized daily events retold effectively could be analyzed and more importantly could become graded essays if presented along with the appropriate theory. Eber Hampton (1995) was a revelation, and I quoted him in every text I wrote:

> Memory comes before knowledge .... Every person's life contains experiences and memories of these experiences. The way it works for me is that I forget those things until I unwrap them, until I actually roll out the sacred medicine bundle of my life and look at those memories. I pick them up and touch them and feel them. And each memory gives me knowledge. (p. 53)

Hence, I used and reused a series of short and concise stories based on childhood memories to discuss issues of othering, altruism, and whiteness. My peers and my professors congratulated my powerful narratives. I was proud of my stories. Once a story was edited, I did not dare to alter it, nor seek alternative meanings other than the one I had first assigned to it. I tended to reify my texts (Pinar 1994, Conle 1999). Moreover, at the time, I awkwardly manipulated the necessary theoretical framework, and I had difficulty completing rich analyses of stories. Professors' comments on my work underlined a certain superficiality of my arguments. The following examples illustrate these characteristics.

Altruism was the subject of a mid-term paper in which I reviewed some childhood memories of what appeared to be altruistic gestures. The argumentation, however, was not an effort to understand compassion, but rather to demonstrate how these stories hid other motives–such as a need for public recognition, a taste for competition and a need to please my parents. I explained that there was much to learn from my narratives when in fact I was working on discrediting the events I was retelling. The whole exercise served only to allow myself to reprehend myself for being an oppressor in a Freirean sense and to portray my incapacity to engage in altruistic action. Moreover, I did not reach an enriching conclusion; I simply encouraged people to reflect on their life in general. "Only a thorough self-reflection on their status and their contribution to the dominating system can lead oppressors to truly want to challenge the unjust social order in which they live." But then, in a rather confusing manner, I inferred that the oppressed group is responsible for the needed transformative action: "... it would be a contradiction if the oppressor would initiate and execute the transformation without the oppressed group being trusted and at the lead of the operating change." In the last paragraph, I systematically summarized the essay as follows:

> From my juxtaposed childhood memories clearly emerge the impact of the dominating values internalized at a young age. In events that appeared altruistic, I fostered standards of social appreciation and competition. My desire to outshine others and my need for my father's approval tainted my actions that were no longer selfless. Through stories, I questioned my altruistic behavior and used Freire's ideas to explain hidden motives.

The problem is that I accusingly questioned my childhood memories but I did not make fruitful connections with my present situation. I never explained what I understood through the exercise that would potentially affect my way of being today.

This need for self-reflection appeared repetitively in my conclusions. In another paper, once again using childhood memories, I discussed relationships with the Other.[5] I exhibited various situations in which I encountered the Other as a child. The whole essay is based on a powerful article by David G. Smith (1996). In the last part of the essay I maintained:

> [T]o identify the Other as a negation of my Self as I did in the introduction is a futile duality. As exposed in my narratives, my identity is a construct of my encounters with the Other. If a new Self is created by the merging of the Self and the Other, the Other still remains a different entity.

I failed to see, however, that we are also the construction of our relationship with the non-Other, the private, the personal (Grumet, 1988). The main conclusion was once again about introspection: "Without a thorough analysis of these relations [between Self and Other], my presence in class could only make the Other more racially and culturally alienated." Nowhere in the essay did I manifest a significant engagement in that reflection. I did not suggest desirable action to take nor did I indicate the impact of the essay on my relationships with the Other. Reflection in and of itself seemed to be the magical remedy. Indications of possible directions the reflection should take and details of what I believed was worth reflecting upon were absent from all my work in that phase. It was as if simply advising reflection was enough to prove my growth through the writing of those essays.

My experience in an Inuit village in Québec is revisited in another paper. Compared with the previous essay discussing teaching Inuit students, this text avoided criticizing the students and their environment. In this second essay, I no longer blamed the Others and the system; I was the only one responsible for what I considered to be a total failure. Freire's work was the theoretical framework that brought me to analyze concepts of race and marginalization of difference. I condemned myself for not understanding the Inuit culture and for naïvely imposing my Western ideas about education. In an effort to compensate for the horrible picture of myself I was depicting, I told a few success stories in which I looked conscientious and professional. As for the other texts from that phase, I referred to Tompkins (1998), who worked in Inuit villages, to once more insist that I must cogitate over my values and my beliefs: "[T]here is this mandatory reflection prior to any involvement with native communities." Despite the fact that my advice about reflection had become more nuanced, I remained vague about the outcomes of my new understanding and how it could lead me to engage in transformative action.[6]

During this phase of passionate criticism of my self, I was very outspoken about any situation that I judged unfair and unethical. Moreover, I saw everything I had done before I understood critical theory as wrong and harmful. This self-flagellation was a reaction to a new understanding of critical theory. I was no longer an observer of the society and making criticism; I had realized my role as a member of institutions (schools in this case) who perpetuate an established order that is insidiously unjust. I felt overwhelmed by the task of becoming an agent of social reform. Advocating personal reflection and expressing loud criticism was a catharsis of some of the inner struggle I experienced.

Then, my coursework began to lay out perspectives progressing towards a more thoughtful ideal. The next comment was a response to a few quotes presented in class regarding the study of lived experiences. It announced that I was moving away from the passionate criticism of myself and engaging in a new kind of reflection:

> Understanding, knowing, thinking, learning, thoughtfulness. My mind is running like runners at the Olympics. Always thinking and rethinking about what I should be thinking. How do I get influenced? What do I choose to believe? How much really changes when I understand something I previously did not understand? Reflecting on what I do is a full time job! The danger is to reflect to a point where one loses track of reality. My recent encounter with Critical Pedagogy and Curriculum Theory was like a bomb in my flower scented bubbly bathtub. It led me to believe that everything in my life has become *critical*. There is racism in every public place, jokes turn into derogatory remarks, doubtful gestures are discriminations and everyone seems to have a Machiavellian hidden agenda. How can I find a desirable balance between reflection and *Zen living*?

The tension was clear and I sought a way to reach calmer waters, a contemplative stability of the mind. I did not want to return to the denial of responsibility, but I also wanted to reduce the exaggerated intensity of my reactions to social injustice. Zen living represents for me the finding of an inner peace which is empowering and which can support my desire to make this world a better place.

A QUEST FOR A BALANCED AND THOUGHTFUL CRITICALITY

Studying interpretive inquiry research methods, I encountered an alternative manner to reveal meaning. Unwrapping childhood memories was a debut in interpreting experiences, but I still had to learn how to use those interpretations to make meaningful changes. A methodology professor required that I explain the beliefs I brought to the study and how these beliefs might affect my work. My answer in a memo projected my changing opinions on the need for reflection and personal growth:

> Since I was a teenager, I have strongly believed that a fulfilling life can only be lived when someone strives to improve themselves. I always question what I do and how I could have done better. Honesty with myself is a key component in this process of becoming a better person .... [However,] sometimes this idea of *always wanting to improve* turns into *wanting more* and prevents me from being content with what I have achieved so far in terms of personal betterment.

I call this third phase a quest for a balanced and thoughtful criticality because it is an ongoing process in which I look for equilibrium between expressing criticism and effective introspection. I previously advocated contemplation but I never presented examples of my own self-study. I denounced difficulties and often blamed myself for them, but I did not suggest how I personally could do things differently. In a thoughtful criticality, though, inner peace emerges and allows genuine caring.

For instance, in a short reflection on required course readings, I describe my present teacher self using three sculptures of a woman. My concluding questions engage the reader in self-reflective work much like I now do myself. Here is an excerpt:

Voluptuous *nanas* in colourful lingerie move graciously with Nikki de Saint-Phalle. Their breasts swollen, ready to burst are the ultimate symbol of nurturing children. The learning souls seek abundance near me. The vibrant colors dance on the nana's body and fascinate the young eyes. Dynamism and joyfulness is the air, I wish to exhale. The women covered by cartoonish corsets unveil an inviting vulnerability.

Set in hard stone, barely emerging, Henry Moore's reclining woman complies in an immutable comfort pupils can lean on, sit on, stand on, dance on. The teacher in an infinite patience will support the children, providing them with a strong and reliable place to grow. The authority of the stone will set the framework, like landmarks, that children find so reassuring.

The muse of Brancusi observes with her wide eyes. Her head heavy with wisdom and ideas must be held with the left hand of creation. She shares her knowledge and explores with her students. She observes and adapts her message to each individual. Left alone, she worries about her children, do they need me? She offers her entire Self to education; nothing remains but the head and the creation.

These three women are part of a unique self: me. The abundance, the pleasure, the stability, the patience, the wisdom, the caring. The analysis of these works of art leads to a confronting conclusion: as a teacher, I am the mother figure in its most patriarchal[7] definition. This exercise now requests questioning over this mother-teacher role that I so easily slip into although I never longed to carry an infant. Is it the repression of a desire or rather, that my motherly impulses are fulfilled in a classroom setting? Could it be that I wish to re-enact a blissful childhood in which my own mother was an important actress? Am I reproducing a female tradition dictated by male power or am I embracing and celebrating motherhood? Moreover, is this mother-teacher model empowering me and more significantly, am I empowering my pupils with this nurturing behaviour?

In this text, I described the various aspects of my teaching self and that led me to recognize that I portrayed myself as a mother teacher. I drew connections with patriarchy, and I questioned how that image affected my teaching and my students.

It was not in the scope of that assignment to directly answer the critical questions on paper, but these were used to fuel class discussions. Nevertheless, it shows that I was not simply denouncing an issue and that I was profoundly involved in seeking deeper understanding about my motherly practice and my role in reinforcing patriarchal models.

Reading about curriculum theory, I was encouraged to investigate how the private aspects of my life affected how and what I taught (Grumet, 1988). In class, we had discussed the meaning of how we chose to dress in response to readings from Weber and Mitchell's book *Not just any dress: Narratives of memory, body & identity* (2005). That evening, I meditated on how I wished others would perceive me and how I would dress accordingly. I wrote an essay on the significance of colourful shawls I regularly wear:

> When I got up that morning I knew I would wear my red cashmere shawl. I was doing an important presentation on the situation of endangered languages as part of a graduate course. My focus was on the poor state of the First Nations, Inuit and Métis languages in Canada. Red called for urgency. I wanted the audience to be awakened to the fate of indigenous languages and cultures. The simple flowers embroidered on the shawl could remind someone of First Nations leather embroidery although the piece came from Pakistan. That added to the seriousness of my argument .... I wrapped myself in it, covering my entire upper body; I was suddenly wide and imposing, just like a powerful mother. I had authority, people had to listen.

The essay continues on, deconstructing several meanings I attributed to my shawls. I wondered what my shawls could invoke, how they represented my identity, my character, and my mood. Through that text I looked into the meaning of appearances and how my clothing triggered responses from the people around me. This kind of reflective process is beyond simply condemning opinions based on appearances; it fosters a productive reflection that is simultaneously personal as well as connected to its context in the interest of eventual transformative action.

A text I wrote on images of the First Nation, Inuit and Métis (FNIM) people is also representative of this third phase. I finally abandoned disjointed stories of childhood memories and found an effective way to weave in my experience to illustrate my opinions. I maintained that our identity construction depends on the images surrounding us. I did more than just encourage the readers to reflect; I took them through a reflection on false stereotypical images, homogeneity of FNIM images, their fixity, and the romanticized aspect of the FNIM culture. The conclusion was based on Freire's request for solidarity with our students. I wrote:

> The need to question my preconceived ideas concerning the First Nations, the Inuit and the Métis cultures motivated the elaboration of this essay. I believe that a profound reflection on the evolution of my identity is necessary to understand the curriculum baggage I bring into my classroom. Reading Paulo Freire reinforced my conviction of the necessity for the establishment of meaningful and liberatory collaboration between my students and me. If I carry the non-Native colonizing past, my Inuit students suffer from the

consequences of sustained oppression .... This act of love [suggested by Freire] can only happen if I work to deconstruct stereotypes of the First Nations, the Inuit and the Métis living in my mind and to circumvent romanticism about Indigenous cultures.

In this essay, I was clearer about the discursive ideas I now adhere to, and I engaged in a discussion about the FNIM images that forced me to re-evaluate elements of my teaching practice. After several rewritings, this text was published (Desautels, 2007) and will hopefully have as much critical influence as a text can be expected to have.

LAST THOUGHTS

The quest for thoughtful criticism is the consequence of first denying my role in changing our world and then passionately criticizing my environment and myself. It is also an outcome of my effort to move away from that feeling of stagnation I had in my most recent years of teaching. I notice a peaceful atmosphere in my latest texts. They are still very novice scholarly papers but they reflect my progress towards that inner peace necessary for any social engagement. Teaching, after all, is about caring for human beings and their experience of the world. Critical theory did rock my world, but now I seek still waters, so I can paddle effectively towards a world of justice and love.

ACKNOWLEDGEMENTS

I wish to thank Mela Sarkar and Frances Helyar for their help in editing this essay. Their friendship is precious. I also take the opportunity to thank the professors who have crossed my path and guided me towards a generative practice of teaching.

NOTES

[1] Narrative inquiry is based on the view that human beings, individually or socially, shape "their daily lives by stories of who they and others are and as they interpret their past in terms of these stories." (Clandinin et al., 2007). People leading storied lives, through narrative inquiry, study how they experience the world. Jean D. Clandinin and Michael F. Connelly are the pioneers of the field (see their 1990 article in the *Educational Researcher* for a concise overview of their work). The contribution of researchers like Fowler (2006) and Conle (1999, 2000) is significant specifically for the methodology of personal narrative inquiry (as opposed to the study of other people's narratives). Stephen Crites (1971) presented a crucial essay on *The Quality of Experience*, and *The Method of Currere* by William F. Pinar (1994) is also an important pillar of narrative inquiry along with Gadamer's concepts of hermeneutics (1975).

[2] The method of *currere* is the study of educational experience as explained by Pinar (1994). Individuals are encouraged to review their past experiences, to relate these to a possible future in order to understand their present situation and their actions. Ultimately, individuals through this process seek to understand relations between curriculum of institutions such as schools and life history in the interest of self understanding and social reconstruction.

[3] The courses were entitled: "Seminar in Curriculum Inquiry," "Policy Studies in Education," "Issues in Educational Studies," "Foundations of Curriculum," "Critical Issues in Second Language Education," "Critical Pedagogy and Interpretive Inquiry."

[4] Soon after that essay, I abandoned the Karen project after my main contact was recruited away by another humanitarian organization.

[5] In this case, the Other was either non-white, a student with different religious background, a person physically challenged or someone not speaking my mother tongue. The idea of the Other refers to people a person perceives as different from oneself. In her essay *Strangers to Ourselves*, Julia Kristeva (1991) offers a rich reflection on the subject.

[6] Transformative action in this context refers to a cooperative approach to the elaboration of culturally appropriate solutions to various educational issues and socio-economic injustices. Collaboration between Inuit and non-Inuit should lead to concrete action towards the progressive transformation of problematic situations. Freire (2000) presents a good example of transformative action.

[7] Traditionally, in patriarchal social arrangement, men are responsible for the welfare of the community, and women are in charge of daily household chores. Women's ability to nurse their children is particularly celebrated and so is their affectionate and mothering nature while their capacity to make political, economical and social decisions is denigrated. Feminist movements strongly question such abusive social structures. To read about the mothering nature of teachers, consult Madeleine R. Grumet (1988).

REFERENCES

Annahatak, B. (1994). Quality education for Inuit today? Cultural strengths, new things, and working out the unknowns: A story by an Inuk. *Peabody Journal of Education, 69*(2), 12–18.

Clandinin, J., Pushor, D., & Murray Orr, A. (2007). Navigating sites for narrative inquiry. *Journal of Teacher Education, 58*(1), 27–35.

Conle, C. (1999). Why narrative? Which narrative? Struggling with time place in life and research. *Curriculum Inquiry, 29*(1).

Conle, C. (2000). Thesis as narrative or "what is the inquiry in narrative inquiry?" *Curriculum Inquiry, 30*(2).

Connelly, M. F., & Clandinin, J. D. (1990). Stories of experience and narrative inquiry. *Educational Researcher, 19*(5).

Crites, S. (1971). The narrative quality of experience. *Journal of the American Academy of Religion, 39*(3), 291–311.

Desautels, A. (2007). Hunting down indigenous stereotypes through introspection. In D. Macedo & S. R. Steinberg (Eds.), *Media literacy: A reader*. New York: Peter Lang.

Fowler, L. C. (2006). *A curriculum of difficulty. Narrative research in education and the practice of teaching* (Vol. 17). New York: Peter Lang.

Freire, P. (2000). *Pedagogy of the oppressed* (30th anniversary ed.). New York: Continuum.

Gadamer, H. G. (1975). *Truth and method*. New York: Seabury Press.

Gamelin Kamanos, A. (2005). The sand diaries. Visions, vulnerability and self-study. In C. Mitchell, S. Weber, & K. O'Reilly-Scanlon (Eds.), *Just who do we think we are?* (pp. 183–192). London: Routledge.

Giroux, H. (1990). Reading texts, literacy, and textual authority. *Journal of education, 172*(1), 84.

Grumet, M. (1991). Curriculum and the art of daily life. In G. Willis & W. H. Schubert (Eds.), *Reflections from the heart of educational inquiry: Understanding curriculum and teaching through the arts* (pp. 74–89). New York: State University of New York Press.

Grumet, M. R. (1988). *Bitter milk: Women and teaching*. Amherst: University of Massachusetts Press.

Hampton, E. (1995). Memory comes before knowledge: Research may improve if researchers remember their motives. *Canadian Journal of Native Education, 21*(Suppl.), 46–54.

Kristeva, J. (1991). *Strangers to ourselves*. New York: Columbia University Press.

Ministère de l'éducation du Québec. (1998). *A school for the future: Policy statement on educational integration and intercultural education.* Québec: Gouvernement du Québec, Ministère de l'éducation.

Mitchell, C., Weber, S., & O'Reilly-Scanlon, K. (2005). *Just who do we think we are? Methodologies for autobiography and self-study in teaching.* New York: RoutledgeFalmer.

Pinar, W. F. (1994). *Autobiography, politics and sexuality: Essays in curriculum theory, 1972–1992.* New York: Peter Lang.

Rasmussen, D. (2001). Qallunology: A pedagogy for the oppressor. *Canadian Journal of Native Education, 25*(2), 105–116.

Smith, D. G. (1996). Identity, self, and other in the conduct of pedagogical action: An east/west inquiry. In W. F. Pinar (Ed.), *Contemporary curriculum discourses: Twenty years of jct. Counterpoints: Studies in the postmodern theory of education* (pp. 458–473). New York: Peter Lang.

Smith, L. T. (1999). *Decolonizing methodologies: Research and indigenous peoples.* England, UK.

Tompkins, J. (1998). *Teaching in a cold and windy place: Change in an Inuit school.* Toronto, Canada: University of Toronto Press.

KEVIN B. O'CONNOR

7. CHALLENGING PARADIGMS

Deconstructing and reconstructing my positionality as a non-Indigenous researcher

QUESTIONS FROM ACADEMIA

I returned to McGill University to pursue my graduate studies in education, which focus on curriculum studies, after spending ten years teaching in Whitehorse, Yukon (1996-2005). This teaching experience focused mainly on developing experiential programs[1] developed to engage disenfranchised students–many of whom were First Nations. I was initially greeted by the academic community with much interest in my experience and work in experiential learning and its place in Indigenous[2] education. Many of my colleagues and professors took the time to discuss the subject and listen to my story. Yet as time progressed and my research interests started to evolve, I began to encounter sometimes subtle and sometimes blatant warnings from concerned colleagues of my positionality as a "white guy" interested in Indigenous issues. The more extreme responses were: "You can't do this work, you're not Indigenous." Over time I came to understand the primary questions: "Why are you interested in Indigenous education?" and "What are your motives as a non-Indigenous researcher?"

My initial reaction to these questions was one of puzzlement–in my teaching positions up north my motives had never been questioned before and, while my work had not been unchallenged, no one before had questioned my motives. Puzzlement was followed by resentment. Resentment that I was being asked to justify my passion and ten years of hard work in which I had tried to help a group of students achieve success within a system that was failing them. Now I was being asked to justify my motives for this work which seemed to me to be very transparent and straightforward.

I had spent ten years creating and teaching experiential learning programs to secondary school students in Whitehorse and outlying rural communities for the Yukon Department of Education. These programs rely on the use of experiential and place-based models as effective tools in delivering culturally relevant curriculum to students through: projects, experiences in the field, and research, in an engaging and hands-on manner. Specifically, I developed two experiential programs that integrate multiple subjects into semester-long holistic models. Even now, as I pursue my graduate studies, these programs continue to operate, and I continue to participate as an educational advisor in the North.

A.H. Churchill (ed.), Rocking Your World: The Emotional Journey
into Critical Discourses, 67–80.

I returned to academia to expand my knowledge base with regards to experiential and place-based education, and to research its impact in Indigenous education. Therefore, the answers to the question about what motivated me to pursue education topics in Indigenous education seemed very simple to me: I had taught Indigenous students for ten years, and I concluded that the regular school system in the Yukon was failing many students, but most importantly Indigenous students who seemed to be most negatively affected. I was fortunate to be involved in research and development of experiential programs that addressed many of the needs of the Yukon First Nations, and I witnessed the success of some Indigenous students as these programs were being implemented. I then returned to academia to help promote this type education at the post-secondary level so that new teachers could be exposed to this "alternative" style of education. To me, it seemed simple and clear.

Many of the people who questioned my intentions were non-Indigenous, and I resented their implications that I had a hidden agenda or that because of the colour of my skin I had no understanding or privilege to speak about Indigenous education.

After leaving my position in the Yukon and returning to McGill, I began working with various Indigenous bands and teachers across northern Canada (Yukon First Nations, Cree, Dene, and Inuit) as a consultant and teacher-trainer with regards to implementing experiential and place-based programming in schools. The people (mostly Indigenous) whom I worked with in the North rarely questioned my positionality and, except for some white guy jokes, were most interested in my experience in alternative education and not my colonial heritage or the colour of my skin. Yet the academics in the ivory tower questioned my involvement. I was confused and became very frustrated.

With the support of my supervisor, I began my Master's degree journey in answering the questions posed to me that sought specifically to better understand my interest and motivation as a non-Indigenous person in Indigenous education and research. I started to answer these questions first by trying to better understand them. I did this by looking at a number of texts that deal directly with three main concerns.

Politics of Knowledge

Colonial structures have been in existence for over ten decades and support positions of power and dominance that favour these structures are politically motivated. Smith (Maori)[3] (1999) refers to colonial influence as "colonization of the mind" (p. 59); a system of organization, classification and promotion of a new pro-colonial form of knowledge that attempts to abolish old conflicting practices and to promote power and domination by the ruling nation. It is a concept similar to Richard Darville's "social organization theory" (Campbell & Gregor, 2002, p. 54) that is best described as the process of gaining and controlling power through organizational forms of knowing or more simply put, "power through knowledge."

Cook-Lynn (Sioux) (1996) speaks to the political structure involved in research as she quotes Dr. Beatrice Medicine (Sioux), an anthropologist and scholar:

> Native people living in the contemporary world are usually the last to know and have something to say about what is being published concerning us. This is whether the work is in history, anthropology, psychology, education or fiction. Recently, much social science or grant applications have emphasized that the projected research is a result of 'tribal council approval'. In many cases, these councils do not inform the poor and powerless people in the hinterlands of the reservations, who are the captive objects of such studies. (Medicine, 1979 cited in Cook-Lynn, 1996, p. 67)

The present dominant research ideology tends to put the accumulation of Western knowledge ahead of the interests of the Indigenous person being studied. In the last five decades, researchers have been governed by the values and systems of the Western academic structure. Taking the stance that the Western way represented a normal, rational and true form, researchers entered Indigenous communities and judged them lacking in many of the so-called canons of civilized behaviour. These political institutions are guided by Western social beliefs that diffuse the notion of differing cultures and thus lead to failing grades for many Indigenous communities when compared to Western standards. As long as researchers report back to a colonial-centred institution that diminishes the values and beliefs of Indigenous people on the basis of comparison that aligns difference with a failing effort, there will remain what Alfred North Whitehead describes as "misplaced concreteness" (Deloria, 1997, p. 221).

Weber-Pillwax (1999) refers to a similar action as "unconscious irresponsibility" (p. 37); the basis for excusing callous and unlawful acts by researchers against Indigenous peoples. "The commonly accepted explanation for these 'irregularities' in conduct is always couched in terms that imply a misunderstanding of a good intent, therefore, it is argued, since there was no malicious intent, what we have is a case of unconscious irresponsibility. So easily is the criminal rendered innocent and the victim(s) powerless!" (Weber-Pillwax, 1999, p. 37). No matter what legitimate motives are present, it is difficult to deny the pressures involved that may affect the social and political perspectives of the benefactors (Weber-Pillwax, 1999). "Research is not an innocent or distant academic exercise but an activity that has something at stake and that occurs in a set of political and social conditions" (Smith, 1999, p. 5).

As I began to appreciate the complexity of how knowledge is produced through research and the power that the researcher has in deciding what knowledge gets produced, I began to appreciate the importance of questioning the motivation of outsiders doing research and the potential impacts this research can have on a community.

Impact of Research

As I explored critical discourses further, I came to appreciate how the impact of research at the community level must be explored. This is a crucial theme that must be recognized as many researchers, similar to federal and provincial government agencies such as social services, are in and out of family homes and communities. Researchers from different projects and research teams can create a revolving door of intrusion, without showing any "collective responsibility" for the blanket effect their involvement has upon the social and personal lives of the participants and their community. In some cases, this has created a deep sense of resentment on the part of the participants towards any form of research or scholarly involvement in Indigenous communities (Smith, 1999).

Alfred (Mohawk) (1999), speaks with a Kwa'kwala'wakw woman with respect to social workers in Indigenous communities. She uses the analogy of a bike wheel and the placement of its spokes with respect to the many social problems and their supposed solutions. She argues that there is a need for everyone to understand where the spokes need to go, with each person responsible for the replacement of at least one spoke. If this occurred, a collective solution could be found. She blames social services for creating more spokes and placing them all on one side of the wheel, fragmenting the process. She reminds Alfred that they are not Indigenous spokes, and they are all on one side of the wheel. Unless the Indigenous community is involved holistically in the process and their input is valued, then the social issues that the social workers are there to address will continue (Alfred, 1999). This scenario can easily be extrapolated to researchers; it speaks to the confusing effects outside involvement can have on the Indigenous community if external values, beliefs and structures are imposed.

Ego-centricity of the Researcher:

I am intrigued by a letter referenced by Cook Lynn (Sioux) (1996), in which a teacher from Columbus, Ohio, wrote to the Indian Historian journal in response to an Indigenous criticism of the controversial novel *Hanta Yo* by Ruth Beebe Hill:

> What are the motives of a White teacher of Indian Lit? Some possible motives occur to me: one is nostalgia for a lost world in which virtuous people lived in close harmony with nature and the holy; another is that a study of Indian history with its tale of betrayal and genocide is useful as a form of protest against oppression ... [to] reveal the dark side of American history and give the lie to unqualified celebrations of the American way; also, in an era of disillusionment with American values, many Americans are groping for new ones. What it all adds up to is that American Indians are called upon to prove some pet thesis. (Teacher cited in Cook Lynn, 1996, p. 74)

Deloria (Sioux) (1997) describes a similar concept, through the perception of the anthropologist who mistakes the natural hospitality of First Nations toward a stranger as an endorsement of academia, approval of the researcher or support of the work. "What she (the researcher) experienced was simply the hospitality of Indians toward a stranger. You can bring almost anyone into an Indian community and Indians will greet him, feed him, invite him to ceremonies, and spend time with him" (Deloria, 1997, p. 218).

A final misconception held by researchers is what is best described as "delusions of grandeur". Researchers in Community Action Research can often fall prey to a false feeling of leadership and hence control that ultimately has the researcher believing that the process relies heavily upon the researchers involvement and decision making abilities (Hagey, 1997; Smith, 1999). This leads to an arrogant approach to research, as many researchers think that the process begins and ends with their involvement without much regard for the benefit and direct involvement of the community upon which the research was based. While referring specifically to anthropologists, Deloria (1997) comments:

Anthros expect Indians to have the same perspective as they do, to have an objective culture that can and must be studied and that Indians themselves will study. The anthros' belief no doubt comes from the extreme materialism that has always been present in Western civilization and from their individual experiences in college and graduate school, when they had to study hard and long to master the rudiments of another culture. But knowing what others have observed about another culture does not mean that the scholar emotionally understands that culture, and this point many anthros miss completely. (p. 218)

This emotional understanding comes from the notion that all human beings within their specific cultures have a story that tells of their own lives as they know, see and remember them. These stories reflect human experience, and that experience governs how one formulates meaning. This lived experience is emotional; it is emotional because we are emotional beings who feel. Emotion is a way of being that guides us (Hampton, 1995). Therefore, to truly understand and make meaning of an experience, one must be affected emotionally in some way.

Having tried to explore and understand these concerns in a more complex way, I now undertook the task of trying to position myself within the web of their implications. Rather than accept my initial, simplistic, somewhat defensive, response that of course I was doing what was best for the people whom I was interested in helping, I now sought to develop a more complex understanding and appreciation for the potential perils of the path I was choosing.

This lead me to develop my own understanding about how I would come to view my involvement with Indigeneous research and my motives for working with Native communities.

PERSONAL HISTORY

In order to develop this understanding, I have spent time reflecting on my own history in the North and the feelings I have developed towards my work. While teaching in the North, specifically in the Yukon Territory, I had the opportunity to teach many students of different cultures and backgrounds. This cross-cultural exposure brought with it the challenge to effectively relay the curriculum in a meaningful and engaging manner to meet the wide range of learning styles, cultural, and social conditions.

Appreciating Colonialism's Impact on Education

It became evident from the beginning that many of the students, particularly those of Indigenous descent, showed a real disassociation with the current content and delivery of the curriculum. The present public educational system lacks culturally relevant programming and fails to provide meaningful and motivational experiences to help the student engage in the learning process.

Through my experience as a teacher and curriculum developer involved with Indigenous communities, I have gained some insight into some possible reasons for disengagement within these specific communities. As I began to review previous research, I uncovered findings that resonated with my experiences and beliefs.

The lack of Indigenous cultural knowledge and perspectives in the school curriculum has been identified as a significant factor in school failure amongst Indigenous students (Cajete, 1994; Curwen Doige, 2003; Kirkness, 1998; Wilson & Wilson, 2002). These findings have prompted calls for an increase in research that addresses the need for Indigenous cultural knowledge to be part of the public school curriculum in order to enhance and support classroom learning for Aboriginal students. It is also important to discover effective ways that dominant-culture (English or French) teachers can integrate such cultural knowledge into their teaching of the regular curricula of public schools (Kanu, 2005).

Angayuqaq Oscar Kawagley (Yupiak), an Indigenous educator, co-director of the Alaska Native Knowledge Network, and faculty member of the University of Alaska School of Education, explains the dilemma of Indigenous education as follows:

> The incursion of Western society on Indigenous peoples brought about many cultural and psychological disruptions in the flow of life in traditional societies. Since the inception of modern education in the villages, the curricula, policies, textbooks, language of instruction and administration have been in conflict with the Native cultural systems. The modern public schools are not made to accommodate differences in Native worldviews, but to impose another culture that is Western. This has had a confusing effect on the Native students. Alienation and identity crisis of youth and their continual search for meaning are a condition of Native life today. New images of modernity collide with traditional symbols, values and beliefs. (cited in Emekauwa, 2004, p. 3)

As I acknowledge the influence colonial forces and Western-style practices in educational institutions have had upon Indigenous identities, I enter my research path with the recognition that I am also a product of those colonial forces, whether

I am cognisant or not, and bring an identity and a certain way of thinking that may not always be consistent with Indigenous worldviews.

I will refer to my position as "non-Indigenous researcher." While I may be White, I am Canadian, of Irish descent, a proud Quebecer, English Montrealer and Northerner with a specific past and identity that aligns me with much more than "whiteness," as I believe it is the people, communities and environments that surround us that create a sense of place in which we define our identity. This principle is what guides the practice of place-based education.

Several scholars (Steinhauer, 2003; Wilson, 2005) have used the term "white" as a justification for strict and defining classifications of entitlement towards cultural understanding and participation. They call for the exclusion of those who do not possess membership within specific cultural and racial borders. This is an important term to address as I pursue Indigenous research as a non-Indigenous person. Therefore I use the term "non-Indigenous" as I acknowledge that my genetic heritage does not involve a Native American association.

With this developing appreciation for the complexity of my positionality as a "non-Indigenous" researcher and the tangled web in which that placed me, I began to seek a deeper and deeper appreciation for my motivation. To do this I continued to try to understand my memories of my work in the North. I did this work in the spirit of Hampton's challenge:

> Memory comes before knowledge. Every person's life contains experiences and memories of these experiences. The way it works for me is that I forget those things until I unwrap them, until I actually roll out the sacred medicine bundle of my life and look for those memories. I pick them up and touch them and feel them. And each memory gives me knowledge." (Hampton, 1995, p. 53)

To follow this advice, I attempt to "unwrap" my lived experience through a process of reflection that involves acquiring knowledge from memory. This allows me to better understand my motives, be respectful of the values of others and create a positive relationship with the participants and the communities involved with the research activities. The following two narratives are reflections of my past teaching experiences. To protect the privacy of the individuals, all names are fictitious.

My First Class

I begin by returning to a distinctive memory that involves my first full-time job as a teacher. I was a Special Education teacher responsible for a diverse class of students who were diagnosed with a wide range of educational and psychological issues, from Fetal Alcohol Syndrome to schizophrenia. I was completely unprepared to address many of the cultural and social issues that affected the Indigenous students in a Western-style public school. One student's story stands out. I still remember the day I read Randy's background history and information. I was shocked that the administration would place a student with no major learning disabilities in my class. Other than his residency at the local detention centre,

Randy's previous history in school seemed quite "normal." I was told this followed protocol and to prepare a place for him in my class.

It is still gut wrenching to recall how Randy naturally tried to disassociate himself from the other students who suffered from psychological and developmental disabilities. For instance, for his work area he chose a large storage closet and, desperate for social interaction, he would dart out the door with his "guard(ian)" in tow to find other Indigenous students when the school bell rang.

I was shocked and was left feeling very naïve when he told me how he purposely and selectively broke laws that would eventually bring him to the "local youth jail" and consequently my class. A warm place to sleep, three meals a day and lots of things to do was his take on being in jail. He was from a remote community that he wanted to leave, and therefore getting arrested and removed from his community and placed in the local jail was his way of meeting his needs.

As I began to integrate myself more into the school population, I realized Randy was not in the minority and that his story was similar to that of many other Indigenous students. As I worked with Randy on his Individual Education Plan, I realized that other than a class on Athapaskan Language, the school provided very little Indigenous knowledge or culturally implicit activities for Indigenous students to access, nor any real process to ensure cultural context in the curriculum. My relationship with Randy and other Indigenous students who followed him had a tremendous impact on my critical awareness of the lack of current educational practices in many public schools that address Indigenous students.

Experiential Programs

As my teaching career progressed, I was fortunate to be involved in the development and delivery of semester long experiential educational programs. These were originally developed to address the lack of engagement of predominantly Indigenous students in the secondary school system. The students were selected based on their lack of motivation and engagement within their present educational environment. One of these students, Tony, was an Indigenous student from the local Yukon First Nations band. He arrived the first day with two of his cousins. I had been briefed about their families' unstable history and previous "issues" with the system. Tony came with minimal reading and writing skills and, to this day, I am amazed at how students like Tony can manoeuvre their way through the educational system without any effective support at addressing those learning skills.

Tony thrived in the outdoors. He spent most of his time trapping, hunting and just living in the open air. He was a proven leader when it came to many of the program's activities that integrated curriculum with local community-based projects and outdoor excursions. But he was also seen as an outcast as his two cousins were not impressed by his willingness to participate in the activities and would mock him constantly about his so-called "wannabe-whiteness." Many of the non-Indigenous students left no place for him either, as he was not a great reader or writer, and was naïve when it came to social norms or the "cool" factor of the typical teenage student.

Nevertheless, Tony spent most of his time at school that semester and participated in most of the school projects that were held outside of school time and on weekends. He was only required to participate in one project, yet he was usually the first to arrive. This was a drastic change from previous semesters at the public school where, I was told, his low class attendance was a major issue. He went on to enrol in the next year's experiential program and continued on the same path of success.

When he reached the last year of his schooling, I was teaching a program designated for high academic achievement students who had shown previous success but who had lost their path while navigating adolescence. Despite the suggestions of many teachers and administrators that Tony lacked "educational skills," I accepted him into the program. I believed the program was designed to suit someone like him as it integrated academic subjects into extended field trips that visited numerous communities and post-secondary institutions.

While Tony and I both recognized that academics would be a serious challenge for him, the many integrated components and life skills associated with this program were beneficial to him. Again, he had to deal with the scrutiny of his classmates as he struggled with most of the academic requirements. Yet when the class moved out to the field, he became the natural leader. Though he failed some of his courses that semester and learned that he had no interest in the pure and applied sciences, he graduated from high school and is currently enrolled in college with the aim of becoming a professional guide when he graduates. He hopes to bring people out on the land possibly for hunting or fishing trips. He feels a strong connection to his culture's traditional ways and wishes to teach others and to continue the traditions his grandparents taught him.

Tony and others who followed him proved to me that there is a place for the Indigenous student in the Western-style school system, *if* the system is willing to acknowledge the student's cultural differences and provide a medium to access cultural knowledge and contextualize activities. Through our many talks, Tony also helped me understand some of the difficulties and barriers many Indigenous students face within the school system and outside. The social aspects of being an Indigenous student within the present educational setting are complex and debilitating for many. Tony reinforced my belief that experiential and outdoor education models can have a positive influence on Indigenous learners in the educational system, while incorporating traditional knowledge and integrating subjects and the connection to place as major components into the curriculum.

RECONSTRUCTING MY POSITIONALITY

Developing Reflexivity

As Indigenous researchers, we must have a clear understanding of the world view that grounds our work. With that world view embedded, we can choose the research methods, tools, or techniques that we will use. (Steinhauer, 2003, p. 78)

As a non-Indigenous researcher, I also believe there is a need to practice this principle. The narratives told in this chapter explain my motives in promoting experiential and place-based educational strategies that integrate traditional knowledge and also provide contextual learning and engagement.

My time spent with Indigenous students like Randy and Tony gives me a better understanding of the social and educational issues faced by Indigenous students in the present educational system. It supports the notion that a lack of Aboriginal knowledge and cultural initiatives has resulted in student disengagement (Curwen Doige, 2003). Many Indigenous students see no relevance in the present curriculum that separates knowledge into parts (Cajete, 1994). The current system also does not present contextual programming, which in turn leads to a sense of disassociation with the curricular content and its meaning. Indigenous ways are different from those of Western knowledge (Kirkness & Barnhardt, 1991; Hampton, 1995). Western knowledge separates "those areas called science from those areas called art and religion. The native knowledge base, on the other hand, integrated those areas of knowledge so that science was both religious and aesthetic" (Cordero, 1995, p. 30). This form of integration provides the basis for constructivism and experiential learning.

"Researchers need to have a critical conscience about ensuring that their activities connect in humanizing ways with the Indigenous communities" (Smith, 1999, p. 149). I believe this process begins with respect. When I refer to the notion of respect I mean to not only show manners in the traditional way of "please and thank you." "Respect means you listen to others' ideas that you do not insist that your idea prevails. By listening intently you show honour, consider the well being of others, and treat others with kindness and courtesy" (Cree elder quoted in Steinhauer, 2003, p. 73).

RECONSTRUCTING MY POSITIONALITY

The next theme of questions posed by some concerned professors challenged my understanding of the field I was entering: "Did I completely understand that I would most likely not be welcomed into the 'Indigenous Education' community?"

As a budding academic who had aspirations of eventually reducing my involvement in the world of self-employment and contracts to pursue an academic job at a post-secondary institution, this had tremendous implications for my advancement. I was warned of a possible lack of publications and employment and the constant scrutiny that surrounded a non-Indigenous academic in the field of Indigenous education. I was even offered other fully-funded research projects that did not involve Indigenous issues to pursue in my doctoral studies. It was positioned as having to make a choice between two paths: taking a simple more straightforward non-Indigenous path or taking a more difficult path that would have me directly involved in Indigenous education. Again, frustrated but determined, I chose the latter.

As I have acknowledged in this chapter that my genetic heritage does not have any Native American blood, I believe it important to address the issue of my race as many (Steinhauer, 2003; Wilson, 2005) have used the term "white" as a justification for strict and defining classifications of entitlement towards cultural understanding and participation.

Race and Culture as Entitlement

As part of Western society, distinctions that differentiate one race from another have traditionally been drawn. This is contrary to Indigenous traditions which see all human beings as equal members in the social reality of the natural world. Alfred (1999) quotes an Indigenous academic Donald Fixico (Shawnee, Sac & Fox, Creek, Seminole) who claims that "white" people can never understand Indigenous values because they "come from a different place on earth." Fixico says: "Anglo-Americans and natives are fundamentally different. These differences in world-view and in the values that go with them mean that there will always exist an Indian view and a White view of the earth" (cited in Alfred, 1999, p. 20). The concept of differing world views imposes important questions for non-Indigenous researchers like myself who search for my place within the context of Indigenous research. Steinhauer (2003) suggests that "white" society holds a very different world view than Indigenous traditions and therefore non-Indigenous researchers have a theory of knowledge that conflicts with Indigenous epistemologies which would in turn lead to harmful outcomes in research.

I refuse to accept a "predetermined" view of the world that dismisses free will and critical thinking. If we agree with Fixico and Steinhauer's view of cultures and values, then we are predetermined in our place and action, and our view of the world is preordained. The notion of change outside the rigid borders of one's culture would be impossible. Alfred (1999) also rejects these assertions by suggesting there is a real danger in subscribing to the notion of fixed views and cultures that cannot change. He responds:

> Fixico's polarization of Indian and European values suggests he believes that white people are incapable of attaining the level of moral development that Indigenous societies promote among their members with respect to, for example, the land. Not only does this dichotomization go against the traditional Native belief in a universal reality, but it offers a convenient excuse for those who support the state in its colonization of Indigenous nations and exploitation of the earth (p. 20, 21).

I am not a "wannabe-Indian who is caught up in some Indigenous Jesus movement, or some self-righteous piety ... that commissions everyone to be spiritual whether they understand it or not" (Deloria, 1997, p. 213). Instead, I have principles that are similarly aligned with various Indigenous traditional teachings.

Connectedness

Through my experiences I have developed a respect for and an affirmation of an interconnectedness among all living things. I am in accord with Smith (1999) who claims that many minority group researchers value the importance of making connections and affirming connectedness. "Connectedness positions individuals in sets of relationships with other people and with the environment. Many Indigenous creation stories link people through genealogy to the land, to stars and other places in the universe, to birds and fish and animals, insects and plants" (Smith, 1999, p. 148). This notion of connectedness is one that I hope to acknowledge in many facets of my research. It will be a crucial theme as I endeavour to pursue research methodologies that seek community participation in all aspects of the research process that propel the participants towards empowerment. "Connecting is related to issues of identity and place, to spiritual relations and community wellbeing" (Smith, 1999, p. 149).

The concept of connectedness also drives my interest in experiential learning and the need for an integration of Indigenous traditional perspectives and cultural knowledge into Indigenous schools. Experiential and place-based education connects place with self and community. Through the integration of subjects and relational forms of knowledge and perspectives, students learn about themselves and their place in the natural world. I believe this process would be effective in addressing some of the issues that lead to the disengagement of Indigenous students in the current educational system.

One's "story"–each person's lived experience–is the basis on which one's identity is formed and creates the lens through which the world is seen. My story is connected to place, as we seek, create and define ourselves in terms of what is understandable and attractive. Instead of creating a false sense of membership and divided unions I think we need to start acknowledging the lived experience and communal influence that bring us together through similar social values.

REFLECTIONS

My initial resistance to the questioning of my positionality was most definitely spurned on by my own ignorance. While I acknowledged my colonial heritage, I tried to disassociate myself from it and concentrate on improving things in the present–which, I am told, is a typical "male" response. I realize now that those questions posed to me by my colleagues–such as "Why are you interested in Indigenous education?" and "What are your motives as a non-Indigenous researcher?" and "Did I completely understand that I would most likely not be welcomed into the 'Indigenous Education' community?"–were not to be felt as criticisms or seen as the basis to divisional walls between races but as a vehicle for my epistemological evolution as a non-Indigenous researcher.

I benefited tremendously from addressing these questions. The journey informed me of the specifics of the history of Indigenous education, the differing values held within not only Indigenous and non-Indigenous knowledge systems but also between Indigenous systems themselves that include the conditions, rights, and way of life of many groups, cultures, communities and peoples. It also provided me with the tools to understand my evolution as an educator and put together the fragmented pieces of my experiences that determine my worldview so that I was able to make some sense of my deep commitment to Indigenous Education. This critical journey also helped me develop an epistemological humility that I believe will serve me in fostering a better understanding of and relationship with other people and groups. My intentions on the other hand have not changed; they are however more informed, and therefore have a better chance of achieving success.

I do not want to leave this point without acknowledging my position of privilege. I understand because of my colonial heritage I can speak to these issues with some "ease" and have the option to take "the easier path" if I wish while others do not have that freedom. But I do not believe that my privileged position should deter my ultimate goal of working with other educators in improving the educational setting for Indigenous students.

I acknowledge that I am non-Indigenous, yet I have a story that includes an Indigenous context and lived experiences with Indigenous people. I am also cognizant that I am a product of the colonial forces that have traditionally dismissed Indigenous methodologies in exchange for the dominant Western paradigm. My interests as an educator are in addressing the lack of engagement of Indigenous students in the current education system. This path is not an easy one.

NOTES

[1] *Experiential Education* is the process of "learning by doing" which begins with the learner engaging in direct "experience" followed by reflection. Experiential education is a practice through which a learner constructs knowledge, skill, and value from direct experiences (Dewey, 1938). This definition embraces constructivist learning theory as well as the traditional practice of learning by doing. Experiential education is the process of actively engaging students in an experience that will have real consequences (Tyler, 1949). "Experiential learning" can be thus defined in terms of an instructional model, which begins with the learner engaging in direct "experience" followed by reflection, discussion, analysis, and evaluation of the experience. The term "experience" is understood to represent "a fact or state of having been affected by or gained knowledge through direct observation or participation" (Merriam-Webster, 1993). A further more contextual description will follow in the chapter.

[2] "Indigenous" refers to the conditions, rights, and way of life of many groups, cultures, communities and peoples who have a historical continuity or association with a given region or parts of a region before its subsequent colonization or the formation of a Nation-State. I do not wish to insinuate by the use of a single reference that Indigenous people can be classified by one term that excludes each group's specific and particular identity. I have learned that not only are there definite relations and nuances within Indigenous nations but they are explicitly specific within each community and reserve. The historical specificity and variability of culture and its synchronous interaction with many other diverse environmental and social structures create specific identities amongst groups that are not to be trivialized by a single term.

[3] The reference to tribal affiliation is done to respect and honour each person's heritage as an Indigenous person. Please refer to "Indigenous" footnote for further explanation on this subject.

REFERENCES

Alfred, T. (1999). Peace. In *Peace, power, righteousness: An indigenous manifesto* (pp. 1–39). Oxford: Oxford University Press.

Cajete, G. (1994). *Look to the mountain: An ecology of Indigenous education*. Durango, CO: Kivaki Press.

Campbell, M. & Gregor, F. (2002). Finding a place to begin. In *Mapping social relations: a primer in doing institutional ethnography*. (pp. 11–25). Auroa: Garamond.

Cook-Lynn, E. (1996). The relationship of a writer to the past: Art, a literary principle, and the need to narrate. In *Why I can't read Wallace Stegner and other essays: A tribal voice* (pp. 63–77). Madison: University of Wisconsin Press.

Cordero, C. (1995). A working and evolving definition of culture. *Canadian Journal of Native Education*, 21 (supplement), 28–41.

Curwen Doige, L. A. (2003). A missing link: Between traditional Aboriginal education and the Western system of education. *Canadian Journal of Native Education, 27*(2), 144–160.

Dewey, J. (1938). *Experience and education*. London: Collier MacMillan. Chicago: The University of Chicago Press.

Deloria, V. (1997). Anthros, Indians and planetary reality. In T. Biolsi & L. J. Zimmerman (Eds.), *Indians and anthropologists: Vine Deloria Jr. and the critique of anthropology* (pp. 209–221).

Emekauwa, E. (2004). *The star with my name: The Alaska rural systemic initiative and the impact of place-based education on native student achievement. The case for place-based. Rural trust white paper on place-based education*. Washington, DC: The Rural School and Community Trust.

Hagey, R.S. (1997). The use and abuse of participatory action research. *Chronic Diseases in Canada, 18*(1): 1–4.

Hampton, E. (1995). Memory comes before knowledge. *Canadian Journal of Native Education*, 20: 46–54.

Kanu, Y. (2005). Teachers' perceptions of the integration of aboriginal culture into the high school curriculum. *Alberta Journal of Educational Research, 51*(1), 50–68.

Kirkness, V.J., & Barnhardt, R. (1991). First Nations and higher education: The four R's-respect, relevance, reciprocity, responsibility. *Journal of American Indian Education, 30*(3), 9–16.

Kirkness, V.J. (1998). Our peoples' education: Cut the shackles; cut the crap; cut the mustard. *Canadian Journal of Native Education, 22*(1), 10–15.

Merriam-Webster. (1993). *Merriam Webster's Collegiate Dictionary. Tenth edition*. Markham, Ontario: Thomas Allen & Son Limited.

Smith, L. (1999). *Decolonising methodologies: research and indigenous peoples*. (pp. 58–77 & 142–162) United Kingdom, England. Zed Books.

Steinhauer, E. (2003). Thoughts on an Indigenous research methodology. *Canadian Journal of Native Education, 26*(2): 69–81.

Tyler, R.W. (1949). *Basic principles of curriculum and instruction*. Chicago: University of Chicago Press.

Weber-Pillwax, C. (2001). What is indigenous research? *Canadian Journal of Native Education*, 25(2): 166–174.

Wilson, S. (2005). Self-as-relationship in Indigenous research. *Canadian Journal of Native Education, 25*(2), 91–94.

Wilson, S. & Wilson, P. (2002). Editorial: First Nations education in mainstream systems. *Canadian Journal of Native Education, 26*(2), 67.

Part III: Teaching with a more critical gaze

BRAD J. PORFILIO

8. FROM WORKING CLASS LIBERAL TO TRANSFORMATIVE SCHOLAR-PRACTITIONER

Struggles and successes amid the newfound status quo

It has been nearly nine years since I started my journey to become a critical scholar, practitioner, and citizen. In the spring of 1999, I entered the Sociology of Education doctoral program at the University of Buffalo with a pedestrian understanding of the relationship between knowledge and the existing hierarchical social and economic relationships (Weiler, 2005, p. 3), of the role schools and other social institutions play in perpetuating institutional forms of oppression across the globe, of how my own experience as a White heterosexual male affords many unearned privileges in my inextricable web of social relations, and of how to "teach and use oppositional discourses so as to remake ourselves and our culture" (Shore, 1999). Although I had some brief exposure to critical scholarship (for instance, I read Freire's *Pedagogy of the Oppressed*) during my training as a secondary social studies teacher in 1997, neither the coursework nor the fieldwork in urban schools and communities prepared me to hold a vision that the "purpose of education in an unjust society is to bring about equality and justice" (Lee, Menkart, & Okazawa-Rey, 2002, p. VIII). Rather, the school of education's chief focus was to prepare the next generation of teachers to employ behavioural techniques to survive their first few years in K-12 classrooms and to internalize a series of disconnected facts in order to pass a battery of state-mandated examinations that are required for obtaining teacher certification. On the other hand, critical discussions relating to how North American schools serve the interests of the most powerful social groups at the expense of minoritized[1] populations, how they generate structures, practices, and rituals bent on keeping the larger power structure in place, and how they perpetuate false narratives, such as the myth that North American society is democratic and fair and the idea that people succeed in North America solely by effort or merit, were absent. Suffocating this type of oppositional thought meant that neither my fellow pre-service teachers nor I would challenge the classist, racist, sexist, and homophobic status quo in secondary classrooms (Chomsky, 2004).

Since I occupied a privilege position in terms of my race, gender, and sexuality, I did not recognize the urgency to further explore how to connect Freire's revolutionary project to guiding my K-12 students to "read the word and the world" or to reformulate my self so as to become an individual committed to humanizing education and the wider world. Sadly, inside of the classroom, my pedagogy consisted of putting adolescent students in cooperative learning groups with the chief aim of looking at history through multiple lenses. Outside of the

A.H. Churchill (ed.), Rocking Your World: The Emotional Journey
into Critical Discourses, 83–98.

classroom, I remained passive in the struggle to "link social change and education to the imperatives of a critical and global democracy" (Giroux, 2005).

Although my graduate work helped me come to grips with the fact that my skin colour and medium build heterosexual body–not my effort or intellect–were instrumental in allowing me, rather than many of my minoritized working-class friends, to become a "successful" student and "escape" the poverty, blight and crime that riddled the working-class community where I grew up ("Little, Italy" in Niagara Falls, New York), the same academic preparation did not prepare me for the resistance I would eventually encounter as a critical pedagogue from students, colleagues, and administrators alike. Nearly nine years ago, I felt obligated to teach mainly White pre-service and in-service teachers about what I had not been taught in my teacher education program about the nature of schooling, society, inequity, and social justice. I was emotionally drained and disillusioned after my first foray in "teaching to change the world." Rather than consulting scholarship or conversing with colleagues as to why White pre-service and in-service teachers resist the transformative agenda put forth by critical pedagogues, I blamed myself solely for failing to generate the educative experiences and producing the classroom climate necessary to foster their personal and intellectual transformation. I was dejected because the students' failure almost assuredly meant their classrooms continued to be or would become spaces for reproducing the larger institutional arrangements in society, instead of serving as learning communities predicated on finding ways to "empower the powerless and transform existing social inequalities and injustices" (McLaren, 2006, p. 186). Moreover, I was perplexed as to why the course had an entirely different effect for a significant amount of my students; the course ensured they developed the critical capacity and enthusiasm to excavate systemic inequalities and injustices in schools and the wider society.

My mentors at the University of Buffalo, unfortunately, never shared their stories or talked about the opposition critical scholar-practitioners face in academic institutions. Consequently, I was also not prepared to deal with the emotional and social fallout of occupying an oppositional identity to the dominant academic culture. At times, occupying a critical subject position in academic circles has positioned me to remain silent on certain issues and has made me very reticent to share my feelings, research interests, or teaching experiences with my peers or the administration, since I have found the academic world to be openly hostile or indifferent to radical pedagogy or transformative research endeavours. This has been a major factor why I have left three tenure track positions over the past seven years. I have been continually searching to join an academic community that provides intellectual and emotional support for critical theorists, rather than researching and teaching amid environments predicated on conforming to the dominant approaches to teaching and learning, and producing and consuming knowledge purely to keep students happy and maximizing profits for the CEOs of higher education.

The purpose of this chapter is to capture what has resulted since I reconstituted my *self* and joined other radical scholars and practitioners in the struggle to create a democratic social order–a society predicated on the ideals of justice, liberty, and equity. The narrative put forth will capture the impact of occupying a critical, often oppositional subject position with my friends, colleagues, and students. The first part of the chapter will map my transition from doctoral student within a progressive Social Foundations department, to contingent faculty member at a liberal arts college, to a tenure-track teacher-educator within two commercialized fast-track teacher education programs. Here I document the challenges and struggles I faced since venturing out of an environment that supported a critical analysis of the relationship between schooling and society and one which promoted educational initiatives geared toward fostering social justice in schools and society. The second part of the chapter will look beyond the purview of the university, as I pinpoint how relationships with family members shifted since becoming a critical scholar-practitioner. The chapter will conclude with several success stories I have had as a critical pedagogue and scholar.

FROM DOCTORAL STUDENT TO CONTINGENT FACULTY MEMBER: THE MANY STRUGGLES OF A NEOPHYTE CRITICAL PEDAGOGUE

After becoming grounded in much of the scholarship in the social foundations of education and serving as a research assistant for a scholar who was committed to improving urban schools and communities, I recognized the immediacy to contribute to the "process of critical world making, guided by the shadowed outline of a dream of a world less conditioned by misery, suffering of deceit" (Kincheloe & McLaren, 2000, p. 303). To this end, I felt I could make my contribution to this radical project most immediately by exposing in-service and pre-service teachers to revolutionary scholarship configured by leading transformative pedagogues, such as Kincheloe, McLaren, Steinberg, Spring, Giroux, Said, Apple, Anyon, Dei, and Sleeter, and by inoculating my teaching with an emboldened sprit, which has the potency to push in-service and pre-service teachers to ratchet a revolutionary brand of pedagogy within K-12 classrooms (Kincheloe, 2004, p. 4). Despite the prospects of receiving a low wage and mentoring 65 White pre-service and in-service teachers during a six-week period, I jumped at the opportunity to teach two graduate sections of educational foundations at a small liberal arts college. I was elated that I could finally contribute to the transformative project.

The dominant student population in the school of education reflected the student population of the remaining academic disciplines on campus; it was upper-middle class and White. Although I had done some cursory readings in relation to the struggles that crop up when teaching White pre-service and in-service teachers, how the large social structure operates to afford White citizens unearned privilege and entitlements in schools and society, how structural forces and systemic barriers gel together to perpetuate a racial, class, gender, and sexual hierarchy in North America, and how there is an immediate need to rebuild our social and economic institutions so as to create a social system predicated on the ideals of justice, equity, and democracy, I naively believed that my students would not resist having their views of North America's social system, of the functions of schooling, and of the nature of their lived experiences, challenged. However, I soon learned that I was way off mark with my pedagogical expectations.

While there are numerous reasons that my teaching was rejected, I want to discuss one in some detail. For some of the students, the form of masculinity I performed[2] short-circuited them from taking seriously my role as an instructor as well as the course content. At this point in my career, I was in my late 20s and dressed very casually to teach. Shorts and polo shirts were my pedagogical attire. Several students had internalized the notion that older White men with Ph.D.'s are the only ones capable of being experts in their chosen field of studies and possess the skills and knowledge necessary to design syllabi, evaluate their work, and provide a thoughtful presentation of the course material. This mindset became evident during the first days of the semester, when I overheard students saying I "look cute" because I wore a backpack and reminded them of their "collegiate sons" who attended this academic institution. Furthermore, my body made them skeptical that my voice could carry much resonance in the field of education because I, unlike almost all of the instructors in the teacher education program, had not spent 20 years in the trenches of elementary and secondary classrooms. Several students attempted to mock my analysis of what social, economic, and political factors braid together to shape life within contemporary classrooms by asking repeatedly during class discussion "how long I was a classroom teacher." This occurred in spite of the fact that I outlined my pedagogical experiences at the beginning of the course, and referenced my K-12 classroom teaching and administrative experiences throughout the term.

Honestly, I did not handle the situation well. I did not ask students why they had a problem with my lack of teaching experience or being taught by their "son." As a contingent faculty member, I did not want to generate large waves and felt it was in my interest to avoid needless conflict with students. Instead, my response was to call on students who only wanted to share their insights on the course material and their experiences as schoolteacher, parent, or student and let those who resisted my analysis of what shapes classroom life remain silent. However, the failure to address the issue of why I was equipped to teach the course started to wear on me. I did not want to teach class. I was dejected because I realized these students were not ready to transform themselves and join the struggle to remake the world. I blamed myself for my students' negative attitude, as I lacked the insight to reflect upon how our bodies impact students inside and outside of classrooms, especially for teacher-educators who go against the grain of what is typically taught in schools of education or in the liberal arts and sciences.[3]

On the other hand, a group of eight pre-service teachers did engage seriously, for at least part of the course, with the course material and often shared their insights and experiences surrounding schooling, teaching, and society. Since they had not spent several years teaching amid the status quo, they were initially open to learning the course content. However, this course was the students' endpoint before they engaged in student teaching in the fall term, which meant they had previously completed the eleven required courses to obtain a MS education degree and secondary certification. By the end of the second week of class meetings, it became obvious, echoing Macedo (citied in Kincheloe, 2004, p. 36), that their previous coursework had "stupidfied" them.[4]

They had, for example, a difficult time accepting the fact that North American powerbrokers purposely generate unjust practices and policies to ensure that many urban youths provide a cheap source of labour for business leaders, are shunted into military units and prisons, and lack confidence, courage and forums to speak out against how the larger social structure perpetuates their own marginalization as well as the marginalization of millions of women, men, and children across the globe. They became visibly upset when their classmates named the many unjust practices and inhumane conditions associated with racialized and class-based schooling in urban North America. They felt students and their parents should not use the debilitating form of schooling as an "excuse" for not performing well academically, and claimed urban children could overcome the obstacles through "hard work and effort."

Several of their classmates and I questioned them about their contentions that urban youths have the power to pull themselves "up by the bootstraps" and hurdle the numerous obstacles that often lead to their marginalization in schools. For example, we queried whether, during their childhood, they faced the same structural conditions that urban youths typically encounter in their schools and communities. We also asked whether it is fair that our government leaders enact policies that ensure White youths garner more educational resources than their Black and Latino(a) counterparts.

The students evaded these questions, since their racial class status undoubtedly shielded them from: attending under-funded schools; teachers and administrators viewing them through the prism of debilitating, racialized, ethnic and class-based stereotypes and from living in blighted communities marred by poverty, violence, and crime. Instead, they provided examples of famous people, such as Oprah, Michael Jordan, and Bill Cosby, who faced obstacles similar to those faced by today's urban youths, but possessed the work ethic to transcend their social class status. They also claimed that our schools and social institutions are continuously improving, and implied it was just a matter of time that urban residents will bask in the "freedom and opportunity" afforded in North America (Sleeter, 2002, p. 38). The students reacted in a similar fashion during the remaining part of the course. Their disillusionment and guilt merely grew as we pulled back the covers of how the North American social system functions to privilege them and their family members, at the expense of our environment and the majority of the world's population.

My stint as a contingent faculty member was short-lived. The administration did not invite me back to teach courses during the fall semester. They opted to judge my teaching effectiveness by the bottom line–that is, my teaching was viewed as ineffective because the student satisfaction survey indicated I "upset too many customers." This occurred despite the fact that the same instrument indicated nearly half of the students spoke highly of Educational Foundations, stating that it was their "favourite course" and they had developed "a new way of looking at education and the world."

Being fired was a tumultuous experience. I had the uneasy task of trying to explain to my wife and parents why some students and the administration questioned my competency as a pedagogue and a scholar, while I was concomitantly searching for answers to the same questions. I was baffled as to why students who occupied the same racial status reacted so divergently to my teaching and the coursework. I also questioned why, as a former White pre-service and in-service teacher, I did not have the same negative reaction to ideals espoused by critical pedagogues.

The teaching experience also made me question whether it would be better to take a more traditional approach to teaching and conducting research. I began to doubt whether I would be able to revamp my pedagogy and my scholarship so as to allow me to conduct research and teach for personal and social transformation, and in the process, satisfy enough students and administrators to keep a job in higher education. After several discussions with my wife, faculty members, and friends from graduate school, who also were fairly new to the world of critical theory, I decided to continue to identify myself as a critical scholar and a radical pedagogue. Though, I realized that, in the future, I would face an uphill battle to leave positive marks on most of my students and to win approval from colleagues and administrators for my brand of teaching and the trajectory of my research.

REVITALIZING MY PEDAGOGY AND RECONSTITUTING MYSELF: A CONCERTED EFFORT TO BE A CRITICAL PEDAGOGUE

Within two weeks of learning about my dismissal, a fast-track teacher education program decided to take a chance that I would not upset too many of its customers. I was hired as a tenure-track assistant professor. The hiring signalled I would mentor and educate students very similar to the in-service and pre-service teachers I had worked with in the summer. For the next six years, I would have the opportunity to reflect upon ways to retool my pedagogy–to ensure it prepares White in-service and pre-service teachers to be agents of social transformation inside and outside their classrooms.

My ability to guide my in-service and pre-service teachers to develop a "social activist persona" (Kincheloe, 2004, p. 4) did not happen overnight. It improved only after much reflection on my summer teaching experiences, after many conversations with former students, critical scholars, and family members, and after conducting research on White pre-service teachers' views of schooling, technology, and cultural diversity. To guide my students to understand how schools and the larger world functions to perpetuate their privilege and the marginalization of Other's marginalization, I found it imperative to familiarize myself with the generative themes that play a central role in my students' view of self and Other, in generating their social relationships, and in the development of events that transpire within their social worlds. Since the vast majority of my students hailed from Canada, I became equipped to understand their worlds by supervising student teachers in Canadian schools, by examining scholarship that focuses on issues of class, race, gender and sexuality in elementary and secondary schools in Canada and in other Canadian social institutions, and by scouring newspapers and periodicals that capture what is mediating events in Canadian classrooms.

I also felt the urgency to tap more concrete teaching resources that pre-service teachers could employ in their classrooms to guide our youths to become active in the struggle to democratize their schools, communities, and the wider social world. In addition to *Rethinking Schools* magazine and *Teaching Tolerance* web resources that I used as an adjunct instructor, I found the cultural texts and cultural work of some contemporary punk rock and hip hop pedagogues to be invaluable resources for schoolteachers. The alternative subcultures can help youths make sense of self and the larger world, provide them one of the few commentaries left on racism, sexism, and classism (Runell, 2006), and give them, echoing Freire (2005), "a passion to know" what steps must be taken to build a more humane society" (Malott & Porfilio, 2007, p. 590). Likewise, the internet has also been a fruitful space to expose students to how the neoliberal assault is damaging all social life as well as to provide alternative dreams of living in a society that is predicated on justice, democracy, and equality (McLaren, 2005; Porfilio & McClary, 2004; Saltman, 2004). Many instructional designs, critical commentaries, and transformative projects are located on critically-oriented websites, such as Media-awareness, Workplace, Z-net, Edchange, Nycore, and Radicalteacher.

Through my growing connections with critical scholars, I learned that my pedagogy would improve if I provided outlets outside of the graduate seminar for students to reflect upon salient issues and questions tied to becoming a critical pedagogue. In this vein, my students joined an online forum, *"Knowing Our Students, Knowing Ourselves" (KOSKO) Project*, which consisted of pre-service teachers from colleges and universities located across the United States. The participants discussed various issues related to social justice, equity, and diversity in education. However, the online dialogues were most fruitful because they ensured that my students possessed an ecumenical understanding of what causes the opportunity gaps in education, and how educators and their students can take action to close these gaps. Finally, by building alliances with other critical scholars, I have been able to extend the learning of transformative education for my students. I have orchestrated several international symposiums on promoting social justice and equity in education, held several brown bag seminars on the same topics, and invited students to attend and present papers and instructional designs at professional conferences.

Although my pedagogy has been continually retooled for the purposes of generating the intellectual skills, pedagogical guideposts, and courage necessary for students to become critical pedagogues, I am cognizant some of my former students did not carry with them a critical stance towards social formations fuelling violence, poverty, and hate in their communities, in their classrooms, and in other social contexts across the globe. Some of the resistance lies in my former students' preconceived ideas about the nature of Canadian society. For instance, many of them entered the graduate seminar with the notion that Canada has historically upheld its legal pronouncement of promoting cultural diversity and respecting the rights of citizens within its social and economic institutions.[5] Many students also had a difficult time accepting the fact that Canada's multicultural policies and initiatives have functioned for the past 35 years to "subordinate minority needs to the 'greater good' or to 'national interest'" (Fleras & Kunz, 2001, p. 19). Moreover, as I illustrate below, my former students' resistance to critical pedagogy was tied to the practical, commercialized nature of their teacher education programs.

WORKING AMID THE STATUS QUO: STORIES FROM FAST-TRACK TEACHER EDUCATION PROGRAMS

Even with the continual evaluation and reshaping of my pedagogy, the commercialized and practical nature of my students' teacher-education programs made me question exactly how many of my students entered K-12 classrooms prepared to dismantle pre-existing, asymmetrical institutional arrangements in schools and the wider society (Porfilio & Yu, 2006). The most obvious impediment to preparing schoolteachers to remove unjust practices and barriers in schools and society was the colleges' "customer-friendly approach" to learning. During a given term, most students took 18 graduate credit hours and completed numerous observation hours at area schools. This was done in a two-day-a-week schedule, so that students were given the option to earn their teaching license and MS of Education degree without giving up their full-time jobs. Certainly, this arrangement allowed the universities to feed their coffers by maximizing enrolment. However, students' intellectual development suffered. Since they had little time to reflect upon course material, they often focused their energy on learning practical information that would allegedly help them survive during their first few years in K-12 classrooms, such as learning classroom management techniques or creating unit plans. What they often failed to intellectually grapple with were the cornerstones of "racism, classism, sexism, equity, and social justice issues" (Horton & Scott, 2004). This is just the type of reflection that may parlay into developing skills for implementing transformative education in K-12 classrooms.

The colleges' drive to increase profits also impacted the graduate coursework earmarked to educate students about the social, historical, and cultural dimensions of schooling and the tenets of critical pedagogy. Like most schools of education, contingent faculty was the most dominant staple of teacher-educators within the two fast-track programs. Not coincidently, amongst a barrage of information that is inline to perpetuate the status quo, my students learned from my contingent colleagues that they should foster multicultural education by cooking and eating "ethnic foods," by dressing up in the "official garb" of ethnic minorities, and by promoting and celebrating Black history month or the alleged "holidays" of minoritized people.[6]

Behind the scenes, so to speak, the commercial and practical ethos of the two teacher-education programs braided together block policies and practices that would build programs based on a shared vision for a just society (Derman-Sparks, 2002, p. 2). For instance, a few years ago, my colleagues and I were invested with the power to design the teacher education department's mission statement. After some prolonged discussion on this topic, a socially-progressive colleague and I suggested that the document should reflect the aims of educating reflective practitioners who are prepared to eliminate the opportunity gaps in education and who are able to promote social justice and equity in their classrooms. Eight of the eleven remaining faculty members responded negatively to our suggestions. Three former school administrators felt that we would be merely treading water by attempting to teach future teachers these skills. They claimed only "principals or superintendents and people within higher education have the power" to make systemic change occur. Four former schoolteachers felt expressing our desire to promote social justice and equity in our program was redundant. They claimed that this was already done in our department and was reflected in the mission statement in the department's claim to produce schoolteachers who employ "caring teaching techniques in the classroom." To close out the discussion, another former principal/superintendent claimed the social justice language was not needed. He believed, incorrectly, that our graduates necessarily promote social justice by teaching children "how to read and write."

Our suggestions were voted down. As a result, the mission statement sent students and the wider community a wrong message, signalling "caring" teachers have the power by themselves to eliminate unjust practices and systemic barriers that have perpetuated opportunity gaps in North America's education system for the past 170 years. Moreover, the discourse generated during the meeting indicated our graduates had been (mis)educated by many of their professors on several important levels. They probably learned that our youths disengage in the schooling process because they lack a firm command of the English language, instead of being trained to see the pernicious impact that poverty, racism, sexism, classism, and homophobia have on students' social and educational performance. They probably learned that administrators are only capable of directing policy and making important classroom decisions, instead of being exposed to the cultural and intellectual work of schoolteachers who are generating instructional designs, engaging in cultural work in their students' communities, and supporting policies and practices that ameliorate our schooling structures. They probably learned to value the importance of how to teach in the classroom, instead of seeing the benefits associated with authentic learning communities that are aimed at teaching students about what historical and social forces give rise to the events shaping their immediate realties.

The impact of teaching and conducting research amid commercialized fact-track teacher education programs for an extended period left me very cynical that critical pedagogues have the power to overcome the institutional constraints that block a revolutionary agenda from taking hold in schools of education. Unlike some of my former critical colleagues and friends who abandoned teaching and conducting scholarship in a critical manner due to the continual challenges they faced from students, colleagues, and administrators, as stated earlier, I reached out to other critical scholars who were grappling with similar issues at their academic institutions. Several of us have joined together to conduct research and share our oppositions and concerns in relation to how schools of education are blocking future and current teachers from learning from critical scholars and examining the ideals of critical pedagogy. This has left me hopeful that our intellectual work and teaching have the potency to radically change the world and has also provided me emotional support when confronting the semiotic machines in the academic world linked to breeding commercial and traditional teaching practices over progressive policies and practices designed to improve schools and the wider society (Carlson, 2008). At the same time, I took it upon myself to find a job at an academic institution that is more concerned with creating an environment dedicated to promoting social justice and critical thought within its community rather than operating to fulfil the market-driven needs of students and to maximize profits.

CRITICAL SCHOLAR-PRACTITIONER MEETS THE CONSERVATIVE PARENTS:
CONFLICTS WITHIN THE FAMILY

Ever since I have consciously taken up a critical subject position towards the larger social and economic structures that perpetuate institutional forms of oppression across the globe, I have faced open resistance from family members who occupy subject positions inline with keeping in place social and economic arrangements that benefit the few at the expense of many. For instance, I have had clashes with my mother and stepfather over what factors account for increasing poverty, gang activities, violence and blight within their decaying deindustrialized community. They get upset when I call them on "blaming victims"–impoverished residents, senior citizens, working-poor families, and urban youths–for the debilitating conditions permeating their neighbourhood. Despite their resistance, I attempt to make them see the current sociohistorical reality of how deindustrialization, the globalization of capital, and neoliberal policies and practices seamlessly merge together to leave their community, as well as many other post-industrial communities in North America, in decay (Porfilio & Hall, 2005). I also have pushed them to reflect upon how skin colour has given them unearned privilege in their community compared to their minoritized counterparts. It has played a pivotal role in shielding them from becoming scapegoats for the denigration of their community, as many minoritized citizens are viewed as "up to no good" or deviant by many police offers, White citizens, and education personnel. It has also ensured they are not living in poverty, unlike 70% of the minoritized population in Niagara Falls, New York, who must deal with this stark social reality (Porfilio & Hall, 2005).

Ironically, my family has also felt the deleterious impact from the corporate conspiracy to hijack all of our social life for the purpose of maximizing profits (McLaren, 2005). During the early 1980s, my mother and stepfather were blindsided by the first wave of deindustrialization to hit their community. For over four years, our family struggled to remain economically afloat, as my stepfather lost his permanent position at an automobile plant in western New York. In addition, corporate greed is also tied to the several bouts of cancer that both of my parents have experienced.

My parents both worked at manufacturing plants and were forced to toil near chemicals and other toxins buried on the plants' premises. They also were exposed to numerous toxins and hazardous waste emitted in the air, buried underground, and placed in landfills by corporations in the Niagara region. The industrial violence also impacted many residents near my parents' home, as many of my parents' friends and their family members were stricken with cancer, birth defects and other medical disorders. Russell Mohkiber (1995), whose mother lived one block from where I grew up, also recognizes the impact that industrial violence and corporate crime has had on this community:

> The industrial corporations back home in Niagara Falls, on the other hand, have taken a toll. After my father died at a relatively young 52, my mother decided to uproot her young family and leave the city, in no small part because of the industrial violence inflicted on the city residents by polluting corporations. While we were in Niagara Falls, two of my first cousins, who were brother and sister, died at the age of five and six from leukemia. Since we left, one cousin died from Hodgkin's disease at the age of 31. Another cousin died from a rare form of brain cancer at the age of 35.

Recently, with my mother's latest bout with cancer, my parents have acknowledged that corporate greed is linked to some of the economic and medical problems they have faced in their lives. Yet, they have not made the connection to how corporate greed is responsible for the proliferation of crime, poverty, and other social dislocations in their community. Rather, they still tend to blame the Other for the inherent by-products of our unjust economic and social systems.

My parents have also clashed with my critical view of the US government's alleged war on terrorism. They, like nearly half of the US population, merged 9/11 with Iraq (Feldman, 2003). However, they, unlike most of the US population and peoples across the globe, continue to openly support America's "unending terrorism" across the globe (Rouleau, 2007; Feldman, 2003). They have been duped by the Bush Administration's rhetoric that America's war against terrorism is designed to protect them against fanatical Muslims who "hate freedom and wish to destroy democracy" (McLaren, 2002, p. 328). They have continuously dismissed the idea that 9/11 attacks were a "gift for neo-conservatives" (Rouleau, 2007).[7]

My parents' disdain for my views on 9/11, US foreign policy, and on what ought to be done to eliminate imperialism, violence, and xenophobia spilled over during a presentation I gave in 2006. My mom attended this presentation that focused on utilizing hip hop and punk rock subcultures to guide our youth to understand the material world, which includes a critical recognition of what gives rise to world violence, racism, sexism, poverty, and xenophobia. She was shaken by the presentation. She quipped, incorrectly, after the teaching demonstration, that I am "too liberal" and vowed never to attend another presentation.

Since my mom's encounter with her liberal son, our family discussions are generally vapid. My parents no longer inquire what I teach to my students, discuss the social problems percolating in their community, or discuss the US government's "war on terrorism." It seems clear to them that we may never eliminate the gaps in how we view our experiences, view the nature of our social and economic institutions, and view what gives rise to institutional oppressions.

THE IMPORTANCE OF CRITICAL PEDAGOGY AND THE VALUE OF SELF-REFLECTIVE NARRATIVES: LOOKING BACK AND HEADING FORWARD

As I have shown above, occupying a critical subject position within commercialized/ practical teacher education programs as well as within my own familiar circles for the past seven years has wrought conflict and tension on the job and at home. However, I am willing to take the bumps and bruises that one necessarily encounters as a critical scholar-practitioner. I believe that through teaching for social, cultural and economic transformation, engaging in research designed to eliminate societal oppression, and through working with other social advocates to ameliorate schools and society, the dream to build democratic social and economic institutions will be reached during the 21st century.

There are many signs in my own social world that my teaching and research are serving as building blocks to "create a just, creative, and democratic society" (Kincheloe, 2004, p. 21). For instance, the empancipatory light flickers when my former students email me to tell me they implemented instructional designs that position our youths to understand how past historical injustices are linked to systemic forms of oppression at today's sociohistorical moment, position students to feel comfortable to stand up to those who foster hate and hostility in their schools and communities, and position them to understand what constitutive forces breed violence, poverty, sexism, and racism across the globe.

It happens outside the graduate seminar when I witness my students conduct a presentation to demonstrate how Bush's No Child Left Behind Act (2001) has perpetuated more opportunity gaps in our educational system, or when I witness students on campus call on school administrators to widen the scope of the school's social justice mission so as to expose how North America's institutions inherently function to create division amongst its citizens and to ensure poverty and urban blight surrounding the immediate campus is eradicated. I also see the possibility for social change when I hear alternative narratives during the research process. For example, I conducted a two-year qualitative research study to unearth pre-service teachers' perceptions and experiences in relation to computing technology and male-centred computing culture. Through the open dialogues and one-on-one and focus group interviews, several pre-service teachers came to a newfound understanding of how systemic barriers, gendered stereotypes, and unjust practices often marshal unjust relationships between the sexes in everyday life. They also made the vital connection that social and economic inequalities could only be dismantled if they themselves create classroom climates designed to educate our youth to think critically about the nature of their social worlds. They also envisioned how computing technology could actualize their transformative visions within the elementary classroom.

After writing this narrative, I recognize more fully the power critical pedagogy can have on one's life. This project has helped me pinpoint the impact my doctoral training has had on altering my views of self and Others, of the nature of research, of the purpose of schooling, and of my role as educator and citizen within this unjust society. The reflective process also left me more cognizant of how the "hidden curriculum" within commercialized and practical teacher education programs functions to keep in place hegemonic teaching practices, relationships, and structures, while concurrently sealing off oppositional ideas and practices that might generate a movement to democratize institutions of learning as well as other oppressive structures. Yet, without this form of research, I may have never realized the various ways I forged pockets of resistance amid the status quo. The constant retooling of my pedagogy helps undo some of the damage inflicted on my students due to practical and commercial nature of their college teacher education programs. Teaching amid the status quo I have concocted ways to guide more and more future teachers to embrace the tenets of critical pedagogy and institute teaching strategies and lesson plans configured to create a democratic social reality in the 21st century.

However, the road to criticality will only be widened if critical scholars continue to bring awareness and take action against the neoliberal assault of higher education. As my narrative captures, commercialized policies, logics, and practices are antithetical to broadening the movement to democratize our social, economic, and political systems. The neoliberal assault on higher education is becoming more virulent, as the ruling elite has stepped up its efforts to eliminate any oppositional ideas or movements that question the value of market forces guiding our social and economic relationships. Recently, several critical scholars, who hold positions in higher education, have been attacked by the reactionary Right. It appears the political and economic elite will now stoop to any level to keep in place the institutions and ideologies that maintain their privileged positions. For instance, they have encouraged current students to secretly audiotape their teachers (Fassbinder, 2006). Such tactics are reminiscent of the anti-Communist witch hunt of the 1950s organized by Senator McCarthy, which targeted the entertainment industry and which used its House Committee on Un-American Activities to terrorize the political Left.

I have suggested elsewhere[8] how critical scholars, students, and citizens can build a counter-hegemonic movement against the neoliberal agenda. One integral part of this process must involve critical-scholar practitioners engaging their autobiographic roads to criticality as well as documenting the struggles, challenges, and success stories associated with occupying a critical subject position. If this occurs, critical scholars and students contemplating joining the revolutionary movement may be better prepared to subvert the policies and practices propagating the commercial ordering of our world as well as feel more inspired that their efforts will translate into developing a society predicated on the ideals of justice, democracy, liberty, and equity.

NOTES

[1] The term minoritized is borrowed from Solomon et al. (2005, p. 166) to document that Whites "are a member of a racial group however their racialization affords them benefits that are seldom available to minority groups."

[2] Many scholars have illuminated the socially constituted nature of gender. The process occurs as one's self operates through various discursive systems and learns whether its socially constituted performance is deemed acceptable by different social actors (or audiences) who embrace certain forms of masculinity or femininity over others. Over the past several years, I have attempted to reflect on how my gendered body has impacted my life, my relationship with students, and Others. My reflection also takes inventory of whether my performances have made audiences question the value of embracing debilitating forms of masculinity, such as being aggressive, competitive, and overly ambitious, which are considered the most socially acceptable for men to perform within the various social contexts that I have traversed. Therefore, I believe that re-inventing masculinity in more humane ways is an essential component to democratizing the world.

[3] Many critical pedagogues have documented how university students use their race or sexuality to discount their work as merely being a feminist "who is out of control" or a visible minority who is "mad at the world." To further examine how gay and lesbian and racial minority female professors have been harassed, silenced and victimized inside universities, please examine De Castell & Bryson's (Eds.) Radical In<ter>ventions: Identity, Politics and Difference/s in Educational Praxis. Albany, NY: SUNY Press.

[4] They were inculcated, just as I was by teacher educators, into focusing on "rearranging the physical layout of the classroom, the format of the curriculum, lesson planning and behavioural objectives," instead of examining "how both the school purpose and teacher/student identities are shaped vis-à-vis larger social-political and cultural formations" (Kincheloe, 2004, p. 36).

[5] Carr and Lund (2007, p. 3) further detail that Canadian resistance and denial of its legacy of oppression is rooted in "the complex, and often antagonistic, relationship it has had with the United States since before Confederation." Canadians have become self-assured that Canada does not have the "endless visible warts, including a long history of racial tension and civil rights struggles." (p. 3).

[6] For instance, some faculty members felt schoolteachers should instruct young children that Thanksgiving reflects peaceful coexistence between First Nation's people and the dominant society during the Colonial Era.

[7] According to Rouleau, the 9/11 attacks were "an invitation to roll out their programme of imperial expansion: occupation of Afghanistan and Iraq, as a prelude to the invasion of Iran; reinforced military presence in central Asia and the Gulf; control over oil resources; replacement of regimes refusing to bow to the new international order. All of this to be done in the name of the 'global war on terrorism', which would be total and endless."

[8] To further examine what steps are needed to create a counter-hegemonic movement against the commercialization of schooling and other social contexts, please examine Porfilio, B. & Yu, T. "Student as Consumer": A Critical Narrative of the Commercialization of Teacher Education. Journal for Critical Education Policy Studies 4(1).

REFERENCES

Bigelow, B., & Peterson, B. (Eds.). (2002). *Rethinking globalization: Teaching for justice in an unjust world.* Milwaukee, WI: Rethinking Schools Press.

Carr, P. R., & Lund, D. E. (Eds.). (2007). Scanning whiteness. The great white north? Exploring whiteness, privilege, and identity in education. In P. R. Carr & D. L. Lund's (Eds.), *The great white north? Exploring whiteness, privilege, and identity in education* (pp. 1–15). Rotterdam: Sense Publications.

Carlson, D. (2008). (In press). Neoliberalism and urban school reform: A Cincinnati case study. In B. Porfilio & C. Malott's (Eds.), *The destructive path of neoliberalism: An international examination of education*. The Netherlands: Sense Publishers.

Cervone, B. (2004). *Recognizing the knowledge of young people: An interview with Michelle Fine and Maria Elena Torre on youth action research*. Retrieved September 1, 2001, from http://whatkidscando.org/archives/featurestories/Cinterview.html

Chomsky, N. (2004) *Chomsky on miseducation*. Lanham, MD: Rowman and Littlefield.

De Castell, S., & Bryson, M. (Eds.). (1997). *Radical In<ter>ventions: Identity, politics and difference/s in educational praxis*. Albany, NY: SUNY Press.

Dei, G. (2005, February 19). *Black-focused schools are about inclusion, not segregation. Guelph Mercury*. Retrieved April 30, 2007, from http://fcis.oise.utoronto.ca/~gpieters/afrocentricschools/acschoolnews2.html

Fine, M. (2004). *Echoes of brown: Youth documenting and performing the legacy of brown v. board of education*. New York: Teachers College Press.

Fassinder, S. (2006, June 4). *The "dirty thirty's" Peter McLaren reflects on the crises of academic freedom*. MR. Magazine Retrieved August 4, 2007, from http://mrzine.monthlyreview.org/fassbinder060406.html

Feldmann, L. (2003, March 14). *The impact of Bush linking 9/11 and Iraq. The Christian science monitor*. Retrieved September 1, 2007, from http://www.csmonitor.com/2003/0314/p02s01-woiq.html

Fleras, A., & Kunz-Lock, J. (2001). *Media and minorities: Representing diversity in a multicultural Canada*. Toronto: Thompson Publishing.

Freire, P. (2005). *Teachers as cultural workers: Letters to those who dare teach*. New York: Westview Press.

Giroux, H. A. (2005). Cultural studies in dark times: Public pedagogy and the challenge of neoliberalism. *Fast Capitalism, 1*(2). Retrieved September 1, 2007, from http://www.fastcapitalism.com/

Horton J., & Scott, D. (2004). White students' voices in multicultural teacher education preparation. *Multicultural Education*. Retrieved September 2, 2007, from http://findarticles.com/p/articles/mi_qa3935/is_200407/ai_n9414143

Juskalian, R. (2007, September 16). Review: Slavery is shockingly alive and well today. *USA Today*. Retrieved September 16, 2007, from http://www.usatoday.com/money/books/2007-09-16-nobodies_N.htm

Kincheloe, J. L. (2004). *Critical pedagogy primer*. New York: Peter Lang.

Kincheloe, J. L., & McLaren, P. (2000). Rethinking critical theory and qualitative research. In N. K. Denzin & Y. S. Lincoln (Eds.), *Handbook of qualitative research* (2nd ed., pp. 279–314). Thousand Oaks: Sage.

Lee, E., Menkart, D., & Okazawa-Rey, M. (2002). Introduction. In E. Lee, E. Menkart, & M. Okazawa-Rey (Eds.), *Beyond heroes and holidays: A practical guide to K-12 anti-racist, multicultural education and staff development* (pp. VII–XII). Washington, DC: Teaching for Change.

Malott, C., & Porfilio, B. (2007). Punk rock, hip hop, and the politics of human resistance: Reconstituting the social studies through critical media literacy. In S. Steinberg & D. Macedo (Eds.), *Media literacy: A reader* (pp. 582–592). New York: Peter Lang.

Malot, C. (2006). Schooling in an era of corporate dominance: Marxism against burning tires. *The Journal for Critical Education Policy Studies, 4*(2). Retrieved January 10, 2008, from http://www.jceps.com/index.php?pageID=article&articleID=58

Marx, S. (2004). Regarding whiteness: Exploring and intervening in the effects of white racism in teacher education. *Equity and Excellence in Education, 37*(1), 1–13.

Macedo, D. (1994). *Literacies of power: What Americans are not allowed to know?* Boulder: Westview.

Mokhiber, R. (1995). Soft on crime. *Multinational Monitor, 17*(5). Retrieved August 4, 2007, from http://multinationalmonitor.org/hyper/issues/1995/05/mm0595_09.html

McLaren, P. (2006). *Life in schools: An introduction to critical pedagogy in the foundations of education* (5th ed.). New York: Allyn & Bacon.

McLaren, P. (2005). *Capitalists and conquerors: A critical pedagogy against empire.* New York: Roman and Littlefield Publishers.

McLaren, P. (2002). George Bush, Apocalypse sometime soon, and the American imperium. *Cultural Studies-Critical Methodologies, 2*(3), 327–333.

Ng, R. (1997). A woman out of control: Deconstructing racism and sexism in the university. In De Castell & Bryson's (Eds.), *Radical in<ter>ventions: Identity, politics and difference/s in educational praxis* (pp. 39–59). Albany, NY: SUNY Press.

Porfilio, B., & Yu, T. Student as consumer: A critical narrative of the commercialization of teacher education. *Journal for Critical Education Policy Studies, 4*(1). Retrieved June 3, 2007, from http://www.jceps.com/index.php?pageID=article&articleID=56

Porfilio, B., & Hall, J. (2005). "Power city" politics and the building of a corporate school. *Journal for Critical Education Policy Studies, 3*(1). Retrieved June 22, 2005, from http://www.jceps.com/index.php?pageID=article&articleID=38

Porfilio, B., & McClary, G. (2004). Future teachers confront globalization: A critical approach to "good citizenship" in social studies education. *Electronic Magazine of Multicultural Education* [online], 6(1), 17 paragraphs. Retrieved December 1, 2005, from http://www.eastern.edu/publications/emme/2004spring/porfilio_mcclary.html

Rouleau, E. (2007). *Terrorism: The chosen tool of the weak against the mighty does global war on terror mask a new imperialism?* Z-Net. Retrieved June 20, 2007, from http://www.zmag.org/content/showarticle.cfm?ItemID=13017

Runell, M. (2006, September 12). *Hip hop education 101.* Vibe. Retrieved October 8, 2006, from http://www.vibe.com/news/online_exclusives/2006/09/hip_hop_education_101/

Saltman, J. K. (2004). Coca-cola's global lessons: From education for corporate globalization to education for global justice. *Teacher Education Quarterly, 31*(1), 155–172.

Shore, I. (1999). What is critical literacy? *Journal for Pluralism, Pedagogy, and Practice, 4*(1). Retrieved June 4, 2007, from http://www.lesley.edu/journals/jppp/4/index.html

Sleeter, C. (2002). Teaching whites about racism. In E. Lee, E. Menkart, & M. Okazawa-Rey (Eds.), *Beyond heroes and holidays: A practical guide to K-12 anti-racist, multicultural education and staff development* (pp. 36–44). Washington, DC: Teaching for Change.

Sparks-Derman, L. (2002). Educating for equality: Forging a shared vision. In E. Lee, E. Menkart, & M. Okazawa-Rey (Eds.), *Beyond heroes and holidays: A practical guide to K-12 anti-racist, multicultural education and staff development* (pp. 2–7). Washington, DC: Teaching for Change.

Solomon, P. R., Portelli, J., Daniel, B. J., & Campbell, A. (2005). The discourse of denial: How White teacher candidates construct race, racism, and "White privilege." *Race, Ethnicity and Education, 8*(2), 147–169.

Weiler, H. (2005). *Theories and practice: Dichotomies of knowledge?* Retrieved June 10, 2007, from http://www.stanford.edu/~weiler/Texts05/CIES_paper.pdf

PRIYA PARMAR

9. THE "DANGERS" OF TEACHING A CRITICAL PEDAGOGY

The dual society, at least in public education, seems in general to be unquestioned.
– Jonathan Kozol
Death at an Early Age, 1964

What good fortune for those in power that people do not think.
– Adolf Hitler

Dissent is the highest form of patriotism

– Thomas Jefferson

I begin my personal narrative with the powerful, and perhaps offensive, quotes above. My K-12 education was a process of *schooling*, not *education*, in which I was indoctrinated and trained to refrain from questioning authority and to passively accept the knowledge transferred from teacher to student.[1] I base this understanding on how Jonathan Kozol characterized education in his first book, *Death at an Early Age (1967)*. It was not until I entered graduate school that I began to understand the purpose of school and the difference between being *schooled* and being *educated*, and why it was so. I now understand what Adolf Hitler meant when he described how he convinced masses of people to believe that the genocide of millions of innocent people was justifiable and in their best interest.[2] I use Thomas Jefferson's famous quote when introducing my students to multiple and alternative narratives that speak and act against the grain of the dominant ideology and culture.

The reactions to these quotes by some students are usually silence, disbelief, and anger that I would actually have the audacity to bring in such bold and offensive statements, especially the quote from Hitler. However, throughout the course of the semester, students become aware, albeit some may still disagree, that what we may have perceived as "common sense" may have been socially constructed or manufactured–the process Gramsci has named hegemony.[3] Students come to understand Jefferson's statement that to dissent is patriotic, and that politics are embedded in institutional arenas and inherent in one's being; in other words, we are all political beings.

These quotes set the tone and tenor of the courses I teach–to facilitate dialogues that encourage students to reconceptualize education, to think critically and

A.H. Churchill (ed.), Rocking Your World: The Emotional Journey
into Critical Discourses, 99–109.

question all ideologies, even mine. As I will explain throughout this chapter, students' worlds, as well was mine, were rocked when realizing that engaging in a critical education resulted in reactionary efforts that polarized my college campus.

My current position as an Assistant Professor of Literacy in the Adolescence Program at Brooklyn College's School of Education has enabled me to teach a variety of courses at the undergraduate, graduate, and secondary high school levels as well as supervise pre- and in-service teachers. Before reflecting on the struggles of teaching critically, I want to give you a brief description of the courses I teach and an idea of my educational philosophy.

I currently teach two undergraduate courses. The course "Art, Philosophy, and Culture of Teaching" links the philosophical, historical, and cultural foundations of education with curriculum and teaching. "Language Literacy in Secondary Education" includes discussions around issues of language development and diversity, and differences between the written word and spoken language. In the literacy course, I provide pedagogical strategies when teaching students of diverse linguistic and cultural backgrounds. I also help my college students identify the relationship between identity formation and reading, writing, and speaking. The theoretical framework that grounds the course is critical theory, specifically critical pedagogy and critical literacies.

I also teach 10th and 11th grade high school students who receive credit towards meeting their English requirements. The stated purpose of the high school course is to help increase interest and motivation in reading and writing, improve literacy rates, and prepare students to take the English Regents examination. I also raise students' critical awareness of the ways in which the popular media shape an individual's conceptions of self and the world. This course incorporates practices of critical pedagogy and critical media literacy and incorporates spoken word poetry to enhance literacy and critical thinking skills. It meets New York City and New York State Standards. The bulk of the course content comprises contextualized examples of the students' lives by encouraging them to bring in texts they listen to or view. These include specific genres of popular culture and elements of hip hop culture to increase awareness and literacy in hopes of inspiring student agency. Similar to my undergraduate courses, my high school students' voices are heard and experiences are validated through the critical analysis of economic, social, and political issues addressed in the classroom, and, for some of my courageous younger students, performed through the power of the spoken word.

All of my courses employ inter-disciplinary, trans-disciplinary, and counter-disciplinary approaches, and I am deeply committed to social change and social justice by engaging in a reconstructivist approach to education advocating social activism and liberatory teaching practices. This is how my teaching expresses critical pedagogy. I see myself as an agent and participant of change, using a dialogical and student-centered approach where students' opinions, voices, and experiences are heard and valued (Freire, 1970; Freire 1973). Encouraging students to employ an inquiry-based approach to learning and asking epistemological questions[4] fosters both critical thinking and intellectual curiosity forcing them to interrogate and deconstruct[5] traditional and non-traditional discourses. Together we interrogate how power and our own belief systems have shaped and constructed our identities. We interrogate and deconstruct how we have been shaped by hegemony and discuss how we can reconstruct ourselves away from institutionalized thinking and positivist teaching practices; hence, students are viewed as producers of knowledge (Gramsci, 1971; Kincheloe, 2004). We achieve this sometimes-difficult task by examining how our own conscious and unconscious biases and prejudices can escalate into detrimental teaching patterns and practices, particularly if critical reflection on or analysis of oneself is absent. This practice exemplifies the difference between being schooled and education.

I have extremely high standards for my students and expect them to take responsibility for their learning. I do this by encouraging each individual to contribute to classroom discussions and by adding supplementary course readings as necessary. My goal is to create a safe learning environment that fosters stimulating dialogue while respecting and valuing diverse views and experiences.

This dialogical pedagogy also means that I must re-negotiate my own position as the professor. I have had to learn to respect and value opposing and dissenting perspectives without punishing students in the form of the grade. This is easier said than done–especially if one is passionate about her views. A dialogic pedagogy is challenging, and at times downright scary, for the professor because this entails student critique and challenge of the professor's work. It means giving up some of the power you hold as the professor–an extremely difficult thing to do!

I have to constantly monitor my own actions in the dialogical process, deliberately and consciously making a concerted effort to remain quiet at appropriate times in order to create a safe space for others to speak with the same passion and rigor that I display. I have learned to step back and appreciate opposing perspectives, respecting those that are well developed and articulated. Not an easy feat when you feel so strongly about an issue. After all, I have been schooled to believe that the teacher is the expert, the all-knowing purveyor of knowledge. Her word is the last, credible word spoken. I have had to learn to un-train or un-condition myself in believing this notion of what a "good" teacher is. As I make my ideological position clear to my students, I require they do the same. I ask them to defend their position as if they were lawyers in a courtroom arguing their case to a jury. I also warn them to be prepared to be challenged by me or their colleagues–that is, after all, the beauty of debate.

Frequent reassurances from me that their grades will not suffer are necessary to ensure safe spaces for critical and stimulating dialogue. I have learned to play devil's advocate, especially at times when opposing views are absent from the discussion. This has been challenging as well because I must consciously think about the issue from the perspective of the Other, one in which I obstinately disagree. Nonetheless, I believe in free speech and am reminded of Voltaire's famous words, "I do not approve of a word you say but will defend to the death your right to say it."

Promoting an awareness and understanding that social and political forces shape the construction and utilization of knowledge has not been an easy feat–nor did I ever expect it to be. My teaching has been labeled "controversial" and "dangerous."

As a result, I have been named as one of the "101 Most Dangerous Academics in America" by conservative author David Horowitz (2006). My first reaction to this label was shock, quickly followed by fear and concern since, at the time the story was revealed, I was an untenured assistant professor at City University of New York (CUNY). When I was a graduate student, I remember being warned by my professors about the implications of teaching a critical pedagogy. I knew that cultural study scholars, especially women and women of color, could become easy targets for discussing controversial issues that challenged mainstream ideologies, but I did not expect to be targeted so quickly and it was overwhelmingly disconcerting!

The allegations made against me and my teaching a critical discourse was distorted, defamatory, and hurtful. They started with the anonymous complaints of several students enrolled in my undergraduate literacy course. Although scores of students vehemently opposed and countered the allegations made against me by writing support letters to all levels of CUNY administration, the unsubstantiated complaints from two students in particular seemed to garner the attention of the press.[6] Once my story reached wider audiences, my research and pedagogy were once again scrutinized and distorted even further. I remember thinking selfishly to myself: "Why me? What I am teaching about is nothing new! There are many more critically acclaimed scholars engaged in critical theory/pedagogy that are teaching and writing about the same issues and more–I learned it from them–why aren't they being publicly vilified?!?!"

Quite honestly, I was petrified and found myself sinking into a playing-the-victim role. Thrown into public scrutiny based on misrepresentations of my work and blatant lies without having a voice to represent myself seemed egregiously unfair. I was naïve and fragile to the harsh politics of the real world and was consumed with fear of the potential consequences.

After regaining my composure and overcoming my fears with the support and strength from my students, colleagues at Brooklyn College, the City University of New York's powerful and political union, the Professional Staff Congress (PSC), and the critical scholars who I once wished were on the chopping block with me, I came to accept the position I was in and attempted to make it work for me by fighting back. Isn't that what my mentors instilled in me?

In fighting back, I was forced to reflect on my pedagogical approach questioning the way I was presenting content: "Did I come off too abrasive or harsh?" "Did I not appear as a credible source to introduce the information even though I cited research and shared personal experiences?" "Was I being too aggressive when challenging my students to think beyond the status quo?" I continue to contemplate the answers to these and many other questions as I learn and grow as an educator.

In terms of my teaching style, my critics faulted me for politicizing education and naming my ideological position in the classroom. They used this as evidence that I was indoctrinating my students. Of politicizing education and naming my ideological position, I am guilty as charged–with no regrets I may add. However, this is simply sound pedagogical practice and, in fact, people who deny the politics of their viewpoints or who do not publicly recognize their ideologies are the ones who should be accused of indoctrination. My academic freedom was under attack and, as a result, my name was publicly slandered due to shoddy research methods published by an author who attempted to bully and silence critical and progressive educators named in his book.[7]

Alternatively, I realized how the politics of education have played a role in my being a target. I had at least four strikes against me: (1) I am a woman; (2) I am a woman of color; (3) I look younger than my actual chronological age; (4) and I did not have tenure. This combination made me both more threatening and an easier target.

My feelings of being mischaracterized have slowly turned into anger due to the defamatory and unsubstantiated claims made of me. Although I do not think I have yet earned the title of "dangerous," I am humbled and honored to be associated with such internationally acclaimed scholars and activists such as Noam Chomsky, Dana Cloud, Angela Davis, Michael E. Dyson, bell hooks, Manning Marable, and Howard Zinn. Therefore, I find myself thinking, "Wow, I'm in very good company, maybe undeservingly." I am inspired by the support and advice I have received from my colleagues and students. I am reminded that when teaching about the history and philosophy of education, Socrates, for example, was put to death for filling young people's minds with "dangerous" ideas; or, how Ann Hutchinson was banished from the Massachusetts Bay Colony for "stepping beyond the bounds of what was allowed for women" when she organized Bible reading groups in her home and taught against the grain of the established religion; and finally, how Frederick Douglass was deemed "dangerous" by his slave master once he learned to read.

It is in this tradition that I would like to be considered "dangerous" or "controversial." My role as an educator is one who facilitates critical consciousness, as I strive to empower my students to think critically, to find their voice, and to become active citizens. Being critical, though, has been an emotional roller coaster of a ride. As I stated earlier, although I was warned as a graduate student of the possibility of being attacked for having progressive ideological thoughts, no one could have prepared me for the onslaught of lies and hate that has engulfed me.

I have debated and struggled whether I should publish my personal story. Advice from both family and colleagues has been mixed. Some advised me not to respond to the false allegations because it would just fuel more fire to my critics' claims, allowing the story to live on. I think about my own position, as an untenured junior faculty member, working for a city university system that undervalues its students, faculty, and staff. Attempting to survive financially is a priority. Living with peace of mind is another priority. My own pedagogical approach encourages my students to fight for equity and social justice, working towards transforming oneself and the education system, starting with one's own classroom.

While I sometimes fear the consequences of teaching critically, I also remind myself: Isn't critical pedagogy about transformation and agency? Wouldn't my integrity be compromised if I remained silent, teaching in a "safe" manner so as not to "offend" anyone? What hidden messages would I be sending if I remained neutral in the classroom? Would tenure even grant me job security given today's attack on academic freedom and the Left? Wouldn't I be a hypocrite if I succumbed to the pressure and advice to "follow the rules," in other words, abide by the status quo, not "rock the boat," and avoid "controversial" topics to create the "quiet" classroom environment that administration value? I know my fears are a conditioned and socialized reaction to pressure from the dominant power structures (for me, my college administration). I know in my heart the answer to my questions and fears: I will not compromise my teaching, or integrity, in order to play it safe and neutral.

Many of my students have expressed that they love the dialogue and debate regardless of one's ideological position and wish they had more of it in some of their other courses. Moreover, debates and dialogical pedagogy provides students the opportunity to perfect their social and presentation skills when attempting to formulate compelling and persuasive arguments of their own. It must be emphasized that critical pedagogy is simply not the bitch and complaint session as it is sometimes perceived. Instead, class meetings are highly structured with rigorous work expectations. Students are required to learn the technical knowledge required of them in their expertise or discipline area. It is my responsibility as a professor to both equip students with the necessary skills to successfully navigate in the mainstream world and workforce and to prepare them to be conscious of the insidious forces that shape and sustain hegemony.

I have been asked many times if I fear for my safety since I was named a "dangerous" professor. As I explained earlier, initially I was consumed with fear–fear of losing my job, compromising my teaching style, and yes, even my physical safety. I received a number of hateful emails containing profane and cynical messages, many from anonymous writers who completely misunderstood my intentions when addressing language and literacy issues.

As Paulo Freire has repeatedly advised in his writings, I have not allowed my fears to paralyze me to the point where I might abandon teaching a critical pedagogy. I rationalize through my fears by reflecting on my own educational experiences, working with New York City public school teachers, teaching NYC high school students, and, equally importantly, listening to the stories my students share with me about their own educational experiences. Students enter my classroom with 12 or more years of "schooling" based in a technocratic educational system in which positivist approaches to teaching have been valued and rewarded. Asking students to analyze and re-think their ideological beliefs is perplexing for some, especially those affirming dominant ideologies.

For example, my undergraduate literacy course introduces students to multiple literacies including cultural literacies. My goal is simply to bring about awareness of and expose my students to the rich cultural and linguistic diversities that exist. What these future teachers do with this knowledge is entirely up to them. In terms of language acquisition, the question I pose to them is "how will you teach your students the standard code [Standard American English] without denigrating a student's home language or dialect?" Put simply, my students and I discuss the meaning of code-switching so linguistically diverse students do not feel inadequate, marginalized, or denigrated in any way. We discuss the many different regional dialects that exist today, ranging from Northeastern dialects to Southern and Appalachian dialects. We discuss how language has evolved historically and more importantly, how Standard American English has evolved to be the present or modern day language of power. We discuss how power in the form of language has evolved historically by analyzing the immigrant experience in terms of language acquisition, oppression, and suppression of home languages with all races and ethnicities (eg. African-American, Italian-American, Irish-American, German-American, Jewish-American, etc).

As an advocate of critical pedagogy, I hope my students will appreciate and value the diverse dialects that exist and welcome these in the classroom in order to teach their future students the "standard code." Otherwise, the rejection of the primary language or dialect may result in silencing and marginalizing students who do not wish to conform to the dominant cultures' values. There is no question that we all must learn how to speak and write in the standard code; however, I have been charged with teaching students that "white English" is the "oppressors' language" and that I "repeatedly referred to English as a language of oppressors and in particular denounced white people as the oppressors." It is both amusing and extremely frustrating to me how my words were so grotesquely twisted and distorted. The references to English as "a language of oppressors" comes from an assigned reading written by distinguished scholar and Dangerous Professor, bell hooks, in response to a poem by the equally distinguished poet and author, Adrienne Rich.[8] I agree with bell hooks, and have my students critically think about, and challenge, the following excerpt that hooks reflects upon: "I know that it is not the English language that hurts me, but what the oppressors do with it, how they shape it to become a territory that limits and defines, how they make it a weapon that can shame, humiliate, colonize."[9]

Another area of my pedagogy that has been attacked is my research on hip hop culture, particularly the use of rap music as a form of critical literacy. Again, I am infuriated at how my pedagogy is misrepresented and mischaracterized by the press. I do advocate for the incorporation of both mainstream and non-mainstream rap lyrics in the classroom as long as a thoughtful critical analysis is done of these texts. I do not support lyrics that are replete with violent and misogynistic messages; rather I encourage my students to analyze, deconstruct, challenge, and re-create these lyrics for any negative contents found within. This type of analysis teaches the necessary skills required by New York State English Language Arts Standards. My students write persuasive arguments, reports, and narratives for or against the messages found in the lyrics. I sometimes have my students translate the lyrics into Standard American English. These exercises are excellent strategies to teach the language of power without denigrating the dialect of either the lyric or the student themselves. Equally important, these exercises engage students in conversations that help them understand why it is necessary to code-switch as well as teaching them to be well-informed, conscious, and critical consumers of media.

Most theoretical texts on critical theory fail to delve deeply into the personal, emotional, and sometimes painful journey of teaching critically. The exclusion of such stories reduce critical theory to just that–theory. The absence of personal narratives, in a sense, results in dehumanization, which is strangely ironic considering one of our main goals is to transform education into a humanizing practice. A wonderful and informative text, *The Critical Pedagogy Reader*, is a necessary read for anyone interested in learning about and engaging in critical pedagogy (Darder, Baltodano & Torres, 2003). One of the closing chapters includes a dialogue between Ira Shor and Paulo Freire discussing the fears and implications of teaching a critical pedagogy. The chapter resonates deeply within me as Shor and Freire share their own experiences, struggles, and fears of public scrutiny by the power elites for teaching critically–in Freire's case, he was labelled as a "bad Brazilian." This chapter names common fears such as pressure from a conservative administration to teach the status quo for fear of being denied promotion or tenure, a pay raise, a desirable teaching schedule; or attacks from ultra-conservative groups; or even one's own students as normal reactions and experiences that come with the territory of teaching a critical pedagogy.

I was also reassured by their candid conversation on the appropriate times to speak and act. I am extremely passionate when addressing certain issues in teaching and am sometimes perceived as being too outspoken in my classes. I have learned to consciously force myself to shut up so as not to dominate the conversations–not an easy feat when you feel like you have so much to contribute! During faculty meetings, however, I find myself a bit more reserved, acting as a sociologist, carefully observing and analyzing my environment before speaking. I have overheard colleagues, both tenured and non-tenured, advise junior faculty to either keep our mouths shut or carefully construct our thoughts before speaking so we do not create controversy or offend the administration and senior faculty who have power to promote us. I have witnessed outspoken critical educators become marginalized by their own faculty because of their brutal candidness in naming social injustices and calling for action. It is most disheartening when you believe your self-proclaimed liberal and progressive colleagues are in full support of fighting for social justice, but when it's time to act, you realize their words were just lip service.

I have also noticed work conditions deteriorate in insidious ways for critical colleagues. Some critical educators are placed under a microscopic lens in the sense that our research and pedagogy are more heavily scrutinized than our less-critical colleagues'. Failure to adhere to administrative guidelines and policies are grounds for punishment in the form of verbal and/or written notices placed in a personnel file. This would not be unfair if not for the inconsistent manner in which it occurs depending on one's ideological position.[10] In their dialogue, Shor and Freire discourage acting and speaking out of impulse and characterize such acts as committing political suicide, particularly if a strong support base is not established. Living in McCarthy-like times, when having tenure is not enough, the label of "dangerous" or "controversial" teacher has its risks, and critical educators must be smart and strategic when teaching.[11] Fortunately, in my situation, most of my colleagues within and outside my department have united to fight the recent attacks on academic freedom regardless of their ideological positions. Shor's and Freire's stories, as well as others, are inspirational and reassuring in knowing that we are not alone in this journey to fight for a socially just society or educational system.[12]

I have been asked in interviews if teaching such "controversial" issues makes me reconsider a career in academia. Despite the highly emotional and fearful journey of teaching critically, I never reconsidered changing career paths. As I grow as an educator, I am dedicated to internal and external growth, which means constantly challenging my own belief system, as well as honing new styles of teaching that engage a rapidly changing body of learners and their various learning styles. I am deeply and firmly committed to liberatory pedagogy and praxis which creates conditions for individuals to self-reflect and become aware that they can be agents of social change, capable of acting on and transforming the world in which they live, teach, engage, and then ultimately pass on these notions to the students they will be teaching.

Despite the "dangers" and risks associated with progressive education, I am still passionate about and dedicated to addressing diversity and social justice, to bringing multiple and alternative perspectives into the classroom–including my own. I will continue to encourage and challenge my students to question texts, even my own. I encourage them to question everything around them and to politicize education because education is a political act. If one disagrees, I welcome them to visit the New York City public school system in which one can clearly observe the economic disparities that exist between neighbourhoods (e.g. availability of resources, physical structure of school buildings, hiring practices, curricular content and pedagogical practices/methods, etc.). These disparities go so far as to resonate within schools in the form of tracking and curricula (specifically, mandated pre-packaged curricula for low-performing schools). The hurdles listed above present difficult challenges for the impassioned educator who graduates from teacher education programs that prepare her/him to implement innovative and creative lessons, especially those addressing social justice and diversity issues. The novice, untenured teacher quickly realizes that s/he has limited voice and rights by virtue of positionality alone, thus many adhere to technocratic teaching methods (aka–"schooling") enforced by top-down administrators in order to maintain job security.

NOTES

[1] Also referred to as the "banking method" of education as termed by Brazilian educator and philosopher, Paulo Freire (1970). The purveyor of knowledge is the teacher transmitting or depositing knowledge into the receptacle or student. The student then recites or spits back the information when told. This is a teacher-centered approach to education.

[2] I wish to make clear that I in no way support the egregious acts committed by Hitler nor do I support any institution or administration that is guilty of the mass slaughtering of civilians, commonly known as "collateral damage."

³ This refers to "hegemony" as termed by Italian Marxist, Antonio Gramsci. The following is a clear definition cited from an on-line website highlighting the work of Gramsci: "By hegemony, Gramsci meant the permeation *throughout* society of an entire system of values, attitudes, beliefs and morality that has the effect of supporting the status quo in power relations. Hegemony in this sense might be defined as an 'organizing principle' that is diffused by the process of socialization into every area of daily life. To the extent that this prevailing consciousness is internalized by the population, it becomes part of what is generally called 'common sense' so that the philosophy, culture and morality of the ruling elite comes to appear as the natural order of things. [Boggs, 1976, p. 39]" (Burke, 1999/2005)

⁴ Epistemology is a branch of philosophy that studies the nature of knowledge and knowing. Questions such as, "What is true?", "Is knowledge constructed or is it inert?", "How do we know?" are but a few of the questions epistemologists ask.

⁵ The term "deconstruction" is associated with influential philosophers such as Edmund Husserl, Jacques Derrida, and Martin Heidegger. Although there is much debate about what the formal definition of deconstruction is, the general meaning behind the term is to break down, analyze, or critique a text, particularly texts and languages originating from Western philosophy, to uncover any hidden or implicit ideas or messages that serve to form the basis for ideas, thoughts, or beliefs (called "ideology").

⁶ I am referring to mainstream press outlets misrepresenting my story. My story was fairly represented by my university's union, the Professional Staff Congress (PSC) newspaper, *The Clarion,* and the American Federation of Teacher's monthly publication, *AFT on Campus.* Websites such as *Free Exchange on Campus* also accurately depicted my story–www.freeexchangeoncampus.org

⁷ In regards to being named in Horowitz' book, no valid research methods were done to substantiate the claims made, and there was no triangulation or attempt to contact me for accuracy. My critics may argue that as an educator, I must transfer knowledge of the "official curriculum" to students in order to prepare them to be successful in the workforce. And as an educator, it may be considered unethical to name my position or reveal my perspective to my students for fear that they will passively adopt my beliefs. Again, this is simply a difference of ideological perspectives and educational philosophies. We must be careful, however, that when naming our position, we also create safe spaces for students to critique, question, and disagree with our position and allow them to name their position without fear of penalty. Dialogic pedagogy values and respects different perspectives as long as the arguments can be substantiated with valid and concrete claims. Naming one's position in the classroom is taking a political stance; remaining neutral is supporting the status quo or official curriculum (Kincheloe, 2004). The official curriculum defines whose knowledge is important or central in learning and whose is subjugated or marginalized. Emphasis is on essential or core knowledge and the development of particular skills, values and morals (Hirsch, 1999; Bennett, 1993).

⁸ bell hooks writes: "One line of this poem that moved and disturbed something within me: 'This is the oppressor's language yet I need it to talk to you.'" (hooks, 2004)

⁹ Ibid.

¹⁰ I want to make clear that I am *not* advocating a complete disregard for administrative policies, especially those that undermine students receiving a quality education. I am referring to minor infractions of the policy. For example, a class meeting is two hours and 20 minutes long. The instructor has accomplished all of her objectives for the evening in one and a half hours and dismisses the class. Because the policy states that students must meet for the full duration of the class for each class meeting throughout the term, instructors are expected to strictly adhere to this policy. But when administration holds some of us to this standard and not others, it becomes problematic and political. In some cases, policy that standardizes (one-size-fits-all) faculty pedagogical strategies is harmful for students. For example, requiring a standardized exam to be administered during finals week for undergraduate students by all faculty and departments is absurd! Education programs across the country teach our students about the value of alternative and multiple assessment tools–portfolios, project-based learning, unit plans, oral presentations, poster boards, and

so forth. When administration requires faculty to provide, each semester, a written rationale to request exemption from giving a final examination or explanation of the alternative assessment being used in place of the standardized exam, political forces are in place. Another example is the handling of student complaints. This is one area that I feel administration should standardize their practice in the sense that if there is a process to be followed, adhere to the process! All student complaints should be addressed, regardless of the professor targeted. I have heard of stories in which administration receives scathing letters about professors from large groups of students but no action is taken due to the personal and/or ideological relationships these professors have with administration. However, if one or two students complain to administration about the "trouble-maker" critical educator, administration is in hot pursuit.

[11] In reference to academic freedom under attack, having tenure does not necessarily provide job security. See the July 2007 firing of tenured, full Professor Ward Churchill, University of Colorado, or the 2007 denial of tenure to Professor Norman Finkelstein, DePaul University.

[12] There are many other noteworthy philosophers, educators, theorists, and activists that have faced public vilification based on their ideological positions and political acts. See Dr. Peter McClaren who was named number one on UCLA's "Dirty Thirty" list by a conservative UCLA alumni group, or any of the profiles of academics listed in Horowitz' "The Professors: The 101 Most Dangerous Academics in America" publication (2006). Historically, some of these revolutionists were imprisoned and exiled. See Antonio Gramsci, Paulo Freire, and The Countess Markievicz. Others were murdered. See Socrates, Che Guevara, and Malcolm X.

REFERENCES

Bennett, W. (1993). *The book of virtues: A treasury of great moral stories.* New York: Simon & Schuster, Inc.

Boggs, C. (1976). *Gramsci's marxism.* London: Pluto Press.

Burke, B. (1999, 2005). Antonio gramsci, schooling and education. *The Encyclopedia of Informal Education.* Retrieved October 10, 2007, from http://www.infed.org/thinkers/et-gram.htm

Darder, A., Baltodano, M., & Torres, R. (Eds.). (2003). *The critical pedagogy reader.* New York: RoutledgeFalmer.

Freire, P. (1970). *Pedagogy of the oppressed.* New York: Seabury.

Freire, P. (1973). *Education for critical consciousness.* New York: Seabury.

Gershman, J. (2005, May 31). 'Disposition' emerges as issue at Brooklyn college. *The New York Sun.*

Gramsci, A. (1971). *Selections from the prison notebooks.* London: Lawrence and Wishart.

Hooks, B. (2004). Teaching new worlds/New words. In O. Santa Ana (Ed.), *Tongue tied: The lives of multilingual children in public education* (pp. 255–260). New York: Rowman & Littlefield.

Hirsch, E. D., Jr. (1999). *Core knowledge sequence: Content guidelines for grades K-8.* Virginia: Core Knowledge Foundation.

Horowitz, D. (2006). *The professors: The 101 most dangerous academics in America.* Washington, DC: Regnery Publishing.

Kincheloe, J. (2004). *Critical pedagogy: Primer.* New York: Peter Lang Publishers.

Kozol, J. (1967). *Death at an early age.* Boston: Houghton.

10. FIRST DANCE

Dance- verb:1. to be an engaged and active critically conscious educator

SHALL WE DANCE?

The year is 2006. Chris Linton[1] is a 28 year-old white male from rural Pennsylvania. He is now an elementary school teacher in an urban charter school in Philadelphia that has a primarily black student population.

The year was 1998. I was a 22 year-old black female from the suburbs of New Jersey. I was a first year high school English literature teacher in a university town classroom in Pennsylvania that had a primarily white student population.

Chris and I have now been friends for eight years. He was my silent partner as I learned to dance in my first year of teaching. In 2006 I found myself having the chance to be the same for him. We decided to meet up a couple of times during that year and talk about what he was thinking, feeling and experiencing during his first year of teaching. We recorded those sessions and talked about them over the course of the year. We had no idea we'd have a chance to tell our story. This chapter is part of the story of how we both learned/are learning to dance: to become engaged and active critically conscious educators. I use Chris' words, some of which are direct quotes from our recorded conversations, as the trigger for my reflections. My reflections will be memories, excerpts from journals and readings from over the years. This chapter is just part of how Chris and I are learning to be critically conscious human beings and by extension, educators and is but one of many of the possible ways to dance. A possible first step? Hear the music.

FIND A TUNE

Ask a child what it means to dance and you may get the response I got when I asked a 5 year-old named Jewel. She thought for a moment and then said, "You gotta hear the music. You gotta move when you dance. And then ... [she stopped and listened to the song currently playing and found a beat] see! Like how I'm moving. And then you move [she pointed to me and literally waited for me to move]. But you gotta be on the beat or your dancing looks weird. Find your beat, Dana." I apologized to Jewel for not being on the same beat that she heard or for finding my own beat. She looked at me as if I was the personification of the "weird" that she had just talked about.

Search for the word *dance* in Wikipedia and you get the following definition:

A.H. Churchill (ed.), Rocking Your World: The Emotional Journey into Critical Discourses, 111–122.

Definitions of what constitutes dance are dependent on social, cultural, aesthetic, artistic and moral constraints and range from functional movement (such as Folk dance) to virtuoso techniques such as ballet … dance can be directly participatory, social or performed for an audience … dance movements may be without significance in themselves … or have a gestural vocabulary/symbolic meaning … dance can embody or express ideas, emotions or tell a story. (Wikipedia, accessed May 14, 2007)

One sentence in particular from the above definition catches my attention: "… dance can be directly participatory, social or performed for an audience." This sentence echoes in my mind as I think back over my conversation with Jewel. What if we replace the word "dance" with the word "teaching" in the definitions by Jewel and Wikipedia? What then are the ways of knowing that we need in order to teach and how is teaching socially situated within the intersecting discourses[2] of participation, social interaction, performance and, I would add, critical consciousness?

Slowly, an idea evolved in my mind as I formulated my thoughts in order to write this chapter. Maybe the concept of "dance" can be used as a metaphor for learning to be an engaged and active critically conscious educator. Extrapolating from Jewel's definition, there are three key actions that should be undertaken in order to "do" dance: hearing, moving, and personally experiencing dance. Next, taking the Wikipedia definition into consideration, I decided to play with the idea that the hearing, moving and personal experience of critically conscious teaching is situated within understandings of critical theory that has, at its foundation, complex understandings of conceptions of social interaction, performance and participation.[3] In light of my failure to dance in a way that pleased my 5 year-old instructor, I remembered that learning to dance could be a struggle; even, or maybe especially, if we think we already know or are conscious of the steps. In fact, it's that initial consciousness that may make it more difficult to learn about other ways of being. But, we can learn the steps. We can learn how to hear, move and try to personally experience as best as possible different ways of being. The dance is tricky, deliberate, often not incorporating the most popular moves. It can be painful and emotionally draining.

This is a dance whose music is inclusive education[4] for informed participation in democratic citizenship—which also acknowledges and actively fights against the competing and horrifically interfering and oppressive music of racism, anti-disability and anti-accessibility policies, classism, gendered bias and harassment, homophobia, ageism, and the vestiges of colonialism, to name a few tunes. This is a dance whose audience, when engaged with and not only instructed to, keeps coming back for more. This is a dance that has the best reception when its first step is humility. This is a dance that requires professionals, not just those who think it looks cool or only feel that it's simply a calling or couldn't do anything else.

And this is a dance that I only began to truly *see* once I looked at someone else trying to learn the steps.

HEARING

Chris:

I see now how much of an influence our own personal history has on how we teach and how we perceive our students. I am an upper middle class white male with three sisters who was raised in a rural community. I come from a nuclear family–whatever that really means. I mean, these labels–they're really entrenched. I went to college and as I started thinking about what I wanted to do when I finished I guess I developed a "save the world" mentality. I got a job with the Red Cross and worked in an after school program for inner city kids. I taught life skills and helped with homework. I really liked what I was doing. But, I started to see that what I was expecting from them–to sit still, listen, and not move around–things in my mind that equalled or were a matter of respect. That was the way I was taught. That is what was expected in my school. That's where my personal history influences my teaching. It's almost like a default way of teaching that I see myself falling back into. So, I think I view the high activity of the kids I teach now in sort of a negative light. Like they're not paying attention because they're moving around or making noise, and so I tell them to sit still. But is that the best way to teach? I don't want to "impose my will" on them, I want to meet them halfway. Or maybe the term is "meet them where they are." But how? And so then the question becomes, if my history is influencing my teaching in just that little area, how do my student's histories influence their learning? How do I find this out? That's an overwhelming question, really. I mean, it's my first year of teaching and I'm six months into this job and I don't know if I'll be like this for my entire teaching career, but teaching right now is a day-to-day thing. Today I feel like I am the worst teacher. I was short and impatient with the kids. Was it because I don't know their histories? Was it my history having too much influence on my pedagogy today? If you had asked me yesterday, I would have said that I felt I did some good things and I was getting a handle on this.

Dana:

As I read over what Chris said, I think back to Jewel's admonition that I hear the music before I dance. The Wikipedia definition noted that "definitions of what constitutes dance are dependent on social, cultural, aesthetic, artistic and moral constraints...." I think back to Chris' voice and face as he spoke the above passage. He was tired. He was questioning. He was worried. Through our conversation it eventually dawned on me that Chris was straining to hear the children–the rhythms and beats–in his classroom. He was realizing, learning and experiencing that what constitutes becoming an engaged and active critically conscious educator is, like dance, indeed dependent on hearing the social, cultural, aesthetic, moral and artistic (among others) constraints acting on the classroom in that moment. He had read about the importance of getting to know his students when he was in grad school, but now he was learning the difference between seeing his students and hearing his students. The students in our classrooms are in front of us everyday. We see them and interact with them but do we hear them? When we close our eyes, what are the rhythms and beats that we hear? What are they saying to us? How do we learn to hear them?

I thought back to the years preceding my first year of teaching. Was it in university where I began learning how to hear? Immediately, I remembered the readings we did in my first year writing class. In my program we had to complete a degree in a content area before we could apply to the teacher education program. So I chose English Literature as my major. I realize not that the moment I read Alice Walker's *In Search of Our Mother's Garden's* (1984) and the poetry of Audre Lorde I began to honestly *hear* my own personal history for the first time. After Alice Walker I read Walker Percy's *Message in a Bottle* (1975/2000) and the essay that helped me evolve a language for what I was *hearing* about my own history is titled "The Loss of the Creature." I read W. E. B DuBois' *The Souls of Black Folks* (1903/1987) and Langston Hughes' *The Ways of White Folks* (1933/1990). I read *I, Rigoberta Menchu* (1983) and I read about the controversies surrounding the book. I saw the contextual complexity of a person's history. Slowly I started to *hear* images and stories that my parents had told me when I was younger. I remembered hearing my father tell me the story of Emmett Till. I remember my mother crying in front of the television when Anwar Al Sadat was killed. I remember going to the music library on campus and listening (again … my mother had played it for me when I was a child) to Billie Holiday singing "Strange Fruit" and really *hearing* the lyrics. Later in my first years of teaching, I would use this song and lyrics as well as the books *Strange Fruit: Billie Holiday, Café Society and an Early Cry for Civil Rights* by David Margolick (2000) and *The Things They Carried* by Tim O'Brien (1990) to help situate my primarily white high school students' introduction to Toni Morrison's *Beloved* (1987). I remember our family watching and then reading Martin Luther King Junior's "I've Been to the Mountaintop" speech. I now realize that at the intersection of these seemingly random moments, my critical conscious was evolving and at the center of this evolution was an emerging understanding of the power of a moment. And like the refrain Dr. King used in his speech, I wouldn't stop there.

Even though I was hearing more clearly and becoming more aware of my history and more cognizant that I had family and friends from different social economic backgrounds, I will admit that I, like Chris would later, wondered how I would be able to teach kids from backgrounds so different from my suburban one. What could I possibly teach kids from urban or rural settings? But, as I pondered this question, slowly, I started to really *hear* what was said to me in classes and meetings at my university: surprised expressions when I spoke "so articulately and clearly" and inquiries into "where [did I] learn to speak that way?" or-all eyes and attention in classes going to me when discussions of multiculturalism and race came up. Around the town I started becoming aware of being followed around certain stores. These are moments when I started to *hear* that while I may have been struggling with "complex and fluid ways" of constructing my identity and developing an emerging understanding of my privilege, that was not what some people heard or saw when I was in their class or in their store. So as I was wondering how I could reach students who had such different backgrounds than me, I had to remember that what some people see when they look at me may fit into their predetermined idea, or tune, of who I am. I slowly began to understand that I had to have a "double consciousness"[5] as DuBois discussed. I now take that a step further and say that we all need to have double, triple, quadruple consciousnesses. The previously mentioned issues of race, class and power create very strong songs in the classroom. So that if I had teachers who had never taken the time to critically examine their history, to hear their history, then the only way they would hear me is if I played a certain song that resonated with the only tune they knew for me. If I was different, then the song was jarring and some didn't know what to do–didn't know how to dance to that song. They responded in default ways. They seemed to only have one consciousness in the classroom context. They couldn't hear me.

MOVING

Chris:

> I know kids need time to be kids, to learn about each other, to socialize and interact with each other. But on top of the curriculum I'm trying to cover, the major tests I have to prepare them for and learning how to effectively communicate with parents, I know I don't provide a learning environment that fosters rich social interaction. I feel that it's not possible to give them that right now. I have to focus on the immediate: preparing for the state-wide test or teaching the curriculum. But I want to move on connecting what the kids learn to their lives. I have gotta figure out how.

After reflecting on what he said, Chris wrote this free association poem and emailed it to me:

A poem can't be written about the noble profession
Summers off
No right to complain about anything
Babysitting, right?
Give 'em a few worksheets and you're good to go
Teach for a few years and you have your plans for a lifetime
Ah, no big deal, they're just kids

Monitoring
Assessing
Sharpening
Correcting
Redirecting

Yelling
Asking (please?)
Telling
Writing
Extinguishing "fires"
Collaborating
Watching
Reading
Cajoling
Walking
Planning
Guessing
Trying
Do you know what each of these words mean?
Do you know what it's like to do each of these everyday?
For 26 souls?
And feel good about it at the end of the day?
Like you didn't snap?
Didn't lose your cool?
You gave attention where attention was due?
You challenged?
You were appropriate yourself?
You modelled what you want to see out of them?
Were you a hypocrite?
Are you being culturally sensitive?
Are you differentiating between different learning styles?
Are you differentiating between boys and girls?
But what about the boy who doesn't act like other boys?
And the girl who doesn't act like other girls?
What do they think of you?
What do their parents say when they get home?
Does being white have anything to do with it?
A man teaching single-parent children have anything to do with it?
Were you clear today?
Are you watching other teachers' kids in the hallway?
Are you watching to see if they have their uniforms on?
Are you consistent?
Can you go home at the end of the day and say that you did well?
These words look melodramatic, crybaby
Everything else you normally have to do to be ready?
Plan your lessons?
Clean up your mess?
Make your copies?
Check your mailbox?
Check your email?

Pick up after the kids?
Get the make-up tests done?
Are you getting through, or are you talking to walls?
Is it exciting for them?
Did you smile at them?
Take attendance?
Grade everything you need to grade and hand it back?
You got all that?

Dana:

It was about the middle of my first year writing class in college that we got the assignment that I feel was the moment where many of the readings, memories, feelings and thoughts racing around my mind converged into a moment of action. I was hearing the music and now it was time to move.

The assignment was to read Paulo Freire's *Pedagogy of the Oppressed* (1970/2000). We were to use Freire's critique of the "banking concept of education"[6] as an analytical lens to explore our lives. We also had to connect this exploration to readings done in class. For a 19 year-old person who felt that she really hadn't been a critical person or had a lot of experiences in her life, this was a daunting assignment. However, I was simultaneously doing classroom observations in my introduction to teacher education class. Because of this assignment and because I was about the same age as many of the students I was observing, I found our conversations were amazing. I started asking what kind of teacher did they think I should be. They were brutally honest and observant. They talked about how for years they had noticed their teachers dealing with many of the things Chris wrote about in his poem. They had been on the receiving end of those musings. And for many of these students it came down to making the curriculum connect with their lives–even in the midst of all that is demanded of teachers and all of the stresses of school life–make it connect.

In my assignment I wrote that this sounded good and was very important but I noted that I had talked to the teachers as well. As I reflect now, I see that most of the teachers echoed Chris' thoughts from the beginning of this section. How do we as teachers acknowledge our histories, acknowledge our students' histories, teach with all of the things Chris wrote about in his poem buzzing around in our minds and also make the curriculum relevant?

When I was 19, I didn't say it like I'm saying it now but the seeds of this song were there. I saw that using Freire's critical analysis of the banking concept education was a way for me to have something to say to all students. I could help make the "rules of game (schooling)" a little more transparent. The next sentence I originally wrote here began, "Irrespective of their race, ethnicity, class, gender, sexual orientation, age, ability," but as I read it over, I see that what I am trying to say is that it is expressly because of these issues that Freire's work is so powerful, so potentially transformative, so moving. Helping students examine their histories and explore their histories is a way to see that the "empty vessel" metaphor so often attributed to our students is indeed an act of violence against them. Helping them examine how their histories, cultures, and social lives intersect and converge on a moment in their education is, in my opinion, part of what Freire was talking about when he discussed the dialectic conversation that should be occurring around issues in education for democratic participation.

What teachers like you, Chris and myself can do is extend this conversation to future curricula we find ourselves having to teach and/or that we create. Extending this conversation to staff meetings, test preparation, classroom management discussions, IEP plans, and parent meetings is what critically conscious teachers can do. I feel that we should be striving to make the "rules of the game" more transparent for all students and teach them how to leverage this knowledge for future success and participation in society.[7] This is a paradigmatic shift from being a conveyer of skill sets to being a critically conscious and active educator. Making the move to this way of being is the next step in dancing.

PERSONAL EXPERIENCE

Chris:

> But these other issues keep ringing in my head. How do we pay attention to our student's histories? How much desire is there in the teacher to learn about and be open to the experiences of their students? If the teachers are not open to it, then they are one strike down, right? And what do I mean by being "open to it?" I mean, in your personal life, are you willing to go out and meet people and have experiences that you didn't grow up with? I think that in the last 10 years I have really stretched myself out a little and have been increasingly open to new experiences. But I also know that that isn't enough. I mean, what the heck do I know about what it means to be African American? There's an idea that people can just choose what they want to do in life. But I know that for my male student who is an African American male, history has put him in a different place than the white male student. The kids may not be aware of this (but I think many are), but it is my responsibility as a teacher to be aware of this. Their parents are aware of this. And what can I say to the parents? What can I say to the African American male student? What do I as a white man know about the struggle of being a black man in America? How can I effectively and truthfully teach them … to … I guess play the game? Or maybe I can help teach them the rules. But is that being a teacher who is trying to make a difference or a teacher who is trying to maintain the status quo? I'm not being an essentialist and I'm not trying to be a neo-liberal. I'm aware of so many things now, but how do I do anything?[8]

Dana:

September 1998
Journal Entry

> ... I don't know what I'm doing here! I am told to ask questions yet I know I can't be open about all of my questions. Feathers get ruffled and people aren't as open as they present themselves to be. I guess I can understand that ... I get so tired of tip-toeing around people ... shaping my words and holding back on what I really want to say. Maybe that's my fault. I am so hyper-aware of being a black woman here. I don't want to be a token! I will not be seen as a victim! I want my teaching to help students see other ways of seeing the world. It's as if I'm an exception and exceptions are tolerated. No, it's not one incident, although the lunchroom monitor incident left me bewildered. How am I supposed to respond when someone says in words they think are a compliment, "I see you all the time and just found out that you are a teacher! And you're black ...." Kids–some are my students!–were around when she said this and they all looked at me. I had to smile. The only thing appropriate I could think to say was as I laughed, "Well, being smart and black isn't an oxymoron." I hope I emphasized 'moron' enough. I just need to get over this and stop being so sensitive. Seriously, grow up. Many before me went through much much worse.

This is the part of the dance that I'm currently working on. Chris and I talk about race and how the politics of identity and critical race theory[9] play out in everyday life; we don't shy away from that really hard conversation. When I was in my first year of teaching, I tried to talk to Chris about what I felt at the school and town I was working and living in. A sliver of those thoughts are evident in my journal entry above. He mentioned to me later that, at the time, he couldn't understand what I was experiencing. He couldn't get it. And how could he? What experience in a predominately white town could he as a white male have that would help him see my situation a little more empathetically? What experiences growing up in a predominately middle class suburban African American upbringing did I have that would help me see my students in an urban or rural classroom setting a little more empathetically? Now, as Chris is beginning to teach in an environment that is very different from the one he grew up in, the conversations that we had years before are coming back. What can he do?

I struggle with these questions. What exactly are my goals? I mean, when do I speak up when I see injustices happening? Every time? How do I learn which battles to fight? How does the experience of my blackness influence my teaching? For Chris, how does the experience of his whiteness influence his teaching? How can he take action that is not tokenistic to help his students, the majority of whom are African American? When should he speak up?

For me, the beginning of an answer to that question happened when I left the United States and moved to South Korea to teach literature and writing classes. I was a fish out of water. I had no superficial cultural affiliations I could fall back on. I had no language, no cultural references, no cultural history to link me to my students. It was in this moment that my writing assignment from five years before (connecting Freire's critical analysis of the banking concept of education to our lives) came rushing back to my consciousness. I had to make sure that my assignments, class discussions, field experiences and casual interactions all resonated with my desire to learn about or more accurately, hear, the histories of my students. I had to be strategic in finding spaces in the curriculum that allowed for opportunities to further develop my DuBoisian double (triple, quadruple) consciousness. I had to get out of my comfort zone. I had to foster friendships and ask the uncomfortable questions. I had to make many, many! mistakes. I started looking up current research on innovations in teaching, curriculum development and culture in a South Korean context. And in doing so, in being proactive about adding to and exercising my critical consciousness, I started to dance. I learned to not dismiss my history and to not only reflect upon it, but be an active reflector for others and start to dance. I had to be proactive in learning how to design learning experiences[10] for and with my students that would allow us to explore different ways of being and knowing. My time in South Korea was a moment of convergence that taught me to dance; to be a critically conscious and active educator. And, I won't stop there.

LET'S DANCE

At the time of this writing, Chris has just finished his second year of teaching and recently tole me that things moved smoother this year. He knows this has to do with many factors, and one thing he noted was that he sees and values the importance of reflection. But equally important is his desire to continue to educate himself and learn ways to act upon his emerging critical consciousness. It was his reflection on the complexity of learning the delicate dance of becoming a critically conscious educator that is having a profound impact on his personal and professional life. Now, how can he take critical consciousness action in his classroom?

And that is the question that we are all trying to answer, isn't it? Learning to dance, to become an engaged and active critically conscious educator is about hearing the music in our lives. Depending on the context, we cannot and should not separate ourselves, our essence, from our teaching. We must always remember that we have to pick and choose our battles. But it is our sincere and humble hope that as you read this chapter, you thought back to times in your life that you may now recognize as moments that have influenced your emerging critical consciousness. The question becomes, what are you going to do?

It was a humbling experience to write this chapter. This reminiscence has made me think of moments in my teaching where I cringe at how myopic I was. I wonder if my dancing is improving or am I still using the same moves as when I first started hearing the songs? Do I dance the way Jewel instructed? It was a humbling experience to talk to Chris and be witness to his struggle. It took a lot of courage for him to be so open and honest with me and to let me write this chapter about him. Being on the outside of his struggle actually helped me to be able to talk about mine. I (we) were able to move beyond simply observing the obvious (he is a white man and I'm a black woman; he grew up in a rural community and I grew up in the suburbs, etc.) to exploring or beginning to explore the nuance and residual interplay of what seems to be obvious within our lives and the lives of our students. And you know, one thing we both realized through this experience is that the moment a student looks you in the eye after you have taken the time to hear them, after you have enacted a pedagogy that moves them and challenges them to take critical reflective action, and after you have participated in their experience, you are not the same. You don't want to be. Yes, there are a myriad of contextual and complicating factors. But as many before me have noted, "We won't stop there." Let's seize the power of a moment. Forgive me, but in the end, I think David Bowie said it best:

"Let's dance."

NOTES

[1] The names Chris Linton and Jewel are pseudonyms.

[2] For the purposes of this chapter, the definition of discourse I'm using is the following: "Discourses structure both our sense of reality and our notion of our own identity. Pecheux's work [with discourses] enables us to consider ways in which subjects can come to a position of dis-identification, whereby we not only locate and isolate the ways in which we as subjects have been constructed and subjected, but we also map out for ourselves new terrains in which we can construct different and potentially more liberating ways in which we can exist." (Mills, 1997/2004: 13). Please see Pecheux, 1982; Foucault, 1970, 1972; Mills, 2004 and Gee, 1999 for more detailed discussions of the term "discourse."

[3] Please see chapter 3 of Joe Kincheloe's *Critical Pedagogy Primer* (2004) for further discussion of the relationship between schools, critical theory and conceptions of social interaction, performance and participation.

[4] By using the term "inclusive education," I am referring simultaneously to the complex, multi-national global inclusive education project and a more simplistic idea that even within the institution of schooling, education can and should be more inclusive of other ways of being. Please see the following works for a broader discussion of inclusion in education as a response to oppressive pedagogies: Slee and Allen, 2001; Oliver, 1996; Gresson, 2004; Meyer, 2008 (in this book); Sterzuk, 2008 (in this book).

[5] Please see chapter 1 of W.E.B Dubois's *The Souls of Black Folks* for a more contextualized discussion of this concept. In the context of this paper, I'm drawing upon DuBois' discussion of "double consciousness" by incorporating this section of his definition: "It is a peculiar sensation, this double-consciousness, this sense of always looking at one's self through the eyes of others, of measuring one's soul by the tape of a world that looks on in amused contempt and pity. One ever feels his two-ness..." (p. 18).

[6] Please see chapter 2 of Paulo Freire's *Pedagogy of the Oppressed* for a more contextualized discussion of this concept. In the context of this paper, I'm using Freire's definition of this concept: "In the banking concept of education, knowledge is a gift bestowed by those who consider themselves knowledgeable upon those whom they consider to know nothing. Projecting an absolute ignorance onto other, a characteristic of the ideology of oppression, negates education and knowledge as process of inquiry" (p. 72).

[7] For more thoughts on this topic, please see Gee and Lankshear (Eds), 2001 and Jenkins, 2006.

[8] For more thoughts on topics raised in this section, please see McIntosh, 1998 and Apple, 2004.

[9]   Please see Collins, 1991; McCarthy and Crichlow, 1993; Nam, 2001; Grande, 2004.
[10] For an interesting and innovative example of designing learning experiences for and with students in
      light of ideas expressed in this chapter, please see Squire, 2006.

REFERENCES

Apple, M. (2004). Creating difference: Neo-liberalism, neo-conservatism, and the politics of
   educational reform. *Educational Policy, 18*(# 1), 12–44.
Collins, P. H. (1991). *Black feminist thought.* New York: Routledge.
DuBois, W. E. B. (1903/1994). *The souls of black folks.* Dover Publications.
Foucault, M. (1972). *The archaeology of knowledge* (A. M. Sheridan Smith, Trans.). London:
   Tavistock.
Foucault, M. (1970). *The order of discourse: An archaeology of the human sciences.* London:
   Tavistock.
Freire, P. (2000). *Pedagogy of the oppressed* (30 Anv Sub ed.). Continuum International Publishing
   Group.
Gee, J., Lankshear, C., et al. (2001). *The new work order.* Westview Press.
Gee, J. P. (2005). *An introduction to discourse analysis, theory and method.* New York and London:
   Taylor and Francis (Routledge).
Grande, S. (2004). *Red pedagogy: Native American social and political thought.* Rowman and
   Littlefield Publishers.
Gresson, A. (2004). *America's atonement: Racial pain, recovery rhetoric, and the pedagogy of healing.*
   New York: Peter Lang Publishing.
Hughes, L. (1933/1990). *The ways of white folks.* New York: Vintage Books.
Jenkins, H., Clinton, K., et al. (2006). *Confronting the challenges of participatory culture: Media
   education for the 21st century.* MA: Massachusetts Institute of Technology.
Kincheloe, J. (2004). *Critical pedagogy primer.* Peter Lang Publishing.
Margolick, D. (2000). *Strange fruit: Billie Holiday, café society and an early cry for civil rights.*
   Philidelphia: Running Press.
McCarthy, C., & Crichlow, W. (Eds.). (1993). *Race, identity and representation in education.* New
   York: Routledge.
McIntosh, P. (1998). White privilege: Unpacking the invisible knapsack. Working Paper 189: White
   Privilege and Male Privilege: A Personal Account of Coming To See Correspondences through
   Work in Women's Studies. Retrieved May 20, 2007, from http://www.antiracistalliance.com/
   Unpacking.html
Mills, S. (2004). *Discourse.* New York: Routlege.
Menchu, R. (1983). *I, rigoberta menchu.* Verso Publishers.
Morrison, T. (1987/2004). *Beloved.* Vintage Publishers.
Nam, V. (Ed.). (2001). *Yell-oh girls: Emerging voices explore culture, identity and growing up Asia- a-
   American.* New York: HarperCollins.
O'Brien, T. (1989). *The things they carried.* Broadway Publishers.
Oliver, M. (1996). *Understanding disability: From theory to practice.* London, England: Macmillian
   Press Ltd.
Percy, W. (1975/2000). *The message in a bottle.* Picador Publishers.
Slee, R., & Allen, J. (2001). Excluding the included: A reconsideration of inclusive education.
   International Studies in Sociology Education, 11(2), 173–192.
Squire, K. (2006). From content to context: Videogames as designed experience. *Educational
   Researcher-AERA, 35*(8), 19–29.
Villanueva, V. (1993). *Bootstraps: From an American academic of color.* National Council of Teachers
   of English.
Walker, A. (1984). *In search of our mother's gardens.* Harvest Publishers.

CARMEN LAVOIE

11. ACTIVISM WHERE I STAND

Moving beyond words in graduate education

"Philosophers so far only interpreted the world. The point is to change it."

Karl Marx

Karl Marx, Paulo Freire, bell hooks, Ruth Frankenberg, Peter McLaren...all looking over my shoulder as I write this chapter. After endless hours of reading their work for my doctoral studies, these authors now live in my apartment, in my computer and in my mind behaving as unruly stewards to the ideas rattling around. Sometimes they wring their hands impatiently and look begrudgingly at each other or at me. They are dissatisfied. They did not intend for me to read for hours, days, months on end. These critical theorists are interested in social change and the transformation of injustice and oppression. So then, why was I, a student of critical perspectives, preoccupied with books and theory?

BEFORE GRADUATE STUDIES

Before I started doctoral studies, I had a strong sense of my identity as an activist. For a number of years, I was employed as a community organizer in low income urban neighbourhoods, working with residents on issues of local concern. I was also an activist in my own community, involved with local feminist organizations and campaigns against poverty and free trade. These groups struggled against the dismantling of state-run social services and against the erasure of government accountability measures. We called attention to corporations that were oblivious to local needs and to the working conditions of their employees. Such efforts brought about tangible benefits for those affected by injustice and restored some of the social welfare measures hard won by previous generations.

Despite the success of these activist efforts, I felt a nagging concern. I realized that in all the hours spent strategizing how to "make the world a better place," there was little time to discuss and debate what this meant. Time was continually swallowed up by the frantic pursuit of activist goals rather than reflecting on and understanding the significance of our efforts. With each social justice campaign, my feelings of concern grew. I was unsure how my personal privilege might be contributing to inequality or how the group efforts might be compounding the injustice I had hoped to change.

When the opportunity to do doctoral studies came along, I jumped at it. Although this decision meant leaving my community and my work, I was excited at the prospect of learning about my role in the transformation of an economic and

A.H. Churchill (ed.), Rocking Your World: The Emotional Journey into Critical Discourses, 123–131.

political system that I increasingly saw as unjust. Unfortunately, my preoccupation as a community organizer with social action and transformation was soon replaced as a doctoral student by a preoccupation with theory and reflection.

GRADUATE STUDIES

Several of my instructors in graduate studies were well versed in critical theory and deeply committed to social change. I remember feeling excited in my first year courses when classroom discussions opened my eyes to different forms of dominance, resistance, and routes to social change. My understanding of power and transformation deepened, as did my understanding of my own position within those relationships. Unfortunately, this classroom focus on injustice and social change did not translate into opportunities for activism.

As a graduate student, it soon became apparent that, on the one hand, I was expected to learn and reflect on my own relationship to injustice and issues of power while, on the other hand, there was little support for me to act upon these ideas. Activism has never been coordinated, facilitated, or even suggested during my doctoral education. An education in critical theory that does not integrate action with reflection in course content or student assignments, in my mind, is not consistent with the theory it espouses.

Action and reflection in theory

Paulo Freire, a central figure in critical theory literature, writes insightfully about action and reflection in his book *Pedagogy of the Oppressed*. In his work as an educator in Brazil, Freire realized that both reflection and action were necessary for social change to occur. Reflection brings about an understanding of power relations, including one position within those power relations, and action puts those ideas into practice. The result is a dialogical process in which reflection and action occur in concert, each changing in response to the other. This process is often referred to as praxis. Put simply, praxis is taking ideas about injustice in the world and acting on them in daily life. Then our actions can inform the ideas from which they came.

By disregarding action in graduate education, the dialogic between action and reflection becomes largely a conceptual pursuit. Graduate students become merely vessels of ideas about social change rather than its practitioners. As Freire tells us, this is antithetical to the process of social change. Without a dialogical process of action and reflection in graduate education, the learning process is conceptually severed from systemic injustice and is irrelevant to the social movements critical theory aims to support.

In the last four years of my doctoral studies, I have had time to reflect on the depoliticizing culture of graduate education. After jumping through many of the requisite hoops in graduate education and participating in many academic forums, such as seminars, conferences, and hiring committees, I now see that praxis-based graduate education conflicts with academia's long-standing fixation on intellectualism and individualistic measures of success.

Intellectualism

Upon entering graduate studies, I had to quickly orient myself to a plethora of theoretical perspectives and debates in my discipline. I spent my time reading, analyzing, and discovering the nuances and perspectives of different writers within critical theory. I read Marx to understand how structures constrain human consciousness, and I read Gramsci to resolve some of the limitations of Marx. I read Freire to understand liberation in practice and then read Foucault to put the notion of liberation into question. I read, read, and read! Then I spent endless hours synthesizing this material into academic pieces of writing. I had to learn to discern core ideas and then apply and organize these ideas into a cohesive and comprehensive piece of writing. These intellectual exercises–that is, my ability to understand and articulate theory–would dictate my early success in graduate studies.

This focus on intellectualizing in graduate studies overshadowed the emotional demands of graduate student life and learning critical theory. In addition to the psychological impact of long hours of studying, social isolation, and academic pressures, I had an emotional and visceral response to learning material that examines oppression. Learning material that implicated me in systems of domination and subordination often resulted in highly charged emotional reactions. As I became aware of these emotions, I was motivated to think about issues differently and to get involved in activism. Unfortunately, this window into activism passed by, unacknowledged by graduate education. The focus was instead on intellectual pursuits. The potential for action remained untapped.

Theory helps me to consider why things are the way they are and how they might be changed. It often provides a framework for challenging practices and thus is an important gateway into understanding oppression and the routes to transformation. My concern is, however, that the value placed on theory and intellectual pursuits in graduate education depletes the energy and focus students can give to community activism and negates the reciprocal relationship between the two. This emphasis on intellectualism, combined with individualistic measures of success, stifles the interest students feel toward activism when learning critical perspectives and detracts from the goal of social change.

Individualism

From the start, much of my work as a doctoral student has been in isolation. I spend most of my time in the halls of the library or sitting at my desk amidst piles of paper, staring at a computer screen. This isolation reached an extreme when, in my second year, I had to write an exam paper on the contemporary debates in theoretical race literature. Up until this point, I had had little direction on this topic and, while writing this paper, I was not permitted to meet with my supervisor or members of my advisory committee. It turned out to be a daunting task. My initial excitement quickly turned to panic when I realized that theoretical race literature crosscuts many disciplines, with ranging degrees of abstraction and application. With little guidance on how to manage the literature and few suggestions on where to begin, I quickly became overwhelmed and, at times, veered off course from my assigned task. In my experience, this individualistic approach to learning and teaching in graduate education did more to foster anxiety and self-doubt than expand my theoretical understanding or develop my confidence in academic pursuits.

Such individualistic approaches to graduate education also pit students against one another. Students are less likely to work together when success depends upon demonstrating familiarity with the scholarly literature, getting credit for your ideas, or surpassing the level of your peer's written work. As a graduate student I have found that I am often isolated, engrossed in the requirements of my doctoral program, cut off from the views and ideas of others who are also pursuing their doctoral degree. Were it not for the commitment of my peers to overcome such divisive and individualistic approaches to education, I am not certain I would have persevered through the early phases of my doctoral studies.

This individualism within graduate education is rooted in the overall culture of academia. Presentations and publications demand isolated modes of intellectual engagement and a focus on personal success. As a graduate student, you quickly realize that scholarships, grants, hiring, and tenure are largely determined by your publication record, particularly in peer-reviewed journals and not your involvement in committees or your contribution to local social movements.

This focus on individual achievement within academia ignores the interdependence necessary to formulate ideas, write a dissertation, or finish a doctorate. It disregards the extent to which students (and faculty) depend on peers, family, friends, and relationships to push through and finish the sometimes monumental task of writing papers, exams, or a dissertation. As a result, students may feel inadequate when they seek the support of others or when they dialogue with their peers in order to learn and progress in their research.

TAKING ACTION

Graduate education that emphasizes individualism and intellectual pursuits without opportunities for activism contradicts the critical perspectives I found in books, scholarly journals, and the classroom. A commitment to social change and emancipatory goals is often somehow lost in graduate education, put aside for intellectual discussions and success as an academic. In living this contradiction, I felt the disappointment of critical theorists whose writings focused on issues of power and processes of transformation. I felt the disappointment of those I had known as a community organizer who were faced with daily injustice and inequality. I feared my own inaction and subsequent contribution to a system that I saw as fundamentally unjust. This was not the life I envisioned for myself. I found myself in a crisis of reflection, painfully aware of my own privilege and responsibilities yet situated outside an activist agenda.

After months of sitting in a university classroom feeling uneasy about the disconnect between reflection and action, I decided to act. A friend recommended I get involved in a local coalition of women's groups that was planning a large one-day awareness-raising event about violence against women. I was relieved that her suggestion helped me find an outlet for my activism, and that it was a comfortable fit with my own personal commitments. I did not have much time (or receive much recognition) for activism as a graduate student, so I was happy to piggyback onto an existing group's efforts. I went to meetings; recorded and distributed meeting notes; promoted the event; and helped with the preparation and serving of food. I assumed my background in social work and critical theory would provide me with the necessary political analysis to participate in group activities and help me to move smoothly through the ins and outs of group process. Unfortunately, however, my role as an outsider to the campaign meant I was unaware of the group's history and the issues that lay beneath the surface. At one point, my meeting notes stirred up tensions in the group: some felt I did not fairly represent divergent views, and I was accused of favouring some members over others. My lack of understanding had unwittingly exacerbated political tensions at a time, unfortunately, when key to the success of the event was group solidarity.

After that experience, it occurred to me that I might have more to contribute if I was part of starting a group. Other students in my class had shared their frustrations with me about the disconnect between classroom activities and community issues so together we formed a group that intended to bridge this divide. We did this by supporting and allying with existing local campaigns: we held a workshop on changes to social assistance in support of a welfare rights group, and we went to a rally for a neighbourhood group that was fighting against the construction of a casino in their area. Many times, however, our meetings did not help the group move forward. It was sometimes difficult to agree on which campaigns to support because we each had our own affiliations, interests, and concerns. Often times many of us found it difficult to feel rooted in the campaign of another group. The absence of a lived connection to the campaigns, I believe, was one of the reasons I lost interest and perhaps one of the reasons the group fell apart.

At this point, I did not know what to do. I thought I was doing everything right: I was taking the analysis I had learned in books and in the classroom and getting involved to create change. It had not yet occurred to me that the barriers I encountered in bringing activism into my life would be an important wellspring for my future activist efforts. In my journey as a graduate student and activist, I would soon find the importance of activism where I stand.

DISCOVERING PRAXIS

As a graduate student, I have encountered barriers to activism. Given my education in critical theory and my identity as an activist, this was unacceptable, and I had to do something about it. As it turns out, I was not the only one who felt this way.

In my second year of Ph.D. studies, I joined with some other graduate students to form a group called "Research as Social Change" (RSC). Since then, we have been working to change university infrastructure in order to facilitate activism through research on campus. Our goal is to create an administrative platform that will enable graduate students (and academics) to engage in collaborative research with local community organizations and groups. In the long term, we hope that any undergraduate or graduate student will be able to undertake community-based activist work as part of a class assignment, paper, or research project.

Even though we are only five active members in the group (with a listserv of over 40), we work across different disciplines and groups (e.g. student groups, community groups, academics, and administrators). Our strategic efforts take place on many fronts:

- We have created an inventory of previous and existing research partnerships at our university to demonstrate their feasibility and the wide-spread interest in these partnerships.
- We have formed allies amongst other student groups, researchers, administrators, and community organizations in order to build a community of people willing to collectively push for change at the university.
- We have conducted a survey of graduate students and summarized their needs and interests regarding community-university partnerships. We are currently developing one for faculty members, and we hope to find the resources to survey community groups.
- We have held events for community groups, graduate students, and academics interested in community-university research partnerships to increase under-standing of participatory models of research.

RSC is currently working with faculty, staff, and administration on an oversight committee that will hopefully lead to concrete changes at the university. In my mind, this project achieves two important goals. First, we are challenging the depoliticizing culture of academia. Our work shifts the focus away from the pernicious individualism in the university toward the benefit of the community as well as the student/researcher. Also, an ethical commitment to social justice is at the heart of this project, forcing intellectual pursuits in graduate studies, such as testing theoretical assumptions, to take a backseat.

Another goal of the project is to remove barriers to activism for graduate students. A platform for community-university partnerships will facilitate trust building and provide the framework for a mutually beneficial relationship. A student interested in working with community groups can do so under the pretext of an established relationship rather than as an outsider. Students can take on small or large endeavours and do so in collaboration with a community group that inspires them, teaches them, and benefits from their work.

Starting up RSC has been a great relief to me. It has eased the anxiety and frustration I felt in those early days of my doctoral education, having to sit for hours reading about social change or listening to others talk about it. And now, when I am completely fed up or drained from working on my dissertation, I can find an outlet for my commitment to social change by meeting with others who share my interest and by working together toward change.

Yet, since starting RSC, I have been advised by well-meaning professors to put aside my activist efforts and concentrate on my dissertation. I have been told to "write my dissertation in a timely manner" and "focus on scholarly publications." That is, after all, how I will demonstrate my aptitude for academic pursuits and improve my chances of getting a university job once I finish my Ph.D. I would be smart to heed their advice if my aim was only to appeal to academic circles. However, my aim reaches beyond that of academia. I entered doctoral education as an activist, and I remain so. Being a "Dr." is not the point; the point is to be a "Dr." who understands change and is part of it.

MAPPING CHANGE IN GRADUATE EDUCATION

Just as activist efforts are inadequate in isolation, so is reflection; intellectual activity without active engagement is only one half of the process of social change. Both are necessary to vent the anger and pain raised by learning about injustice, locating ourselves within it, and witnessing it in the lives of others. Reflection and action together also form a check and balance to ensure our activist efforts match our concerns and personal values and bring about the change we desire.

My experiences also taught me that activist efforts rooted in my own convictions and lived experience brought a deeper understanding of praxis and the dialogic between reflection and action. When I first became involved in activist efforts as a graduate student, my personal detachment from the issues at stake left me feeling more like a spectator than a participant, and this diminished my ability to contribute and stay involved. Only when I considered my own experience, and the issues that confronted me, did I begin to journey through meaningful reflection and action. My own feelings, emotions, and struggles became the basis of my activism and the dialogic relationship between action and reflection moved from the abstract to the profound.

Unfortunately, finding this connection between reflection and action can be difficult in graduate education. Individual success and intellectualism are often the only sources of recognition in graduate education and such academic demands often leave students feeling disconnected from each other and the world around them. Thus, graduate education based on praxis and the dialogic between action and reflection will likely require some effort. I have put together some suggestions based on my own experience to guide other activists and students of critical theory in their journey towards praxis-based graduate education.

Bring life into graduate education (and graduate education into life)

Bringing real world events into the classroom is a quick and easy way to politicize classroom discussions that are generally couched in abstract theoretical terms. This may include discussions of local and international topics or topics inside the university walls, such as students' experiences of graduate education, their department, and the activities of the university. These topics enrich the debate and pull discussions of theory into real world terms so that students engage theory, and an understanding of power and oppression, with something they know and live. In my view, this approach is strengthened by opportunities, such as assignments, placements, or research, that engage community groups and organizations and allow students to see their work put to use. Such collaborations bring deeper meaning to education and provide students with a lived experience of praxis.

Expand opportunities for student dialogue

Students need space to get together, to share their experiences and ideas in order to recognize what they have in common and to foster collective action. Meetings after class, cooperative learning groups, social events, or graduate school "survival groups" are a powerful antidote to the pervasive culture of individualism in graduate education and competition between students. Also, when students work together, there is an opportunity to share skills that are not rewarded in the classroom. This can shift peers' perceptions of one another and build students' confidence. The result is less focus on academic measures of success, such as who has scholarships or publications and who does not, and increased solidarity amongst the group. This solidarity can serve as the basis for future collective efforts.

Understand the university as a politicized site

As activists and students of critical theory, we must understand that the university is a hierarchical institution shaped by historical and contemporary conflict, struggle, and power. Power relations define who gets access to the university and what ideas contribute to our understanding of society, truth, and justice. Recognition of this, and questioning who has power, who does not, and who benefits, points us to the possible sites for change. For instance, once we realize that the university is built on appropriated First Nations land, we understand more deeply the importance of standing in solidarity with First Nations groups. By thinking about the university in this way, we also must see ourselves. Graduate students are a privileged group, often with influential contacts, higher paying jobs, and access to systems of knowledge production. As activists and proponents of critical perspectives, we have a responsibility to understand the implications of this privilege. We have a responsibility to examine how we resist, as well as how we contribute to, the systems of power connected to the university that create and recreate oppression.

Increase accountability to the community

The university holds ties to the surrounding community, ties rooted in history, political networks, or personal relationships that may challenge and/or reinforce existing power relations. Unfortunately, as an institution of status and privilege, universities often perpetuate local social inequalities, for example, by admitting few students of colour or not ensuring access for people with disabilities. However, as students, we can be part of bringing about change on campus, change that benefits the whole community and not just those who are privileged. We can ensure that our universities are part of progressive social change by pushing for ongoing dialogue with local groups, by including applied components in degree requirements, and by collaborating with local groups and organizations to support their transformative efforts. As we see the university as connected and accountable to the local community, we see new possibilities for participation in the local neighbourhood and new possibilities for change.

CONCLUSION

As an activist and student of critical theory, my aim is social justice. I study participatory processes and debate ideas of agency and power with my friends. I try to understand the power relations that bring about exploitation, subordination, and dominance and how I may be complicit. And, I try to change those relations of power. Unfortunately, as a doctoral student, there are few opportunities to be part of such change. Expectations of me as a graduate student focus more on succeeding in an atmosphere of über-individualism and intellectualism rather than applying what I am learning and fighting for social change.

My own fear of complacency, combined with calls from critical theorists for transformation (Thank you Karl, bell, Peter, et al–now please get out of my head), compelled me to act. Ultimately, my activist efforts led to a new student group with allies in the community and across campus and strong prospects for change within the university system. This process of change was not always linear or rewarding–indeed, I sometimes felt confused about my role, and some of my attempts at activism flopped. It was only after I examined my own experience and fought for issues that held some significance to me that my activist efforts were sustainable and appropriate to the context I faced. My journey through action and reflection in graduate education revealed my own experiences as an important springboard for activist efforts. It is my hope that this chapter will provide the foundation for other graduate students to do the same.

REFERENCES

Marx, K. (1886). *XI thesis on Feuerbach.* Progress Publishers.

Part IV: Living criticality

NOAH DE LISSOVOY

12. THE HEGEMONIC CONSENSUS

How "liberal" discourse marginalizes critical activism

INTRODUCTION

My purpose in this chapter is to analyze certain typical responses to, and representations of, radical critique and activism within mainstream "liberal" settings in higher education, as well as to describe what these responses feel like to those who are the object of them. I focus here on exposing strategies aimed at shutting down opposition that threatens mainstream structures of doing and thinking. I also want to suggest some ways to confront these responses from the point of view of those committed to critical political and educational perspectives. My analysis is based on my own experiences as a researcher and teacher educator during my graduate school career. I don't suggest that my reflections can be generalized to all other higher education settings, but I think there are certain commonalities in many such contexts that can make my comments fairly widely applicable.

I focus on liberal reactions to critical activism rather than conservative ones, because within the field of education in the university the former represent more often than not the predominant institutional discourse; in addition, while much is written about the challenges posed by conservative politics, not enough attention has been given to the way that mainstream liberal politics collaborates with conservative discourse in the marginalization of critical perspectives.

My analysis in this chapter rests on the distinction between mainstream "liberal" perspectives and critical ones. The former are in favour of moderate reform, while (consciously or unconsciously) participating in the maintenance of fundamentally dominative social processes and structures of power; the latter are committed to critiquing and transforming these basic processes and structures. The **mainstream liberal politics** I analyze here are organized around several key imperatives:

– a) a commitment to obfuscation in regard to basic theories and principles;
– b) a deliberate unconsciousness with regard to ideological questions; and
– c) a commitment to a positivist orientation toward reality, which sees truth as a matter of arguments over traditionally-defined kinds of so-called "neutral" evidence, rather than as emerging from experience, struggle, and values (Harding, 1997).

I examine here the characteristic ways in which these commitments are expressed in response to radical critique. The political position that I come from, and from which my critiques emerged which are the occasion for my reflections

A.H. Churchill (ed.), Rocking Your World: The Emotional Journey into Critical Discourses, 135–145.

here, is an antiracist, anticapitalist, antipatriarchal perspective, combined in my own particular mix. This mix makes a difference; on the other hand, I believe that the representations and responses I analyze here commonly come up in response to critique from a range of critical perspectives outside the mainstream consensus. In the experiences I describe below, the particular contradiction that was most salient, in terms of the way its representation was controlled and delimited, was that of race and racism. However, similar formations and discourses are encountered in response to critical activism around other forms of oppression as well.

The setting that these experiences and analyses are drawn from is the Graduate School of Education at the University of California, Los Angeles, where I did my doctoral work. The contexts within this school that I describe in this chapter were by and large dominated by a liberal politics and discourse that some might call "progressive" (and others might not), although this perspective was not predominant at all times or places. This is a political formation that is relatively common, even hegemonic[1] (though not uniform), in university schools of education. I believe that most other schools of education in the U.S. would furnish examples and experiences similar to those I consider in this chapter.

It is important to acknowledge that many responses to critical interventions have merit, including those made from a mainstream vantage point. We need to maintain a fundamental commitment to dialogue, which allows us to see the limits and problems in our own positions. Indeed, part of my focus in this chapter is on the way that liberal responses to critique often shut down the possibility of dialogue. It is also important to emphasize that these are my experiences and my reflections on them, and that they are influenced by my own positionality (as White, as a man, as middle class, as a student, among other things), my own ideology, and my own personality. Others who raise similar critiques from different positions, or in different ways, call forth different responses and have different experiences. Both the commonalities and the differences are important.

WHAT DO MARGINALIZING RESPONSES LOOK LIKE?

During my graduate studies, I was hired as a field supervisor for the school of education's teacher education program, which had as a specific mission to form partnerships with inner-city schools as well as to pursue a "social justice" agenda. In addition to working with the specific students to whom I was assigned, and a subject area seminar, I was also invited to be a participant in faculty meetings and a field supervisor inquiry group. Many of the most interesting discussions and difficulties surfaced in the latter meetings, as debates took place about the meaning of "social justice" and what it meant to teach in the context of a commitment to this principle.

I was also hired as a graduate student researcher for an education policy research centre and was assigned to several projects focused on building an "equity" agenda in California in partnership with community groups, politicians, professionals, and other education researchers. In this context, I was a participant in regular team meetings that included senior faculty researchers, centre staff, and other graduate students. These meetings were the occasion for revealing conversations about how to frame campaigns, appeal to different constituencies, and conceptualize educational change. Contradictions between mainstream and critical approaches to these issues were often apparent in these sessions, even if they were often suppressed.

The examples of response to critique that I describe in this section are drawn from the two university contexts described above. On the basis of my experiences as a researcher and teacher educator, I outline **patterns in mainstream liberal arguments** used to defend against criticism: the kinds of strategic rationality deployed to variously block, undercut, refute, or belittle arguments about systematic oppression and the importance of it to analysis and action. These patterns reveal a set of tools for preserving the dominance of mainstream practices and beliefs, as well as a basic philosophical grammar that it is important for critical activists and educators to see and understand. In analyzing these examples and experiences, I have found that they fall into several different categories, and I have organized my discussion below on the basis of these categories which include: **resistance/ blocking, the pretense to neutrality, being "practical", and "evidence" versus experience**.

Resistance/Blocking

As part of the work for the research centre described above, a colleague and I were assigned to prepare research briefs on critical issues affecting students in public education in California, including access to qualified teachers, funding, accountability, and other topics. We found that our efforts in this work to include attention to historical and systematic racism in schools were continually overridden by our superiors. As a result, at one meeting we presented a set of criticisms of the fundamental assumptions guiding the research work that our team was engaged in, focusing on the lack of consideration of culture, race, and experience as mediating the realities of educational injustice (as opposed to the simple quantitative description of resource disparities). We spent a lot of time beforehand in preparation to make sure our arguments were clear, non-confrontational, and well supported by research. After our presentation, we were effusively commended by our superiors, and told that we should "consider writing an article about our suggestions." There was no substantive follow-up to the concerns we raised.

What I have called "resistance/blocking" here includes all those efforts that aim to head off critique and discussion, or to prevent its having any effect. This may seem to be a trivial technique, but it may be the most crucial. Liberal politics is grounded in claims of and appeals to democracy, and this strategy is crucial in policing the boundaries of this "democratic" space. At stake here is a central contradiction in bourgeois politics:[2] the conflict between a rhetoric of dialogue, and a persistent reality in which true dialogue is made impossible (Freire, 1997).

The first form of this blocking is avoiding critical discussions altogether. When discussions are agreed upon, the next line of defense is a refusal to engage. This can take the form of silence, of jokes to downplay concerns raised, or defensive negotiation of each point raised. Finally, if it should happen that dialogue takes place and results in an agreement, the final tactic of resistance is to refuse to act. In another example, which illustrates the latter tactic, a colleague and I in the teacher education program presented an anti-war statement to the director–in the context of recent U.S. aggressions in the Middle East–which was signed by a significant number of staff and students. It was our view that as educators and intellectuals with a special responsibility in relation to young people, it was our duty to express our opposition to unjustified militarism. She promised that it would be published in the upcoming newsletter of the program. Not surprisingly, it was not. The very commonness of these experiences for activists points to the importance of this strategy as a way to marginalize critique.

Pretense to Neutrality

As mentioned above, the teacher education program had as part of its mission a commitment to "social justice." What this meant, however, was never defined. In practice, it was expressed mainly in the program's links with "low-performing" schools in Los Angeles, and in the set of progressive readings to which teacher education students were exposed in the course of their studies. Nevertheless, otherwise the program was characterized by a studious avoidance of efforts to name and confront the actual systematic obstacles in the way of working toward social transformation in education. Indeed, as the discourse of "social justice" proliferates through higher educational institutions, it may partly serve, in its vagueness, as an impediment to a rigorous naming of forms of oppression (De Lissovoy, 2007). As part of the inquiry groups that field supervisors participated in, several of us decided to push the envelope and to argue that antiracism should be an explicitly identified principle within the program's understanding of social justice. We argued that program curriculum, activities, and initiatives ought to be in accordance with this principle. Our view was not that this principle was sufficient in itself as a definition of social justice, but rather that it was a good place to start in specifying the program's social and political commitment.

Interestingly, the objection that we heard from faculty in the program and from our fellow field supervisors was not that such a principle was a bad idea in itself, but rather that it would limit the range of concepts and practices that could be brought to bear in their work by participating teacher educators. I recall some participants becoming quite exercised by what they perceived as an offensive intrusion into the private space of their own values and professional judgment. In fact, to the extent that our aim was to limit the use of racist ideas and practices, this characterization was correct. However, the actual function of this objection was to sabotage our intervention and to continue the dominant process of "silencing" that is pervasive in relation to race and schooling (Fine, 1987), and in this way to refuse any real movement toward an organized antiracist position. Paradoxically, then, the concern that educators in the teacher education program should be able to construct the domain of social justice and the practices it implied in any way that they wished to, resulted in a prohibition on our perspective–the view that social justice implies a collective project of understanding and naming oppression and organizing effective and concrete responses to it.

The liberal pretense to neutrality aims to shut down critique by turning the tables and arguing that such critique is itself oppressive, since it refuses a putatively neutral position, and thus marginalizes the views of those who would disagree. Usually this takes the form of objections that critical perspectives are overly partisan, or that adopting these perspectives would shut down the diversity of views that neutrality protects, threatening the right of individuals to disagree (Benhabib, 1996). The foundation for this strategy is the idea that liberal politics are themselves located at the very centre of the spectrum, and that in grounding and framing discussion in general, they do not in fact constitute a particular politics at all, but rather a universal criterion of fairness. On this foundation, the prohibition on the articulation of other political principles becomes a kind of morality, a protection against the potential injury to the dominant consensus.

Being "Practical"

As part of a larger communications strategy geared toward changing public opinion in relation to conditions and resource disparities, the team that I was working for in the policy research centre was developing ideas for a possible media campaign to raise awareness of schooling issues. In order to show that many students suffered from a lack of resources, the team wanted to combat the idea that low achievement was the fault of students and their families. One idea for a television spot that was suggested in this connection was a sequence that would show a Latino student hard at work on his homework, with the implicit or explicit message that Latino/a students are "just as" diligent and concerned, in regard to education, as Whites. I objected, saying that in taking as a starting point the deficit perspective and discursive racism that casts communities of colour as unconcerned about education, we would be partly legitimizing this racism; in addition, we were not questioning the equation of Whiteness with social virtue and morality. Proponents responded that it was necessary not to alienate Whites, since we needed them on our side. How would we change people's minds, they argued, if we couldn't appeal to them in the first place?

Liberal politics has a theory of opinion, but no theory of ideology:[3] it does not see the latter as a crucial battleground for struggle (partly since to do so would be to risk the exposure of its own ideological foundations). Antiracist, feminist, and socialist politics require a consideration of deep processes, logics, economies, and meanings. To remain, then, always in the domain of the immediate, the practical, and the self-evident is to make critical analysis and dialogue impossible. This doesn't mean that critical analysis is without practical effects, but it does mean that this politics necessarily involves theory—we need to lay bare the organization of domination in this world in order to imagine a different one. Marcuse (1991) demonstrated the tendency of contemporary society to reduce truth and politics to the flat space of the operational—to reduce the range of acceptable problems to those that present themselves as purely instrumental, purely "practical." In education politics, this has the effect of restricting the range of discussion to "what can be done," where this means what can be operated in the realm of official bourgeois practice–in other words, in terms of elections, legislation, court decisions, etc. Analysis and strategy, it is argued, should not alienate those who hold power, and should be organized not on the basis of the most important political or ethical imperatives, but on the basis of what can be "won."

"Evidence" Versus Experience

Much of the work in the equity campaign of the research centre involved strategizing about how to use research to build a case and movement for educational change. However, the sense of what counted as "real" evidence was limited to a positivistic universe of large-scale survey results and experimentally designed studies. On many occasions, I argued that the experiences and expressions of the people who suffered from the conditions we were trying to change should be included in our presentations of educational research evidence. This would have extended the sense of "research" and "evidence" to include both the texture provided by qualitative studies as well as some of the straightforward testimony of parents and community members that we were hearing in the course of our work. Senior members of the team objected that this evidence would be unconvincing and irrelevant, since it couldn't count as the foundation of informed policy-making.

Captured as they were by the need to prevail within an arena of scientific and policy contestation whose terms went unchallenged, these researchers could not see the violence involved in refusing the validity of the feelings and experiences of those who live the difficult conditions we were concerned with. This is not to suggest that experience does not need to be questioned and reflected upon, but rather that it is an important source for science and politics. The marginalizing response I discuss here involves the mobilization of a specifically patriarchal logic. In this logic, emotional understandings and expressions are belittled as being without use or value. Feminist theorists such as Alison Jaggar (1989) have discussed, by contrast, the epistemological[4] authority of feeling and experience. In this regard, this strategy of the mainstream consensus involves two steps: first, characterizing emotional experience as inappropriate or irrelevant, and then, in the language of "research," refusing the understandings it suggests as unscientific or incomprehensible.

WHAT DO MARGINALIZING RESPONSES FEEL LIKE?

While it is important to analyze the arguments that I have discussed above, which are brought to bear in response to critique, it is also important to describe the kind of emotional and affective space that is created on these occasions. Antiracist, feminist, anticapitalist and other forms of critique rupture the normative social expectations and assumptions that surround and underlie day-to-day interactions, even in "progressive" settings. As crucial as the arguments are that attempt to meet these critiques on the symbolic level, so are the ways that this social field reflexively sutures itself, seals itself up and away from the force that threatens it. This is something that is deeply felt and experienced, rather than simply known. Below I describe several important aspects of this experience.

Zipped-Up Space (Alienation)

One of my most common experiences in the settings and on the occasions I have discussed above, when I put forward a critique of problematic assumptions or practices, was a feeling of the space in the room being "zipped up" around the intervention–almost a kind of asphyxiation of dissent and dissonance. This has to do with the discomfort of the participants involved, but it's also important to see this as the collective response of a social field that is threatened. For example, to raise the issue of capitalism in mainstream settings, as I sometimes did in my graduate teaching and research positions, is to cast in doubt the assumptions, vocabularies, and even mannerisms that undergird "normal" interactions. This is partly true even in classrooms, but it is especially true in the kind of work settings that I have described above. When the "matrix of intelligibility" (Butler, 2006) of liberal discourse is threatened, there is an immediate withdrawal from engagement, a smoothing out of the injury, and a sealing and restoration of the normal system. This leaves the critic feeling isolated, denied and refused.

I have often experienced a profound and yet very mundane alienation at these times, as polite (even friendly) as it is violent. The feeling is of being exiled. As the considerations you raise fall away from the sealed space of the liberal consensus, their energy falls back into you, and you see, in the eyes around, that this energy is seen to be a personal property of you. It is constructed as an inscrutable anger attached to your person and not to the world that you are attempting to describe. I know that this alienation is a much more common experience for those who are Black or Latina/o or poor or queer or otherwise outside the "mainstream," and even more so for those who are outside the mainstream *and* actively critical of it. These occasions, then, in my own life, are also opportunities for me to have a better understanding of the experiences of others.

Those who have felt the spaces of alienation I describe here know that, at these moments, the environment acquires a special vividness, perhaps because one is suddenly present to the very precise situation of one's isolated body–at once in relation, and at the same time refused a relation, with those nearby. The shine on a table, a sound through the window, or the flatness of blank walls are all magnified and made meaningful as witnesses, or perhaps as mirrors of the apparent muteness of one's own words. Although these moments are difficult, perhaps we can also take them as instants of heightened aliveness, and in their very intensity, proof of the power and reality of our own critical interventions.

Textures of Power

Another interesting aspect of these critical moments, when the "normal" is potentially threatened, is that the networks and structures of power become especially palpable. When a challenge is raised to a racist representation or assumption, and this challenge is swiftly argued away, or is refused in the quick transition to another topic, or is benevolently entertained and then humorously spun in some innocuous direction, the map of power in the space of the conversation becomes almost a physical thing. One can then feel the reservoirs of power that surround those who are privileged to speak and decide in such settings: the power of institutional position, the power of wealth, class and cultural capital, the power of authoritative, proper (often patriarchal) discourse, and not least, the bright smiling power of Whiteness. In many elite higher education settings, even in education, the majority if not all participants are White. At times of crisis, when norms are challenged, one can feel this Whiteness vibrate and find itself, one can feel a White solidarity crackle like electricity, as bodies stiffen and glances quickly find each other for reassurance and to re-establish the circle of order.

The other side of this is that as participants in settings of privilege, we are always offered, in different degrees, a place at the table and a measure of pleasure in such privilege. In my case, I am offered much more as a White middle-class man. However, at some level, no one who is an official operator of institutional processes is completely outside of these circuits of power: each participates in the status and privilege of employment in higher education. Even as a graduate student researcher, one is continually asked to identify with and support economies of privilege based on the factors I have mentioned–to be, if only for a moment, an expert, an authority, or "in the know." It is important to be aware of what we take and what we refuse on these occasions. Part of the dialectic of resistance is an honesty about our own implication in what we resist, and even of the necessity, to a degree, of those implications. Until we organize an oppositional collective that is much broader than each of us by ourselves, these contradictions will not be fundamentally transformed.

RESISTANT UNDERSTANDING AND ACTION

The responses and reactions I have described above can be difficult and sometimes demoralizing for those who are committed to critical perspectives and to social transformation. However, I want to conclude by suggesting some ways in which we can think about these patterns of representation, argument, and experience that can make them more endurable, and which can also point toward methods of successfully resisting.

Historicizing Experience as a Tool for Resistance

I believe that in the context of critical action against injustice it is helpful in moments of difficulty and disappointment to recall the social and historical background against which these struggles are played out. It is useful to contextualize instances of resistance and response in terms of the class and cultural hegemonies that frame them, and to remember that these political forces and antagonisms are much larger than us as individuals. In this way, we can begin to read those who try to shut down radical critique as representatives of social fractions, and as carriers of particular ideological structures, which have their own purposes and determinations apart from these individuals. Maybe even more important, we can start to see ourselves as representatives as well, as agents of an opposing class and purpose, whose history and destiny is much larger than us and our own personal victories or defeats. This understanding can help to temper our frustration–once we begin to understand and to feel the invisible lines of solidarity that connect us at once to a thousand other sites of struggle.

As Marx shows, it is first of all in capitalism that people begin to assume as a starting point the idea of themselves as abstract individuals. So to challenge the individualism of our experience is itself a key step in struggle. As long as the story is the story of an individual, the dominant forces will always win (which is why it is the job of Hollywood to persistently narrate this fiction). Once we see that even in the most personal aspects of our lives we are fully social beings, we can begin to counter our egocentric (and ideological) attachment to our individual political experiences. We can then understand the link between the polite argument in the conference room and the skirmishes with police in the streets. When it is demanded in a teacher education program that a general commitment to "social justice" be specified, to force the taking of sides in real struggles around racism and class oppression, and when this demand motivates fierce opposition in the name of "neutrality," this is a concrete example of class struggle in action. The discursive resources that are brought to bear in this debate are not simply those of individuals, but belong also to the larger groups and forces these individuals represent (whether they are conscious of this or not). And these arguments are contests with real stakes: their outcomes partly determine the access of teachers and students to very different visions of the world, and to the very different material possibilities connected with them.

Critical Tactics: The Importance of Flexibility

Chela Sandoval (2000) describes how the decolonizing movement of the oppressed involves a special flexibility, which is a capacity of those who have had to be skilful to survive against systematic violence. Rather than being stuck to one position or strategy, this methodology, as she describes it, makes use of **multiple oppositional strategies and understandings** within a consciousness that goes beyond them to a new form. One implication of her work is the importance of not being tied to a single approach, identity, or understanding that would restrict the capacity to resist. In this regard, I think it is important for critical educators and activists to be continually creative in their work. This can mean engaging in multiple (and sometimes even contradictory) forms of intervention at the same time. For example, these reflections suggest the importance of following varied approaches to critical discourse and action, such as:

- a) raising issues formally in official contexts, while understanding the ways in which institutions are constrained;
- b) proceeding autonomously, which is to say beginning independently to implement the kinds of changes that are being called for;
- c) dodging counter-offensives, and avoiding bitter struggles which will be more damaging than they are worth;
- d) using multiple languages of critique, in order to vary the lines of attack;
- e) working outside, i.e. building more authentic resistant cultures and spaces outside of dominant institutional contexts.

The left is sometimes held hostage to its own "language of critique" (Giroux, 2005), and given to a kind of fatalism that can be perversely attractive–the compulsion to go down fighting. We need to be happier, more creative, and more energetic in thinking about the ways we will win, the ways that we will not go down. We need to learn not just to struggle, but also to manoeuvre. I am suggesting an agile opposition that weaves in and out–a moving target that can't be easily pegged and demoralized and immobilized. This is especially important from the point of view of struggle within mainstream liberal contexts. Liberals are master political manoeuvrers, as Malcolm X often pointed out, expert at manipulating the contradictions between political image and reality. We need to learn to out-tactician them from the ground of our own critical politics.

Above all, I believe that faced with the kinds of difficult moments of critique and reaction that I have described in this chapter, we need to not lose that solidarity that keeps critical action and analysis going. We need to not lose that love for each other that keeps us human against the dehumanizing structures, processes, and discourses that oppress society and then construct our resistance as mad, irrelevant, childish or dangerous. That love is our secret weapon. It is secret not because it is hidden, but because to the powerful it is invisible, incomprehensible, or insignificant–this is their constant mistake, the one that undoes them continually. It is also the place and resource that we need to remember and start from. As long as we are strong enough to begin from that critical solidarity, we have already won.

NOTES

[1] Hegemonic here refers to the fact that not only is this political formation common, but in addition it works hard to maintain itself in a position of dominance, and to prevent other perspectives from overtaking it. This term (and the noun hegemony) is used in critical theory to refer to the cultural and political struggle among different forces and classes (and their characteristic ideas) within society. Hegemonic ideas reflect those who win out in this struggle, but they become the norm for everyone, even if they act in the interest of particular groups. See McLaren (1989) for further explanation of this term; Gramsci (1971) is the influential theorist who originally developed this set of meanings.

[2] By bourgeois politics I mean the dominant political culture in capitalist societies, and especially in the U.S. Politics in capitalism, as Marx and Engels (1967) explained, is dominated by the bourgeoisie, or capitalist class, which has an interest in limiting political discussion to topics and arguments that do not call the underlying social and economic systems into question. At the same

time, this class represents the limited debate and democracy that it does allow as a completely full and free space of discussion.

[3] I am using ideology in the sense of the system of beliefs and ideas which individuals use to make sense of their experiences. While liberals are interested in debating competing opinions or strategies, they are less interested in exploring alternative philosophies or systems of ideas which might call some of their own unspoken assumptions about the world into question. However, I believe that true political discussion and struggle involves just such an exploration. Ideologies are not right or wrong; rather, they are particular systems of meaning-making with a variety of political effects. See Althusser (1971) for a very powerful investigation of this topic.

[4] Epistemology refers to the theory of knowledge–investigations of what knowing is, who can truly know, and how knowing happens. While Western philosophy has traditionally reserved true knowing for privileged subjects, processes, and modes (e.g. men, universalizing scientific inquiry, and an "objective" attitude of detachment), feminist philosophers have shown that there are other legitimate ways to know, and other legitimate knowers. For example, emotional experiences can furnish important knowledge of the world, and can therefore constitute an important mode of knowing. In addition to Jaggar (cited in the text), see also Harding (1993) for a fuller explanation.

REFERENCES

Althusser, L. (1971). *Lenin and philosophy and other essays* (B. Brewster, Trans.). New York: Monthly Review Press.

Benhabib, S. (1996). Toward a deliberative model of democratic legitimacy. In S. Benhabib (Ed.), *Democracy and difference: Contesting the boundaries of the political* (pp. 67–94). Princeton, NJ: Princeton University Press.

Butler, J. (2006). *Gender trouble: Feminism and the subversion of identity*. New York: Routledge.

De Lissovoy, N. (2007). Frantz fanon and a materialist critical pedagogy. In P. McLaren & J. L. Kincheloe (Eds.), *Critical pedagogy: Where are we now?* (pp. 355–370). New York: Peter Lang.

Fine, M. (1987). Silencing in public schools. *Language Arts, 64*(2), 157–174.

Freire, P. (1997). *Pedagogy of the oppressed* (M. B. Ramos, Trans.). New York: Continuum.

Giroux, H. A. (2005). *Schooling and the struggle for public life*. Boulder, CO: Paradigm Publishers.

Gramsci, A. (1971). *Selections from the prison notebooks* (Q. Hoare & G. N. Smith, Trans.). New York: International Publishers.

Harding, S. (1993). Rethinking standpoint epistemology: What is strong objectivity? In L. Alcoff & E. Potter (Eds.), *Feminist epistemologies* (pp. 49–82). New York: Routledge.

Harding, S. (1997). Is there a feminist method? In S. Kemp & J. Squires (Eds.), *Feminisms* (pp. 160–170). Oxford: Oxford University Press.

Jaggar, A. (1989). Love and knowledge: Emotion in feminist epistemology. *Inquiry, 32*, 151–172.

Marcuse, H. (1991). *One-dimensional man*. Boston, MA: Beacon Press.

Marx, K., & Engels, F. (1967). *The communist manifesto*. London: Penguin Books.

McLaren, P. (1989). *Life in schools: An introduction to critical pedagogy in the foundations of education*. New York: Longman.

Sandoval, C. (2000). *Methodology of the oppressed*. Minneapolis, MN: University of Minnesota Press.

13. CRITICAL PEDAGOGY AND THE GREAT WHITE HOPE DILEMMA

I asked a friend if she had seen the movie *Freedom Writers* yet. She replied: "No. I refuse to see another Great White Hope Story." I never saw the movie either. It is no secret that the Great White Hope Story is alive and well in Hollywood. I cringe when I watch those movies where the white male coach swoops into the ghetto landscape and gathers the black boys to rally around him using the discipline of basketball or football to convince them to embrace higher education. I scratch my head watching films where the Snow White angelic teacher overcomes her fear of loud hip hop loving students and eventually shows the very ethnic class the joys of English Literature.

Now it seems that I have unknowingly stumbled upon my own Great White Hope Story. It's one thing to watch an archetypal story play out on the big screen and find it ideologically disturbing; it's another thing to discover you are starring in it.

POSITIONALITY

Some people ask me why am I not in Asian or Multicultural studies if I am so deeply concerned with researching multicultural education, diverse scholars and diverse student populations. That question offends me. It suggests that diversity is the primary concern only in certain discourses, whereas it should be one of the primary concerns in all educational discourses. Some people ask me if my white male supervisor can really guide me through these critical discourses given our differences in positionality. I had enough difficulty finding a supervisor that shares the same ideology with me never mind finding one with whom I could share similar experiences based on who I am and what I live. In this point of difficulty, I am confident I am not alone in the minority graduate student community. Questions of positionality, representation, and voice are everywhere in the academy; for some of us these questions are more present and unavoidable and are our concern in all aspects of life even outside academic institutions.

I have also been warned that my voice is in danger of being colonized or harvested by white professors. I would argue that how could it *not* be in an academic system that flaunts its roots in colonialism to begin with. The academy shamelessly supplies us with endless curricula and syllabi across all fields and disciplines where one voice and one positionality are valued and normalized over all others–even while it urges us to be critical educators. It is not the individual

A.H. Churchill (ed.), Rocking Your World: The Emotional Journey into Critical Discourses, 147–156.

white male academic colonizing or reproducing power dimensions. Ironically some of the most outspoken critics of the nature of reproduction of power in education are white men.

But this alone does not change the nature of the institution. The academic institution seems to reproduce the macro power dynamics of the society in which it is embedded. If we were to magically remove all the white male academic figureheads in administration, tenured professorships, and publishing and conference rock stars, I am fairly sure that the majority of those positions would be filled with more white males and these replacements may not necessarily be on the side of the marginalized voice. Positionality and representation is not about the personal or the individual; it is about power in relation to the system at large.

The problem that critical pedagogy faces is that as it seeks to be critical and dismantle power relations, it is caught in an academic and publishing system that is mediated by existing power relations. It is seen as the elite trying to lead the revolution. Of course I do not mean to suggest that critical pedagogy is only meant for those who are marginalized from the mainstream. The oppressors themselves must also be liberated. However, one of the reasons critical pedagogy offers hope to those who have traditionally been disserved by educational systems is that it sees the possibility of transforming education and thus transcending its binding reproductive nature. It is constantly speaking of action, calling us to act upon our critical consciousness. However, it has not yet transformed itself.

I engage with critical pedagogy both intellectually and affectively. I see a conflict between the ideology of critical pedagogy and the positionality of the mostly white men who dominate its sphere. I know ideology matters more, significantly more, than positionality. But I cannot discount how I feel when after many years of education I am still learning from white men and women and in this case learning how to be critical from white men and women. I feel frustrated. I feel hopeless. I feel like can it be possible that we really have so far left to go? Ideology counts but that does not mean we can discount positionality because we do have far to go where it is concerned. I am not frustrated at white critical academics, I am frustrated at a system that allows the constant reproduction of power imbalances to reproduce themselves.

This chapter is not an homage to my love affair with critical pedagogy. I am not here to sing its praises, but neither am I here to condemn it. Put simply there is something amiss about my relationship with critical pedagogy today and this chapter is an attempt to put my finger on it. It is an attempt to retrace my steps and see where I and critical pedagogy went astray. This chapter is about my uneasiness with the representation of critical pedagogy theory today and how we might differently envision a critical pedagogy in the near future.

CRIT PED AND I–A LIKELY PAIR

I naturally gravitated towards critical pedagogy. It seduced me with whispers of the radical and the political in these, at times, stale ivory towers of education. It had me at *Pedagogy of the Oppressed.* Critical pedagogy and I were really quite taken with each other. It was love at first sight. Eventually we even settled into terms of endearment: it became crit ped and I became marginalized student.

Or perhaps it was the other way around. Maybe critical pedagogy naturally gravitates towards students like me. I am after all an unlikely grad student–young, child of Filipino immigrants to Canada, and a product of a strong single mother household. I have always felt like the schools I was going through were not exactly tailor made for someone like me. I knew that much more than schooling took place in schools. School was always a place to learn White Canadian and how to unlearn how I was at home. Thus, I was an easy believer in critical pedagogy. It did not take much convincing on my part. The language of the discourse provided a framework for my already present convictions about schools; critical pedagogy was an ally for me in these ivory towers. It can function as a shield for those who feel like pariahs in their higher academic institutions. To those of us who do not have the cultural capital to feel at ease in an academic environment, critical pedagogy cries out "Don't worry! You belong here too!" When I stumbled upon critical pedagogy in my first years of grad school I clung to it fiercely, thinking it was what was going to help me get through these bleached ivory towers relatively unscathed. Sure I always took a peak at what else was going on in other discourses but in the end I always came back home to crit ped.

When I began my affair with critical pedagogy I felt I needed to trace its roots in an attempt to better understand contemporary scholars and their work. I was pulled to two geographic poles–Frankfurt and Brazil. Ah, the Frankfurt School and Paulo Freire. From the start it was very clear that the Frankfurt School was something I should definitely know about. Critical pedagogy also made it apparent that Paulo Freire would figure prominently in my library. I must admit that the idea of the Frankfurt School did not really pique my academic interest. From what I gathered (as someone just entering the discourse) the Frankfurt School was the grounds for the founding fathers of critical discourses. I was immediately judgemental and thought "powerful white men in Europe laying the foundations for the rest of us," how novel. Much later on, with the help of Martin Jay's historiography of the Frankfurt School, I was proved wrong about my assumptions on the story and experience of those founding fathers. I no longer see the Frankfurt School as some lifeless academic publishing machine from way back when, but I see it through the stories and struggles that pushed those academic minds to create works that continue to push critical scholarship across many discourses.

However in the beginning phases of my introduction to critical pedagogy there was something about Paulo Freire and his writings that reached out to me and pulled me in as a young scholar. He had zeal, he had passion. I read a few of his chapters and I was hooked. Freire's words gave me an outlet, a way to connect my passionate political views with the somewhat bland educational graduate material I was muddling through at the time. Truthfully though it was not only his poetic and incisive writings that intrigued me but also his life. Freire gave my graduate studies in education some colour–literally and figuratively. I clung to him fiercely.

I later had a similar experience when I stumbled upon Renato Constantino's *The Miseducation of the Filipino*. Interestingly our expansive library did not have it and, although I did not think much about it after ordering a copy from a library half-way across the country, when it arrived I read it and I think fireworks went off in my head. Through the words, the thoughts, the subject, all from a Filipino scholar and about the Filipino educational context, I experienced for the first time pride and connection in my academic life. His thoughts on American colonization of the Filipino educational system moved me in so many different ways. It sounds ridiculous I know! But that's what happens when you go so long without seeing someone who looks like you be respected in your field and when you go so long without anybody even talking about your context, your situation. I wanted to talk about it with everyone. The problem was that no one knew who he was. I was struck by how similar his analysis was to that of contemporary critical pedagogues. Constantino's existence assures me of the value of continuing to actively seek out more than just what my syllabus provides to properly ensure that I am getting educated from more than just one corner of the world.

THE PARADOX OF THEORY AND REPRESENTATION IN CRITICAL PEDAGOGY

Raw emotions motivated me to write this and not the theoretical musings to which I have become accustomed to writing in academia. I have become uneasy with the positioning of the white male as the visionary of critical pedagogy. I'm confronted by the paradox of reading and being inspired by critical pedagogy literature that champions diversity and speaks to those who are marginalized, yet the field of critical pedagogy does not seem to boast diversity in its own canon of current and historical writers. This paradox is the gap between the changes that critical pedagogy theoretically argues for in our educational systems and the degree to which critical pedagogy adheres to the static nature of our post secondary institutions. Despite critical pedagogy's whispers of the radical and the political I am stuck in the web of academia, faithfully learning the canon of European white males and now North American white males in order to succeed.

Theories do not float around in the air, opening themselves up to grad students, waiting to be discovered and rediscovered by generations and generations of students. We meet them through the faces and personalities of our professors and through a canon of established authors in the field. When we think of physics we see Albert Einstein's goofy face. Faces, stories, life experiences are always connected to the theories we toil over. Try as we might to avoid the iconography and idolatry of theorists and academics, the cult of the icon persists in academia. Anyone who has been to an AERA session where a well-known academic was speaking is keenly aware of the type of rock star/fan scenario that sometimes plays out in the room. We live in a visual culture of information overload. Students are unconsciously and increasingly consciously seeking mentors and role models in their respective fields; they want to see that someone like them has made it, that someone like them has said and published thoughts that count too. I want to believe that in all of history and even up to today that it must be impossible that almost all of social theory and especially critical discourses were written by mostly white men. What hope do I have as an aspiring academic if I can see no trail blazed before me?

Locating myself between the founding fathers and successful sons

"Founding fathers" is a term that rolls off the tongue so easily it seems the most benign of phrases. I was recently in the audience of an interview where the participant and the interviewer were both well-known figures in the field of critical pedagogy. I sat near the front that day and was struck by how the discourse of critical pedagogy was again being represented by white males whether or not the white males in question felt comfortable with that or not. There were many undergraduates in the audience that day so a rudimentary genealogy of critical pedagogy was necessary to lend context to the speakers. It was roughly explained that if Paulo Freire and the Frankfurt School could be considered the fathers of critical pedagogy, then the interviewer and interviewee could be considered as the sons of this critical discourse. Of course I do not dispute these facts; this is not what concerned me at the time or presently. I was struck by the imagery both in the words and in the visual in front me.

The whiteness of these talks can be deafening; the maleness overpowering. I wonder what it would be like to listen to Paulo Freire and have the room to breathe in a little colour. It may make all the difference in how I experience these things; it may not. It is an odd feeling and an uncomfortable statement for me as many of my doctoral student colleagues and indeed my own supervisor are white and male. Yet at times I cannot fight the power of the visual image and all the cultural capital and historical weight that society attaches to that of the white man. I earnestly try to separate the signifier from the signified because I know that white men cannot be superficially stripped down to existing just as symbols of white oppression. But symbols are powerful forces in our visually mediated society. They will not be easily dismissed.

There is a mantra often uttered in the lecture halls that we should not be consumed by positionality in the face of ideology. This is not a witch hunt. You might mistakenly think that I am caught up in positionality, pointing accusingly at any white male, or woman for that matter, who has achieved academic scholarly success through critical discourses. Positionality only becomes a problem when all the visionaries seem to occupy one position–that is of the white male. I have heard the argument that we must learn the tools of our oppressors; I am not satisfied. I want more. And I have every right to demand more of critical pedagogy. Critical pedagogy needs people like me. If students and aspiring academics like me do not engage in the discourse of critical pedagogy, then where does that leave it? Critical pedagogy discourse needs a diverse base. I am aware that change takes time. But we in the critical discourses must do all we can to put pressure on the current situation and analyze our own role in the cycle of white male domination of our syllabi and library shelves. We can no longer push aside these issues in academia. If we are to be critical of the classroom we must be equally if not more critical of the lecture hall. Critical discourse is in danger of losing authenticity when it is not

' critical of itself. It is in danger of seeing and confronting the political everywhere but within.

WHERE ARE ALL THE BLACK ACADEMICS AT?[1]

In fact critical pedagogy seeks a diverse base. I attended an event at AERA 2006 in San Francisco entitled "Visions from the Visionaries." The panel was meant to address critical pedagogy's direction in the future; it consisted of three men and one woman who was speaking on a male academic's behalf in absentia. I had a breakthrough during their presentation because I experienced a moment where I truly felt that the uneasiness I was experiencing was also being shared by some of critical pedagogy's own leaders. The last speaker bluntly asked why there was such a weak representation of African-Americans at the critical pedagogy sessions at the conference and in the room at the moment. At which point I distinctly remember surveying the audience from where I sat. From what I could readily see, the speaker was correct in his assessment of the audience demographic. The speaker proceeded to emphatically state that critical pedagogy is for diverse scholars–but that despite this fact there was a noticeable absence of black scholars in the discourse of critical pedagogy. To further underscore critical pedagogy's relevance to black scholars, he mentioned W.E.B. DuBois' own relevance in relation to critical educational philosophies and how DuBois' work can and should be considered some of the first published work in the discourse of critical pedagogy. His appeals were heartfelt and I am sure that his concerns were shared with others in the room.

There does seem to be something inherent in critical pedagogy that seeks to touch all populations–oppressed and oppressors, lower class and upper class, and I could go on. At times however comes across as a type of colonizing discourse, an umbrella theory if you will. There were critical discourses that existed before critical pedagogy and there are critical discourses that exist alongside critical pedagogy. It recognizes the importance and relevance of African American critical theories and queer theories but it would like to recognize those theorists as critical pedagogues as well. In a sense it wants to find the critical pedagogue in all of us, which is not of course something it should be chastised for. But critical pedagogy must recognize the discomfort this creates. It is a discourse that at times wants to address everyone and everything from language rights to queer rights to everything in between in the classroom and on the playground. Critical pedagogy could be a powerfully uniting tool; it also can send powerfully dividing messages when critical pedagogy theory and rhetoric appears to only come from the power elite.

Ricky Lee Allen refers to these type of questions in critical pedagogy as "The Race problem in the Critical Pedagogy Community."[2] I wonder, could we broaden that to the "gender problem," the "sexuality problem," the "linguistic problem," the "class problem?" I think we can, and I think the time has come to, start thinking about these problems as genuinely standing in the way of critical pedagogy advancing and evolving as a viable educational theory and praxis for the near future. It seems that in recent years taking stock of critical pedagogy has started with edited collections such as *Critical pedagogy: where are we now?* and *Reinventing critical pedagogy*. In these exercises of taking stock there is a strong cry for more diversity in the theory and better representation; I align myself with these voices. Sadly when these cries for diversity come from new scholars there is a touch of fear, of hesitancy, that accompanies their frustrations with critical pedagogy. What kind of community are we creating and reproducing if there are those among us who are afraid to speak out? I quote at length from Allen's chapter in *Reinventing critical pedagogy*:

> Writing this chapter on the 'race problem' in critical pedagogy makes me nervous because I fear what might happen when powerful critical pedagogy figures read it. As an assistant professor soon to be going up for tenure, I understand the importance of having influential allies; being a radical in academia can be very tricky business. Also, I have learned a lot from these powerful figures. (Allen, 2006, p. 3)

I laughed and worried when I read the above quote. I laughed at the part about "being a radical in academia" because it's ironic that in a theory that is supposed to be radical, you could be fearful of repercussions for being too radical. The truth of that statement is a sad testament to our ability to create a safe community of radical pedagogy in critical pedagogy. I worried because Allen expresses a sentiment that this type of questioning of critical pedagogy may affect his career. As a graduate student, I think I feel a degree of this fear but mostly fear of what my immediate community within my university will say. When I started writing out these thoughts in this chapter I was afraid of what my student colleagues and my professors would think when they read this since most of them are white critical pedagogues. Would I polarize myself in my community? Would people easily dismiss me as a disgruntled graduate student? Would anyone take me seriously?

A MODEST PROPOSAL

Let me venture back to another notable incident during the aforementioned AERA panel. A comment was posed to the panel at large during the question and answer period. An audience member proposed that Western scholars not come to lecture in his country for a year or two. In the time where his country's academic borders would in effect be closed, his country's own scholars could debate and build academic discourse amongst themselves. This would build their scholarly national base and would in turn better prepare them to interact with other international scholars. I was not sure whether his statement was made in all seriousness or was made to bring attention to the impact of Western scholarship on his country. Perhaps the audience member was speaking in response to one panellist's discussion about how he and a group of his graduate students occasionally travel where they are invited to speak to those who are interested in and actively engaged in revolutionary critical pedagogy. Or perhaps he was motivated by more personal circumstances that he did not share in the moment. When I reflect upon that moment I am reminded of Jonathan Swift's brilliant satirical essay "A modest proposal" where he details how and why the consumption of Irish babies would ease the situation of poverty and population rates; as a satire it was not meant literally but to cunningly draw attention to social attitudes and conditions concerning the impoverished Irish population. Similarly, maybe the man's comment was not made in any serious way and he just wanted us to question the impact of the dominance of Western scholarships in some countries.

I looked around to gauge the audience's reaction to the man's question. Many were shaking their head as if to convey that his suggestion was preposterous. Many looked quite frankly stunned. Doesn't he know that at AERA we are all supposed to get along? I myself enjoyed the man's comment, as preposterous as it may have sounded. I enjoyed how he had the courage or audacity to bring up in public an issue that in his world might be brought up quite often in private closed rooms. Of course the question came out of nowhere and may not have been appropriately phrased or posed fairly. We should not be putting each other on trial here; after all, we are all working towards similar goals. But maybe it is exactly because we are working towards similar goals that we should and must put each other on trial.

This brings us back to the question of voice and positionality in critical pedagogy discourse. W.E.B. DuBois had penned thoughts on the politics of education and race that merit a solid position in the canon of educational social theorists (DuBois, 1903). We go on about the Frankfurt School yet we do not recognize DuBois and his writing about schools, students and education until a white man asserts his importance in our critical discourse. The structural systems that govern power and discourse in our society have not come as far as we like to think in regards to diversity in representations. We may all learn the importance of multicultural education and critical analysis of power in education, but we still live in a system of academia where most high level positions are occupied by white males. This drives me crazy. It makes me want to scream with frustration when I see faculties of education where most are white like their mostly white pre-service students who go out to teach classes where they are the minority in number and I am the majority.

THE PROVERBIAL LOOK TO THE FUTURE

If the sociological imagination begins with personal experience but inevitably is completed by an accompanying social theoretical analysis of that experience, then this chapter is incomplete. I had too much personal experience that I wished to spill out onto these pages and although I invariably recalled possible references throughout; I did not defer to them. I am sure it would be a useful tool for all, most of all myself, if I were to revisit this work and deconstruct it from a theoretical perspective. Truthfully I feel as though I am airing out critical pedagogy's dirty laundry here, committing to paper those hushed comments in the conference halls and grad student houses. I realize it is dangerous to leave experience to speak for itself, especially in writing where interpretation is out of the author's hands. But my purpose here is to merely shine a light on the challenges present and looming for critical discourse so that we may overcome these challenges together.

I see possibility in critical pedagogy because it seeks to address education as a whole. It has the scope to see language connected to human rights connected to class connected to media. It can make conceptual connections between education as a historically repressing tool in the developing world to education as a historically class reproduction system in the developing world. It can take many forms and shapes, some more radical than others. But because of its wide scope it walks the line of silencing or marginalizing already existing dynamic discourses in critical theory.

Where does all this airing out of my frustrations leave me? Where does it leave you? Whether or not this piece is read by many or few it was not an easy task to approach and execute. I was afraid to be judged, I was afraid to be misunderstood, but most of all I was afraid of offending white friends, colleagues, and peers. I presented some thoughts on this paper at a graduate student conference with much hesitation. I had some of the piece written and thought it was now or never to see how people would respond. A fellow student whom I rarely speak to came up to me and said thank you because she felt it was something that needed to be talked about in public and written about. The whole day was peppered with similar events with students and professors approaching me and giving me courage with each comment. After writing this I am sure there will be a graduate student out there someday who will read this and be nodding their head in recognition of my frustrations. That is who I wrote this for.

A white colleague and fellow critical pedagogue finishing up her dissertation is about to embark upon an academic career and had an open invitation to help her practise her job talk for a university in an area with a significant First Nations community. She said to the room of people that it was her hope to one day be replaced by a First Nations scholar, that this is what she was working towards. That comment stuck with me and I think encapsulates the challenge and paradox that lies ahead for critical pedagogy. Critical pedagogy must seek to not only challenge but to change the existing power structures in the academy and within itself.

NOTES

[1] Interestingly the following invited panel also took place at the 2006 session of the American Educational Research Association: Paulo Freire Special Interest Group. Invited Panel: Does the Freirean Legacy Leave Racism Unchallenged? Presentation: "The Whiteness of Being Critical Pedagogy and the Absent Presence of Blackness."

[2] Ricky Lee Allen's work engages in many of the same frustrations and fears that my chapter speaks to. I would point readers to his chapter "The Race Problem in the Critical Pedagogy Community" in the edited collection *Reinventing Critical Pedagogy* as well his 2004 essay in *Educational Philosophy and Theory*, entitled "Whiteness and Critical Pedagogy" as good companion pieces to this chapter.

REFERENCES

Allen, R. L. (2006). The race problem in the critical pedagogy community. In C. A. Rossatto, R. L. Allen, & M. Pruyn (Eds.), *Reinventing critical pedagogy: Widening the circle of anti-oppression education.* Boulder, CO: Rowman & Littlefield Publishers, Inc.

Constantino, R. The miseducation of the Filipino. *Journal of contemporary Asia, 1*(1), 20–36.

Dubois, W. E. B. (1903). *The souls of black folk.* New York: Penguin Books.

Kincheloe, J. L., & Mclaren, P. (Eds.). (2007). *Critical pedagogy: Where are we now?* New York: Peter Lang.

JONATHAN LANGDON

14. "COSTLY GESTURES"

Addressing the tension between collaboration and criticality

INTRODUCTION

Since I first entered graduate school in the fall of 1999, I have been struck by how our various disciplines in the Arts, Humanities and Social Sciences shape us into astute critics, able to deconstruct[1] at a virtual glance the oversights, gaps and undertows of bias in the work of others. These skills have led to many devastating and insightful interrogations of the work of established scholars from virtually every possible ideological position. And these interrogations are occurring in virtually every graduate classroom across North America, as well as elsewhere in the world; one can imagine listening across the distance to the cacophony of critical voices in graduate seminars in hundreds of locations both at the very moment I write this and at the very moment you read it. This communality of purpose is the creative and critical spirit that potentially unites us–a sort of "imagined community"[2] of graduate students around the globe. There is also a real danger behind it as this spirit of criticality also carries with it the seeds of a community's–imagined and real–destruction.

Perhaps this vision of a generation of graduate students being united through critical training could be perceived cynically, or perhaps we are simply the product of the postmodern,[3] born into an age where all is negotiable and therefore ripe to be critiqued. Perhaps we are being shaped into a sort of postmodern aesthete-cum-gunslinger, standing in the middle of Main Street, setting up and then shooting down all the straw figures who oppose us.[4] While I have contributed to and have applauded these types of attacks, I have also begun to wonder at their costs–especially for attempts at community building within such a "Western" set-up. For instance, it is rare to find the cowboy movie that values the gang over the lone gunslinger–the one setting out to face the world on his or her own terms. And this type of narcissistic individualism has real costs that go far deeper than mere straw targets.

For our graduate student community, the most visible marks of these costs are written on the faces of each of us as we each turn the muzzle of our deconstructive six-shooter on our own colleagues–shifting from straw targets to real people with real feelings. Somewhere in this shift is the very core of our latter-day western desensitization, where reality seems to dissipate into a cloud of "single-serving" episodes[5] that bear no relation to one another. Some authors have called this "historical amnesia" the victory of hyperreality,[6] where the human cost of systems of power is conveniently forgotten in each New Neoliberal[7] World Order (Semali

A.H. Churchill (ed.), Rocking Your World: The Emotional Journey into Critical Discourses, 157–164.

& Kincheloe, 1999; Rains, 1999). And these single servings certainly carry no guilt and responsibility for whatever hurt they may have caused as community building is sacrificed to winning the latest round of critical Russian Roulette.

Somewhere in this desensitization is the transformation of the academy into a marketplace where individuals rather than communities of practice *own* knowledge and sell it to the highest bidder. And it is the critical-theory-slinger most capable of shooting from the hip that wins the right to know, leaving a trail of targets both straw and real by the wayside. In this new marketplace, criticality therefore becomes not only an analytical tool for discerning the deeper connotations of particular theories and practices, but also, more devastatingly, it becomes a mechanism, or technique, for pulling those ahead of us down and pushing ourselves ahead. This marketplace mentality puts a new twist on Newton's famous saying that we are "standing on the shoulders of giants," if those giants are instead reconceived as those we have pulled down in our critical quest for the top.

In this chapter I want to dwell on the cost of this way of being, not only on a personal level, where people become targets and ideas become tools for advancement, but more importantly on the level of progressive change. Not only should we recognize the costs of this unfettered individualism, but we also need to begin to develop a more nuanced understanding of the "costly gestures" we all make as we enter the critical realm–the gestures each of us is willing to make towards radicalness, towards destabilizing what we have come to know as being true or normal, towards taking action in ways that make each of us, from our respective positions, feel like we are pushing the boundaries of our comfort zone. For criticality is a realm where we may all agree to no longer accept the status quo and we may all wish to contribute to its change, yet we all have vastly different understandings of what this change may mean and the costly gestures we are willing to make to see it come to life. Despite what naïve interpretations of postmodernism may suggest we cannot all be right all of the time; in actively fighting each other, we may all be wrong for all time. In this sense, the chapter before you builds on the notion that we must begin to balance criticality–in our practice, in our teaching, in our theorizing–with cooperation, where we can work together to subvert some of our latter day tendencies to fracture and divide those whose core values are the same as ours.

"PULL ME DOWN" SYNDROME

I would not want to misrepresent our current situation in academia as being something all that new, although it is, of course, new to me as a young person now struggling to become a member of this community of scholarship. On the contrary, I think the effects of criticality as self-advertisement and self-advancement can be seen in many sectors of the so-called progressive movements. Having grown up in a political household where my father, Steven Langdon, was a Member of Parliament for the socialist New Democratic Party of Canada, I have witnessed first hand how the costs of in-fighting can destroy an emerging socialist agenda. I witnessed how failures to build cooperation between the NDP at a provincial level in Ontario and at a national level resulted in the virtual disappearance of the party as a force for socialist change in Canada.[8]

Many times the result of a system where individual critical strength is given precedence over a form of community cooperation is the usurping of the community agenda to suit the individual. In this approach, broad based consensus building is overwritten as the strongest individual makes unilateral decisions for the best interests of all. The tragedy of this situation is that this democracy-of-the-strong–what Jacques Derrida (2003) calls the democracy of "might is right"–is exactly what so many progressive movements are against.

The result of this type of winner-takes-all phenomenon is a hard fought competition for the right to lead. In this intense competition we see the Western gunslinger motif revealed again: a sort of last-person-standing being crowned the winner and therefore the one who is right. And so, out of this situation a pull-you-down syndrome evolves, where anyone who is perceived to be gaining momentum in the progressive movement becomes the target of attack from within the movement itself; if one thinks of the common metaphor of the corporate ladder, where those above step on those below, while those below try to pull down those above, the intensity–as well as the origin–of this mentality become clear. In the case of progressive movements, this type of infighting creates clear moments where the collective best interests of the movements are superseded by the interests of the individual leaders within movements or one group within a coalition's particular worldview.[9]

On a much smaller scale, this same pull-you-down syndrome is in place in many graduate student communities. As a result of the growing cost of education, and the intense competition associated with securing funding, getting published, and finally finding work after graduation, graduate students are pitted against one another virtually from day one of our schooling. Of course, this competitive ethos is at the centre of contemporary educational practice, with its mentality of constant marking and ranking. Yet in graduate school, the community is much smaller, and in many cases the stakes are much higher. And so, criticality emerges as not only a mechanism for showing one's own skills, it also becomes an effective tool for the critical de(con)struction of the competition.

NAÏVE UNCRITICALITY

Upon hearing of and experiencing the potential infighting within progressive movements and graduate communities, the reaction of many both within graduate student communities and within broader communities fighting for social justice is that we must never be critical of one another; we must somehow blindly accept what everyone says as being right and true and valid. I think it is equally dangerous to imagine that each of us has nothing to learn or gain from having our ideas challenged, from learning from new perspectives, from considering positions overlooked before. In her chapter in this book, Elizabeth Meyer notes that when she first came into contact with the progressive ideas of critical theory they included many marginalized groups, yet they overlooked the gay/lesbian/bisexual and transgendered community. She and others leveled this critique against leading writers of critical theory such as Henry Giroux, and the theoretical position shifted to include this oversight. This is reminiscent of Paulo Freire's acknowledgement of his own phalocentrism[10] in *Pedagogy of the Oppressed* (McLaren, 1994). Certainly, critical and progressive movements have much to gain from critical self-reflections that emerge from within their midst. Consider historically how collectives such as the Bloomsbury group, or the abolitionist movement, or the anti-apartheid movement, or the Frankfurt School–the foundation of critical theory itself–were deeply informed by a spirit of critical collaboration. The constant critical self-reflection as well as collaborative interactions within the Bloomsbury group helped its members, such as E.M. Forster, Virginia Wolfe and John Maynard Keynes, to dramatically alter the arts and economic thinking in Great Britain; similarly, the constant critiques as well as collaboration at the heart of the Frankfurt School are what led Adorno, Horkeimer and Habermas and the other members of the school to effectively challenge orthodox Marxism in the academy and, as a result, lay out the foundation of critical theory. Likewise, graduate student communities have much to gain from each other as the process of learning cannot simply be one of naïve uncriticality, where nothing is challenged and no re-articulation of ideas occurs. It is the timbre, the tone, and the manner in which these processes occur that is at stake here. In other words, as graduate students trained in the art of critical analysis, we must strive to achieve the complex balance between collaboration and criticality in order for real sites of mutual learning to emerge.

To give a practical example of the complexity of this balance, a group of colleagues in our graduate class that had started a study group were recently attacked in the broader graduate community for being exclusive. While to the outside observer this group may have appeared as a clique, what was lost in all the attempts at defamation was any sense of where this study group had come from, and its role as an emerging site of collaboration building. The group was started by a number of us who were frustrated with an education experience dominated by professors. We decided to build our own space, open to all who expressed interest: no one was ever refused entry. At the same time we didn't advertise the group because we were worried the meetings could become too big. To avert this, we also suggested to colleagues that they start similar groups, with the aim of creating a synergy of graduate student self-directed learning. We even invited professors to join us, allowing us to learn on our own terms rather than on those of the faculty. The agenda for meetings was always collectively determined, and revolved around both our commitments to gaining better theoretical understandings of issues and a strong desire to debate the practical possibilities of various critical theoretical approaches. In many ways, this book is connected to the discussions that occurred in our study group. Yet, it must be acknowledged that it was and still is just one study group, and is not, nor can it be, an extension of an entire graduate community that numbers into the hundreds. We felt that to transform this type of space into a faculty-wide experience necessitated the active involvement of student government as well as many more members of the broader student community–something we didn't feel should be forced, or was the bottom line agenda of our group. On an individual level, I would have loved to see our graduate community become radicalized to such an extent that we could begin to make our education more responsive to our student-community needs. I know there are examples where this has been done; for instance, the UMASS Faculty of Education involves students in all aspects of curriculum formation.[11] Nonetheless, the tragedy to underscore here is the manner in which the misrepresentation of this study group as a form of exclusive club ended our meetings, drove a wedge deep into our graduate community, and left many of us wondering if building collaborative spaces is really possible.

THE COST OF GESTURES

With this fissure in the graduate community in mind, it is at this moment that I wish to bring forward the key idea behind this chapter: the notion of costly gestures. In essence what I mean by this, and I derive this term from Arturo Escobar's (1995) reading of Foucault, is that we need to understand where someone is coming from before we mobilize our complete arsenal of devastating critical skills to take him/her apart. As I have just noted, this does not mean some form of naïve uncritical acceptance of whatever is said and done, but rather a genuine attempt to see the risks involved when someone takes action . We are not all made to stand on the picket line, and in many cases this may not even be the hardest thing to do: imagine a loved one setting off in the morning to defend a factory job, or a piece of land set for expropriation; imagine the strength it takes to let this person go, to stay back and take care of those who may have to fight another day. There is no way of truly understanding the costs of each of our gestures, yet we must try to open our eyes and hearts to each other, as Paulo Freire suggests when describing why he wrote *Pedagogy of Hope* (1995):

> It (was) written in rage and love, without which there is no hope. It is meant as a defense of tolerance--not to be confused with connivance--and radicalness. It is meant as a criticism of sectarianism. It attempts to explain and defend progressive postmodernity and it ... reject(s) conservative, neoliberal postmodernity. (Freire, 1998, p. 10)

Tolerance and radicalness live side by side, according to Freire. It is only from balancing both of these positions that we can truly understand the damage sectarianism can cause–where divisions matter more than the substance that unites, where perceived motives matter more than what we say we mean. And it is from this balanced perspective–that both accepts who people are, yet also challenges them to do more–that hope is derived. Having an understanding of costly gestures is in fact synonymous with this representation of hope by Freire, as is maintaining a tension between criticality and cooperation.

This is why I think it is important to also understand how cliques within a community can fracture, and can cause jealousy, even though the spaces have been built for collective learning. In this sense, I am trying to understand the position taken by those who actively attacked the study group we put together, and to also recognize the costs of the gestures they made, both to themselves and to our group. For instance, many of those critical of our group saw it rightly or wrongly as an emerging bastion of privilege and were simply trying to live by the creed of critical theory to question power wherever it manifests itself. As a result, our critics did not necessarily see how they were hurting their colleagues with their accusations, or how attacking this space made it far less likely that people would be willing to build collective spaces again and risk similar attacks. Similarly, those who took on leading roles in attacking this space also suffered for their gestures, as relationships became strained throughout the community. If we had all taken more time to understand the costly gestures behind each other's actions, some of this damage may have been averted.

But recognizing each other's costly gestures is not enough. There is a further wrinkle to the complexity of this awareness that must be considered. For, even as we can ask others to be aware of the risks we are taking, we must also accept responsibility for the potential negative impact of our actions on others. Our group obviously caused a sense of exclusion in our community, and, in retrospect, there is likely much more we could have done to make it either more welcoming to other students, or to make more of an effort to help others to begin similar groups. In this sense, recognizing costly gestures cuts both ways. We need to recognize the cost of our gestures on others, even as we strive to see the costly gestures of others. I think the biggest problem in moments like the one I described above is an inability to take the time to see the costly gestures being made from all sides. In a sense, and to return to the opening ideas of this chapter, this is a failure that is embedded in our current system of education that places individual competition over collective cooperation. We have very little language, and very little space to clear the air around these moments of misreading and misunderstanding. And, too quickly, we all reach for the critical soapbox from which we can stand on high and give ourselves an edge in the hyper-individualized world of academic survival. As an example of how bad this fracturing of community can become, during my Master's degree one colleague joked we should turn our saga into a new "Survivor" series, where we would vote one of our classmates out of school each week.

In an alternative world, where the fallout of this situation had been different, and where people took more time to recognize the costs of gestures being made all round, this confrontation over the interpretation of this group could have been the beginning of a new graduate community–perhaps one as democratic as the one at UMASS mentioned above. Certainly, had there been more attempts at mutual recognition, I think the major issues at the core of criticism could have been addressed by using the mechanism of student government to mediate and potentially collectivize our desire for student-led learning space. And doing this in an open manner would have helped all those members of the community quietly feeling excluded to voice their desire for more control of our educational future. In short, with more recognition of costly gestures all round, cooperation and collaboration could have been deepened in our faculty rather than destabilized.

CONCLUSION

Despite what those outside the academy may believe, being in graduate school is not easy. In the era of major competition for funding, publications and teaching experience, the life of a graduate student has become more and more synonymous with metaphors of the market place where only the strong survive. What is especially insidious is to see this logic of competitive practice beginning to heavily influence even those faculties with strong community and progressive agendas. And, it is precisely through the over-developed sway of hyper-criticality that this process manifests itself, as graduate students discredit each other and raise their own stature through the use of critical skills acquired in the process of graduate training. I think we all need to build our awareness of this process, especially as it informs our own actions and the actions of others in our various graduate communities. This does not mean we should somehow silence our critical voices when it comes to each other, or put them aside for a position of naïve uncriticality. Rather, we need to develop our skills as individuals and as communities to recognize the costly gestures made by others and the cost of the gestures made by ourselves. We also need to fight hard to be allowed to build collective spaces where we can learn how to better cooperate while keeping a critical eye out for each other and allowing a dialectic of ongoing learning through a constant exchange of ideas. Taking a note from Vygostsky (1978), we need to consciously build overlapping Zones of Proximal Development (ZPDs)[12] where our synergy of effort to learn can help each of us achieve more than our individual efforts could hope for. This is by no means an easy process, but in our societies where more and more of our common space is disappearing, and where democratic freedom is becoming synonymous with the freedom to become individuals selling our selves and our skills in the inequality of the marketplace, we must fight for the right to learn how to collectively produce and share knowledge and how to collectively act. Democratic practice and democratic learning spaces are not innate to us, and therefore must be consciously built; to do this means we all need to learn to recognize the costly gestures, and to work through the ups and downs of community building. As noted above, groups like the Bloomsbury group and the Frankfurt School went through many ups and downs, as did the abolitionist and anti-apartheid movements–yet all of these forms of collective action dramatically altered the world. This is the true nature of democracy, not–as Derrida (2003) reminds us–the right of might, but rather the transformative process of collective deliberation where might is not right and critical collaboration builds agendas that include the voices of us all.

NOTES

[1] Deconstruct: a term linked with textual analysis of the latent or unstated biases that inform a particular argument or position. The term is most often associated with the work of French post-structuralists such as Derrida.

[2] Imagined community: this is a term derived from the work of Benedict Anderson (1991) and it describes the way that far flung groups of people can feel a sense of community by participating in similar experiences.

[3] Postmodern: both an era, as in that which follows the modern, and a way of thinking–what Jean-Francois Lyotard (1979) calls the postmodern condition: "incredulity towards metanarratives" or cynicism towards the grand concepts of truth in society. Works produced under this "condition" often result in ironic, playful and self-aware counter-commentary on these grand truths.

[4] I owe this imagery to a conversation with Anthony Paré at the American Educational Research Association Conference in Chicago, 2007.

[5] I take this notion of single-serving episodes from the movie Fight Club (1999), where Edward Norton's character makes single serving friends on flights, believing he will never be responsible for what he says to them.

⁶ Hypereality: a term closely associated with postmodern techno-cultural living, where reality and fantasy merge as consumerism dominates life, and consciousness is saturated with a constant barrage of information to the point where it becomes difficult to assess the meaningless from that which has meaning. The term is often associated with the work of Jean Baudrillard.

⁷ Neoliberal: a form of economics founded on the premise that free trade and less government is better for prosperity. It has been widely criticized as putting growth before human need, and has been accused of worsening the conditions of the world's poor rather than improving them.

⁸ The New Democratic Party of Canada went from a national high in the late eighties of over 40 seats in Parliament to less than 20 in recent elections. At the height of this surge of popularity, the NDP led popularity polls at the national level, and won a major victory at the provincial level when they became the governing party of Ontario in 1990. The tension between the federal and provincial levels of the party quickly emerged however as the Ontario NDP made choices that many disagreed with. In the 1993 federal elections, and in subsequent provincial elections, the NDP were eliminated as a force to be reckoned with. Under the recent leadership of Jack Layton the party has begun to rebuild, but the political terrain makes it difficult for the party to gain much ground.

⁹ William Carrol (1995) has discussed how New Social Movements (NSMs) have failed to find a unified position in the aftermath of the collapse of Marxist states. He presents a useful set of interpretations for the reasons behind this factionalism from a Foucauldian and Habermasian perspective.

¹⁰ Phalocentrism: as in centered on the phallus, meaning seeing the world from a male perspective.

¹¹ I owe this understanding of UMASS's approach to student involvement to Bonnie Mullinix.

¹² ZPD: a term derived from the work of Lev Vygotsky (1978), Zone of Proximal Development (ZPD) refers to a way of measuring the difference between what a learner would learn on their own as opposed to in interaction with other knowledgeable peers. In this sense, it can be thought of as a way to be consciously aware of the influence those you surround yourself with have on your own learning and development.

REFERENCES

Anderson, B. (1991). *Imagined communities: Reflections on the origin and spread of nationalism.* London: Verso.

Carrol, W. (Ed.). (1995). *Organizing dissent: Contemporary social movements in theory and practice.* Toronto: Garamond Press.

Derrida, J. (2003). A dialogue with Jacques Derrida. In J. Habermas, J. Derrida, & G. Borradori (Eds.), *Philosophy in the time of terror: Dialogues with Jürgen Habermas and Jacques Derrida.* Chicago: University of Chicago Press.

Escobar, A. (1995). *Encountering development: The making and unmaking of the third world.* Princeton, NJ: University of Princeton Press.

Fincher, D. (1999). *Fight club.* United States: 20th Century Fox.

Freire, P. (1995). *Pedagogy of hope: Revisiting pedagogy of the oppressed.* New York: Continuum.

Freire, P. (1998). *Pedagogy of the heart.* New York: Continuum.

Lyotard, J.-F. (1979). *La condition postmoderne: Rapport sur le savoir.* Paris: Minuit.

McLaren, P. (1994). *Politics of liberation: Paths from Freire.*

Rains, F. (1999). Indigenous knowledge, historical amnesia and intellectual authority: Deconstructing hegemony and the social and political implications of the curricular "other". In L. Semali & J. Kincheloe (Eds.), *What is indigenous knowledge: Voices from the academy.* New York: Falmer Press.

Semali, L., & Kincheloe, J. (1999). Introduction: What is indigenous knowledge and why should we study it. In L. Semali & J. Kincheloe (Eds.), *What is indigenous knowledge: Voices from the academy.* New York: Falmer Press.

Vygotsky, L. (1978). *Mind in society: Development of higher psychological processes.* Boston: Harvard University Press.

ANDREW H. CHURCHILL

15. A CONVERSATION AMONG THE AUTHORS

Perspectives on Writing

INTRODUCTION

Following is a conversation between the authors that occurred after the individual chapters were written. As part of the book project process, the chapters were posted online to be available for authors to read each other's work. An online forum was created for reflections about each other's chapters and the process of writing. The discussion was initiated with the following hope:

> The idea is to capture a conversation here amongst ourselves about some of the main themes that have emerged from writing this book. This will stand in place of some sort of concluding chapter and hopefully serve to spur more thinking rather than create closure. Comments could be of a general nature, refer back to something either you or another author has written, or reflect a new level of insight spurred by this additional opportunity to reflect.

There were four questions to which authors responded. The following are some of their thoughts:

How have you come to understand the importance of affect in your own learning and/or teaching?

> The problem is, it is not important–or, it has not been important enough. It is too easy to deny the relevance of me, my life, my history, my being in the context of academia. I am not suggesting that people in academia are insincere. On the contrary, many hold a deep passion for their work and for the people they encounter along the way. I am suggesting that affect holds little relevance to an academic performance. There are ideas, and the integrity of those ideas in light of other's ideas and in light of history broadly stated. There is not, however, much sign of me (broadly stated).
>
> *Posted by: Carmen Lavoie, July 8, 2008.*

> I agree–much academic work has tried to divorce itself from its humanness in the name of "scientific objectivity" which doesn't work. It just cloaks its biases and emotions in obtuse language to justify them: the science of "race" and "intelligence" are good examples.

A.H. Churchill (ed.), Rocking Your World: The Emotional Journey into Critical Discourses, 165–176.

In teacher education, it is so important that we get to the core of individuals' beliefs and how they FEEL about things. People can "know" one thing and "believe" another and the belief will have the more powerful influence over that person's perceptions and actions. I struggle to keep the emotional present in my teaching, but then you can get accused of being too personal and causing students to go into emotional "crisis." Well, Kevin Kumashiro writes a lot about the pedagogical utility of being in crisis and it is how we support students while they try to work through these crises that really matters. We need to help our students feel present in their bodies and their emotions and to do so, I feel that we need to create safe spaces in our classrooms and model that.

I had a class I taught in the fall ("Diversity in Human Relations") read my piece for this book. It was a risk. Some people thought I was insane to stand in front of a class of students who had just read about these deeply personal, deeply painful experiences of mine. But I thought it was pedagogically important to do so. I ask my students every day to push themselves, take risks, ask questions, and expose themselves. If I'm not prepared to do so myself, then how dare I expect them to?

Posted by: Elizabeth Meyer, July10, 2008.

I strongly identify with both postings and I also wonder if how we construct a "professional" identity in the academy shapes our readiness and willingness to reveal the affective side of our work. I agree with Carmen that many, if not most, in the academy are deeply passionate about their work, yet somehow there's this missing link between this affect and most of the work that is being (re)produced in journals, books, and lectures. As a young scholar trying to figure out how to navigate what it means to be a "young scholar," I receive conflicting messages about where/when/how I can reveal myself in my completeness as a scholar constantly in evolution and constantly being influenced by past events and experiences. I sense that as a young scholar if I veer towards allowing my affect to enter my research and my teaching too much, I can be discounted as lacking a certain amount of professionality, where objectivity is confused with professionality.

Where do I get these messages from? Most strongly, I receive them implicitly from those immediately around me in my academic community. Although there is a small circle of scholars–new and established–around me that do share the same pedagogical openness that Liz embodies, I can recall more examples of professors and colleagues that do not share in that way, their affective dimension was self-silenced. This is not to say that I do not learn from those scholars, I do in immense ways, but in addition to those lessons learnt, is the unspoken lesson that this is what a professor/scholar does: they teach about what they read/research, they rarely teach from their own experiences. Obviously this is riddled with problems because we know that we all are influenced by affective experiences. I also get this message of "objective = professional" from the journal articles and books I read, many times I find myself reading an evocative piece of work and wonder "hmm ... I wonder what they were feeling when they were doing this research, I wonder what compelled them to take this line of research." In short, I model my notion of professional on the implicit, unstated genre of practices concerning academic professionality around me.

Posted by: Eloise Tan, July 14, 2008.

I, too, can strongly identify with all the posts above. Like Eloise, I have a small circle of colleagues who are open and comfortable in sharing personal, emotional experiences with their students. Encouraging this kind of dialogue creates an open, warm, safe classroom environment that humanizes you to your students. I believe this is when "real" teaching occurs (along with, of course, students engaged in rigorous research). But in terms of affect, I think students appreciate the sharing of affect more so than technocratic, positivist styles of teaching that often result in students who are passive, bored, and disengaged.

My undergraduate, students (pre-service teachers) sometimes struggle with the idea of sharing personal and emotional experiences in their future classrooms. They are often instructed to remain "objective" so as not to sway or indoctrinate their students. I, too, have been given that advice from a few colleagues! We discuss this notion of objectivity and what it means to be objective–is it even humanly possible to remain objective? Do our personal biases, values, beliefs, or experiences influence our decisions, thus making it even more difficult to be objective? Does being objective support the status quo? Does being objective and not stating your opinion, really mean that you are, indeed, taking a position? Are you sending hidden messages by remaining objective? The end result of asking these questions? Stimulating discussions, passionate debates, and engaged, interested students!

When Andy sent his prospective to us, I remember thinking, "Wow, FINALLY, a text that will address the emotional and personal struggles–and victories–of teaching a critical pedagogy!" I recall my years as a graduate student studying and learning about critical theory and various issues within cultural studies and only ONE professor spoke about the "risks" involved in teaching critically, specifically the attacks and/or hostile resistance one may receive from both students and colleagues. Gaining and sharing insights to the real personal and emotional struggles critical pedagogues feel while engaging in critical teaching is crucial if we want to survive in the academy where academic freedom and promotion and tenure may be at risk simply due to one's ideological position. This is precisely why this book is a must read for those of us engaged–and those not engaged–in critical pedagogy. It really provides a sense of community in which one can share and relate his/her struggles and pain with others who truly understands the difficulty of teaching such "controversial" or political issues. More importantly, sharing such stories humanizes critical pedagogy as opposed to reading it as simply a theory that has no realistic application to the classroom.

Posted by: Priya Parmar, July 15, 2008.

This is a great discussion. I think it is especially important to emphasize the emotional aspect of criticality, and thinking generally, when folks are not inclined in that way to begin with. For me, an important part of my education and development has been challenging myself to consider the affective dimensions in my own activism, teaching and writing, and pushing myself beyond my initial boundaries in this regard. I think one of the main political tasks, in order to build a radical solidarity, is to break through the dehumanizing impersonality and technicism of the contexts in which we live and work, which are also the mask of more direct forms of domination. This process of critique is what I have tried to describe in my chapter. However, I think we also have to be careful not to fetishize emotion as a kind of pure mode of being or of politics. After all, conservatives also depend very much on emotional appeals, and on inculcating a hostility to analysis and "secular" reason. I like the idea of some feminist (and also Marxist) theorists that the textures of experience (especially of those who are oppressed) are the basis and starting point for radical thinking and doing, but that the feelings and insights that come from these experiences need to be developed, challenged, and made systematic, in order to become actual critical philosophies and political strategies. We also need to break through the reified and privatized forms of affect that are bought and sold in the mass media and the culture industry to get to the collective, dangerous, and generative modes of feeling. I think this book will be a crucial tool in this project.

Posted by: Noah De Lissovoy, July 23, 2008.

How has reflecting on one's own journey (or hearing the reflections of others) been important?

I loved writing my piece. It was one of the easiest (and hardest) things I've ever written. I just sat down and it all poured out. I did a mini excavation of all my journals and papers from those times in my life and looked at them through a new lens. It was really interesting doing this self-study exercise as I had always felt it was a very self-indulgent form of "research." Maybe it is because the first one I read was really awful paper I got at AERA a few years ago, and it didn't make connections to anything that made it useful or interesting for me. I always felt that "self-study" was for those egotists who couldn't find anything more interesting to study other than themselves …? I've since changed my mind.

After working on this piece and studying & working in teacher education for the past 5 years, I've come to realize that this self-study is an essential ongoing process for educators–especially those of us who aim to teach critically and integrate critical pedagogy throughout what we do. It has given me a valuable insight into the important lessons and epiphanies that can happen when we excavate our buried moments and histories and examine our formative experiences and long-held assumptions.

Posted by: Elizabeth Meyer, July 10, 2008.

In a faculty of education we often ask undergraduate and graduate students to undergo the type of critical self reflection that comes out in *Rocking Your World*. I remember having to ask undergraduates to write a critical self reflection in a course and there were a lot of comments like "how is this real work?" and "what does this have to do with teaching?" and "if I don't have a sob story, I won't get a good mark" and, of course, "I have nothing to reflect on." After having spoken to many undergraduates while in this department, there is this sort of "here we go again" feeling when a professor asks them to critically self-reflect.

It's strange that this is an exercise, a practice, that we value so much at the undergraduate level but it is not something that seems to be valued very much at the level of professor scholars. We extol the benefits of critically reflecting to undergraduates because we are adamant it will help them become better teachers, but where is the same push at the university level of teaching?

Reflecting on writing my own story I wrote a lot of uncertain emails to Andy: "Should I use more references?" "Is it too personal?" "Should I write more theory into it?" As Liz said, it was very much an easy/hard piece to write. It was hard because I was being asked to be rigorous about my affect, which is not something I am accustomed to being asked. I asked myself a bunch of times: "this is so personal to me, who else would benefit from it besides me?" The same kind of doubts Liz mentioned about it being self-indulgent flew through my mind more than once. Eventually though, I said to myself there aren't going to be many opportunities where someone will come along and say "Eloise, do you have something to say? Say it here however you like, in whatever kind of language you want and I'll try my best to get others to read it." In the end, I had to get over my hang-ups about what is or isn't useful or indulgent in research and try to think outside those boxes we create for ourselves.

Posted by: Eloise Tan, July 14, 2008.

Writing my story on paper was somewhat therapeutic because as Eloise writes, we, as scholars, are not usually asked to self-reflect as we ask our students to do. Sharing my story and writing about the emotional toll it took on me was like removing a huge weight off my shoulders, a sense of relief in knowing that others out there also experienced similar struggles with their students, colleagues, or society at large. We need to hear more personal stories of our struggles and victories of teaching critically not only to keep sane and survive but to sustain and improve critical pedagogy!!!

On another note, I want to address the hypocrisy of asking our students to critically self-reflect but, we as faculty, not engaging in it ourselves. Critical self-reflection is a difficult process–you have to have tough skin, a strong sense of self, AND humility if you embark on this journey. I am amazed–and saddened–when attempts to self-reflect during faculty meetings fail miserably. For example, so much lip-service is given to issues of social justice and diversity (as often included in many schools of education mission statements) but when it comes to agency and self-reflecting on HOW we address or implement these issues in our own classrooms, we are often met with silence. Or, it is argued that these issues are somehow to be relegated in the diversity and multiculturalism courses! Why is it so uncomfortable to self-analyze and reflect on our own pedagogy but demand our students to constantly reflect on theirs? And when one has the courage to address such issues, especially in my experiences when naming positionality and whiteness, [some] faculty react defensively or the room is filled with an uncomfortable, eerie silence. I suppose it is easier to name and critique others but not ourselves. It really is contradictory and hypocritical to the mission statement we claim to live and teach by.

Posted by: Priya Parmar, July 15, 2008.

Through my research I have come to a deeper appreciation of the importance of story and its undeniable connection to place. I believe this is a framework in which we can begin to understand the confusing and emotional questions of ethnicity and identity. "Our story," each person's lived experience, is the basis on which a person's identity is formed and creates the lens through which the world is seen. This identity is connected to place, as we seek, create and define ourselves in relation to what is understandable and engaging.

The act of remembering is directly linked to our development of knowledge. Ideas and events retained in memory are recorded into words and phrases and their further conceptualization, have an impact upon our identity and influence our perceptions.

By the act of remembering, reflecting, writing and juxtaposing my personal narratives, I was able to make sense of my motives. This process also provides me with a context in which to understand my perceptions and understandings with respect to many facets of my life.

Life stories should not only be narrated but located and this has tremendous implications within the field of critical theory. It is better to make explicit our understandings, beliefs, biases, assumptions, presuppositions, and theories (Van Manen, 2002). We need to continue to acknowledge lived experience as an important facet of learning by incorporating personal narratives and self-study methodologies in the educational system.

In the act of reflecting, we come face-to-face with at least two sides of ourselves: the self-writing and the self who is remembered. Re-membering is self-work; it is the work that must be done on oneself and by oneself, and as such each must come to it on their own. Yet its benefits may be collective (Chambers, 1998). Sharing of values often brings us together, reinforces our beliefs, and creates knowledge that is retained. This is what I consider to be "authentic" education.

Posted by: Kevin O'Connor, July 15, 2008.

How might this book have helped you at various moments in the development of your criticality?

This question makes me wonder what I intended to offer to my reader. I was actually surprised at the responses I got from a few of the people who read a draft of my chapter. They were impressed at how brave I was to expose myself. The courage.

Well, I didn't feel particularly courageous or exposed–maybe because I set the chapter up in a framework which emphasized the unreliability of memory or maybe because I linked my story to a foul-mouthed cartoon. What I wrote was not an objective account of actual events in my past; it was more like a detective story or a forensics narrative: my participation in this human tendency to remember past events in order to explain our present lives.

One of my readers was my brother and I told him how the reaction puzzled me. His field is medicine and he made an interesting analogy between medicine and education: researchers in these disciplines tend to believe they're the ones with the knowledge and that their role is, in many ways, to fix people. When they read an autobiographical story like mine, their automatic response is to say, "That was brave of her to uncover herself in such a vulnerable manner. The poor thing–how can we help her or the likes of her?" But the reaction I wanted from my reader was, "Yup, I can see how I've felt that way as well and how those childlike motivations still push me ...."

As Priya wrote, in order to reflect critically on one's story, "you have to have tough skin, a strong sense of self, AND humility ...." It's not about finding the most heart-wrenching "sob story" (as Eloise's students comment) or a brave game of exhibitionism. To me, critical self-reflection is about accepting that self-understanding and social change go hand in hand (Pinar, 2004); it's about going beyond understanding criticality–it's about *living* it. And once you start reflecting on yourself critically–and I hope I'm starting to–you might be surprised at the layers of deception that you uncover in yourself. Oh yeah, humility is required. But only then can you start to be more understanding, rather than simply critical, of the duplicity found in others.

Posted by: Sandra Chang-Kredl, July 15, 2008.

The participation in this book, be it through the writing of my personal text, to reading other contributors' experiences and interpretations, and also through the passionate and stimulating discussions I have had with our beloved editor, has pushed me in my critical understandings in education.

Pinar (1994) describes a process in The Method of Currere: "the present ... becomes an acting out of the past, the superimposition of past issues and situations and persons onto the present" (p. 22). This speaks to the influence past experiences have upon a person's identity and actions. Be it through lived experience or through story, the construction of reality through these processes develops an understanding of how one knows, sees and acts upon the world. An experience of identity is presented and shaped when past, present, and projected understandings merge into events of consciousness.

I recognize that "history as told" is not always a flawless true reflection of "history as lived," but this should not lessen the need to promote more use of story, as is the case in this book. In fact, it supports the notion that narration, as each individual, community or culture with their own story, is unique and important. These stories come from a human imagination found in each of us that is interesting and intellectually stimulating. Narration is not to be seen solely as a personal act with personal benefits, as sharing our stories and their accompanying interpretations provides the framework for community knowledge. A portion of what we learn is through other people's experiences and their interpretation of those experiences. It is through this very process of sharing stories that sustains the transfer and expression of ideas that ultimately defines us as individuals and the communities we are part of.

Posted by: Kevin O'Connor, July 23, 2008.

I used a draft of my piece in a course I teach called "Self and Other in Education." I found that the article generated interesting classroom discussions. My students expressed some misgivings around the idea that learning to think critically could somehow change or affect their personal relationships. One student explained that she wouldn't be willing to do or say anything that would impact how she got along with her family. Her comment lead to an interesting class discussion about privilege and which groups (dominant) have the luxury to **choose** to think critically. Overall, I feel that the discussion generated by my chapter was worthwhile and I plan to make use of other chapters in future courses but my student's comments also left me feeling slightly concerned that my story somehow provided her with an excuse not to move towards criticality. I still maintain that talking about how our worlds were rocked is useful but I also wonder if I may have unwittingly provided my students with privilege with an easy out.

Posted by: Andrea Sterzuk, July 23, 2008.

Some people believe that an emphasis on the affective will subvert a focus on the intellectual and scholarly rigor and/or critical action, how would you respond to such a critique?

I think that an emphasis on the affective is important for a few reasons. Through my classroom research and teaching of pre-service teachers, I've become increasingly convinced that individual's belief systems and school ideologies inform/influence/construct/create discriminatory practices in schools. I think that intellectual and scholarly rigor and/or critical action are important but I also think that unless people connect their feelings to their thoughts and actions, their ideologies go untroubled and real change can't occur. I think that the kind of change that occurs when feelings are not engaged runs the risk of being temporary. My student teachers read theoretical pieces in my classroom but they are also expected to produce reflective writing that connects theory to their lived experiences. My goal in such work is to interact with their belief systems with the larger goal of disrupting some of the discursive practices that I've observed in elementary classrooms in my research. I don't think change can come simply from thinking or doing. I think that feeling has a large role to play too.

Posted by: Andrea Sterzuk, July 14, 2008.

I totally agree. Just as in your research, I found in my study with secondary school teachers it was their own identities and early experiences in schools that strongly shaped their educational philosophies and what they could and couldn't "see" in their own classrooms and schools. People who have an aspect of their own identity that has given them that double consciousness are so much more tuned in to the oppressive practices of schooling than those who haven't. The majority of current teacher education candidates either haven't experienced such marginalization, or haven't been given the language or the lenses to understand how power and privilege play out in schools. Such knowledge is painful. If you never feel that pain, however you are given access to it, you will never truly appreciate and understand social inequities and systemic oppression. If we want future teachers to work responsibly against racism, sexism, homophobia, ableism and all other forms of social injustice, then they need to FEEL the pinch. Somehow. I believe as Andrea does, to truly MOVE teachers and impact them beyond the 12-14 week semester, we have to teach with emotion and help them feel deeply. Support them, encourage them, but expose them to ideas, knowledges, and experiences that will force them to feel differently about the world.

Posted by: Liz Meyer, July 15, 2008.

Your posts reminded me of some conversations that I had with my students last semester. We were talking about inclusive education and digital technology use in the classroom and one student said, "But Dana, I can read about this till I'm blue in the face. How do I experience it? How do I find out what it's like to be a kid with a learning disability in a classroom?" Another student joined in and said, "Yeah, like, for example, do I have to be learning disabled in order to know what it's like? I can't do that. But I want to help." It opened up a really good discussion about what it means to say that you understand the effects of marginalization and systemic oppression. An interesting comment was then directed my way by a student who had been silent the whole time. He just blurted it out. He said, "But Dana, let's say you have experienced marginalization in some way. What makes you think that your experience helps you see things differently?" This comment brings me back to the topic of this thread and I am now wondering, just how do we define intellectual and scholarly rigor and/or critical action? What is the relationship between them both? Is it about exposure combined with tools for critical engaged action? Both of your posts reminded me of the fact that we as educators are asking people to try to feel or experience the complexity of marginalization, for example, within the institution of schools that are themselves sites of exclusion. And I am apart of this site of exclusion–I'm a teacher and I'm educating teachers to be apart of it. It's an incredibly complex web of relationships ... maybe that is where the intellectual and scholarly rigor comes in ... being able to articulate and then critically act upon this complexity?

Posted by: Dana Salter, July 19, 2008.

I am reminded by how I struggle when teaching about power, privilege, and marginalization. As Liz writes, "If you never feel that pain [marginalization], however you are given access to it, you will never truly appreciate and understand social inequities and systemic oppression." I agree, one cannot TRULY know what it's like to feel marginalized unless it is experienced first-hand. Beyond engaging my students in critical–and HEATED–dialogues on the above named issues, I conduct exercises, unbeknownst to my students, in an attempt to make them experience what it's like to feel marginalized ... even if it's just for a few minutes. Most of the time, these exercises are effective with a few students who quickly catch on to what I'm doing.

I teach a Language & Literacy course to pre-service teachers pursuing a degree in secondary education. Dana's post reminds me of an activity I do when I address the marginalization and frustration special needs students experience in school. The lesson after my students take an exam, I walk in and announce that they will be given a 10 minute pop quiz to help them earn extra points to the exam given the previous class session. I hand out three different versions of the quiz ranging from extremely easy to extremely difficult. The easy quiz simply asks basic questions about "core" knowledge (i.e. name of the current president, NY governor, first president, etc). The quiz usually takes 5 minutes to complete. At the bottom of this particular quiz, there are instructions that require students to "act" impatient and uneasy, to fumble at their seats expressing frustration at the fact that others have not yet completed their quiz. The second quiz is a worksheet with scrambled words and letters. Students must decode the words (purpose is to read the text as a dyslexic student may see it). All students taking this quiz are unable to de-scramble the words in the 10 minutes allotted. The third quiz is comprised of college level physics questions too difficult for students to complete in the time allotted. Although I always have a few students figure out the activity is a hoax, most students, believe it or not, are unaware of the hoax. I have had students feel so frustrated by those few select students taking the first version of the quiz that they completely gave up on completing their quiz. I even had a few students walk out of the class due to the convincing acting displayed by those students taking the first version!! After chasing them down and explaining myself, students reported feeling tension upon learning that there was a pop quiz, frustration or embarrassed for being unable to complete the quiz on time, and anxiety for witnessing others completing the quiz on time, making them wonder what was wrong with them. I then show them the PBS documentary entitled *How Difficult can this be? F.A.T. City–A Learning Disabilities Workshop*. It shows many simulations of what it's like to live in the shoes of a learning disabled student–specifically understanding the frustration, anxiety and tension associated with competing in a standardized curriculum. Although the video is great we do critique it for its flaws (i.e. lack of diversity). The activity, for the most part, works well in sensitizing my students to the needs of learning disabled students.

Another activity I engage my students in when discussing the importance of recognizing and validating the various dialects of the English language is simple but quite effective. We discuss what the "language of success"/ "language of power" is (Standard American English), why and how it was determined to be "standard" and what it "sounds" like giving examples of speakers who speak "correctly" or in the standard code. Since I teach in Brooklyn, many of my students speak a very distinct, rich Brooklyn vernacular that many non-New Yorkers can easily identify as coming from New York. I call on select students to read aloud passages from our reader. As the student reads, I intentionally correct him/her when letters in words are not enunciated enough (i.e. - emphasizing the endings of words, the "g" , "er", "ar" in "ing", "er", or "ar" endings, respectively) or any pronunciation of words that do not adhere to the standard code. Students who have been corrected on the spot have reported feeling embarrassed, inadequate for not being able to speak "correctly," and distracted from the content of the passage just read. While the reader is being corrected by me, we will often hear others laughing or assisting the reader by correcting with me! Most students, reading or not, report little or no comprehension of the text read. They were so busy concentrating on pronouncing the words "correctly," all meaning behind the words were lost. I conduct this exercise to sensitize students to the linguistic and dialectical diversity that exists and the emotional impact of how one is perceived if s/he is not accepted or valued for speaking in the home dialect. We discuss the concept of code-switching and effects to one's identity and self-esteem if one is forced to acculturate in terms of language acquisition (I explain the importance of this exercise in more detail in my chapter).

Again, it's a challenge to "teach" or feel marginalization without experiencing it directly. If we are not living it, we must at least engage in it by taking critical action, otherwise, it is merely reduced to meaningless theory (although I am NOT "dissing" the importance of theory here).

Posted by: Priya Parmar, July 23, 2008.

REFERENCES

Chambers, C. (1998). On taking my own (love) medicine: Memory work in writing and pedagogy. *Journal of Curriculum Theorizing, 14*(4), 14–20.

Pinar, W. (1994). The method of currere (1975). In *Autobiography, politics and sexuality: Essays in curriculum theory, 1972–1992.* New York: Peter Lang.

Pinar, W. F. (2004). *What is curriculum theory?* Mahwah, NJ: Lawrence Erlbaum Associates, Inc., Publishers.

Van Manen, M. (2002). *The tone of teaching.* London, ON: Althouse Press.

ABOUT THE CONTRIBUTORS

Chang-Kredl, Sandra. Sandra Chang-Kredl has worked for a number of years as an educator and administrator in early childhood education. Her research interests include children's films and literature within educational curriculum. She has written a number of chapters and articles on issues of childhood, and is completing her doctorate at McGill University.

De Lissovoy, Noah. Noah De Lissovoy is an assistant professor in the College of Education and Human Development at the University of Texas at San Antonio. His work and writing focus on the investigation of oppression and resistance in schooling and society, critical pedagogy, and the development of contemporary theories of liberatory pedagogy and praxis.

Desautels, Anie. In her research, Anie Desautels uses personal narratives to explore prejudice, racism, and intolerance. Her teaching experience has ranged from teaching primary grades in Thailand, to training teachers in the Karen Hill Tribe in a Burmese refugee camp, to teaching Inuit children in Northern Quebec. She completed her graduate degree at McGill University.

Langdon, Jonathan. Jonathan Langdon is finishing his doctorate at McGill University. A scholar of international development, indigenous knowledge, social theory, and education, his new book, *Indigenous Knowledge, Development and Education* will be published by SENSE Publishers.

Carmen, Lavoie. Carmen Lavoie is completing her doctorate at McGill University in Montréal. She is currently researching the construction of race and ethnicity in neighbourhood community organizing. Her areas of interest also include migrant issues, participatory approaches to research, social work education and effective models of community-university collaboration.

Meyer, Elizabeth J. Elizabeth Meyer is the ePortfolio Manager in the Faculty of Education at Concordia University. She is an international facilitator and workshop leader on topics of bullying, harassment and the related issues of sexism, racism, and homophobia in secondary schools. A former high school French teacher, she is completing a book on gendered harassment.

O'Connor, Kevin B. Kevin O'Connor is an instructor for the Office of First Nations and Inuit Education (OFNIE) and a Ph.D. candidate at McGill University. He worked as a teacher, department head and principal at an alternative experiential secondary school in Whitehorse, Yukon. Kevin is a teacher and consultant with various Indigenous communities across Canada.

Parmar, Priya. Named one of the 101 most dangerous professors in the world, Priya Parmar teaches at Brooklyn College. She is the author of books and articles on issues of teaching, positionality, critical pedagogy, and hip hop as curriculum. The creator of *Lyrical Minded: Enhancing Literacy through Popular Culture and Spoken Word*, she sponsors a yearly poetry slam at the Nuyorican Café

Porfilio, Brad. Brad Porfilio is an assistant professor in the Department of Educational Studies at Saint Louis University. His scholarship and expertise include: urban education, gender and technology, cultural studies, neoliberalism and schooling, and transformative education. An innovative educator, Brad has hosted several conferences on social justice and critical education.

Salter, Dana. Dana Salter is a course lecturer and a doctoral student at McGill University. She is researching the relationships between the in-school and out-of-school learner identity constructions of students diagnosed with learning disabilities as they relate to participation with digital technologies.

Sterzuk, Andrea. Andrea Sterzuk is an assistant professor of language and literacy education in the Faculty of Education at the University of Regina in Saskatchewan. Her research interests include literacy and academic achievement of minority language students, educator language bias, and education in postcolonial contexts.

Tan, Eloise. Eloise Tan is a course lecturer and a doctoral student at McGill University. She is currently working in Montreal schools on a grant engaging hip hop and spoken word as curriculum. A Filipino Canadian, Eloise is engaged in issues of diversity and equity, especially in areas of identity and schooling.

ABOUT THE EDITOR

Churchill, Andrew H. Andrew Churchill is a former high school administrator, who is currently a writing instructor in the McGill Centre for Teaching and Writing. His areas of research include school policy considerations relating to cyber-libel, cyber-bullying and Internet harassment as well as adolescent literacy practices. Most recently, Andrew worked for the Quebec English School Board Association as a consultant for their Internet Task Force. In this role, he conducted and analyzed large scale survey work of students, parents and teachers to assess their attitudes and beliefs about the Internet and other technologies vis-à-vis its impact on student learning and school communities. Currently Andrew is building on this work to develop curriculum which brings student on-line literacy practices into the classroom.

Lightning Source UK Ltd.
Milton Keynes UK
177866UK00005B/15/P